HOOKED

Clare Gee was born in Africa in 1977 and was sent to live in North Yorkshire with her English father when she was five. Aged 16, she moved to London, where she descended into a life of drink, drugs and prostitution. After a period of rehabilitation, she rebuilt her life.

HOOKED

Confessions of a London Call Girl

Clare Gee

MAINSTREAM
PUBLISHING

EDINBURGH AND LONDON

First published in Great Britain in 2010 by
MAINSTREAM PUBLISHING COMPANY
(EDINBURGH) LTD
7 Albany Street
Edinburgh EH1 3UG

ISBN 9781845966034

This book is a fictional account loosely based on the life, experiences
and recollections of the author. Dates, places, sequences or the detail of
events have been changed for artistic purposes and/or to protect the
privacy of some. Most of the people in this book are entirely fictitious

The author is donating a portion of the royalties
from this book to a children's charity

A catalogue record for this book is available
from the British Library

Typeset in Futura and Granjon

Printed and bound by
CPI Group (UK) Ltd, Croydon, CR0 4YY

15 17 19 20 18 16

This book is dedicated to Mark Herris Ibson, Ibo, the Great Ibster.
You have proved to me that unwavering love can exist.

Hooked *adj.* physically dependent; enthralled, attached, gripped by

*

ACKNOWLEDGEMENTS

Heartfelt thanks to my agent, Isabel Atherton at Creative Authors, whose passion and professionalism are immeasurable, and to Bill Campbell for recognising a good thing when it's staring him in the face! Thank you to Emily Bland for the book cover design. To all the staff at Mainstream, thank you for your hard work, especially to Claire Rose, of whose meticulous eye for detail I am in awe. I will never understand how you do it. Loulou Brown, without you I'd have cracked before I'd really begun. I will never forget your support throughout. Thank you to Kathrin Wagner, Penny Bowden and Leo Tennant for your beady eyes. Kisses to Katharine Scott, Neil Bond and Christian Gerling, without whom the book would have taken a lifetime to write. Thanks to Nirpal Dhaliwal and Tim Bates for giving me the confidence to start, and to James Duffett-Smith for your legal help. Thank you to Western Counselling Services for guiding me into sobriety. Where would I be now without you people? (Don't answer that!) And Rex . . . I hope your faith in me is being proved right. You helped save me from myself. I will never forget all you have done for me. Thank you. Finally, loving Jill Scott for her album *Who is Jill Scott?*, which kept me company during those many lonely and pensive nights writing *Hooked*.

Daddy Dogle Jude, you laid my foundations, of which I am proud. I thank you for cradling me, teaching me, keeping me and above all loving me. I love you. I always did. I always will.

M, you stayed, we made it, we three. I love you for loving Daddy as you do, and I love you for just being you.

CHAPTER 1

AUGUST 2003

I lifted my arm slightly to see if I could smell the perspiration that was streaming from the pit. I could. A musky scent and stale deodorant. I looked back at my husband, to whom I'd just said goodbye. What he didn't know was that I had three kilos of weed strapped to my stomach. I wanted to walk back outside Gambia's Banjul airport and dump it, but it was too late.

In that moment, I was so anxious I couldn't decide if I wanted to shit or vomit. I clung to my Chloé bag and subtly pulled at my kaftan to make it billow out.

'Next, please,' a voice called. It sounded distant. I was sure I was about to faint. I was unsteady on my feet and I gasped for air in an attempt to keep upright. Thank God it was a man in charge of the scanner. At least I could flirt with him to try and distract him from the guilt that I felt sure was etched on my face. Charm certainly didn't guarantee anything. I could only try to use my femininity and make him like me before it occurred to him to disapprove of my hairstyle or my choice of clothing or some other equally banal thing and he decided to interrogate me.

My heart was booming. I was convinced that the security guard could hear it. I smiled. He looked at me and nodded with a straight face. *Does he know something? Has he been tipped off?* I was shocked that he hadn't smiled back.

He waved me through the metal detector and it started screeching.

HOOKED

I froze. I gritted my teeth. My throat tightened. Sweat tickled my forehead. The alarm was condemning me with its rhythmic song, and for a second I imagined surrendering. It crossed my mind that it was either that or I would faint and it would all be over. The authorities would stretcher me out of the airport and into prison.

'Step back and walk through again, please.'

I did as I was told. The alarm continued.

'That's odd,' I said, bluffing, looking directly at the security guard to see how concerned he appeared to be.

It's all fucking over. They've got me. I could feel my pulse throughout my body.

'Are you going to London?'

He's knows, he knows. He's trying to work out where I'll be getting imprisoned.

My mouth was dry. 'No, I'm not, but I'm *from* London. I couldn't get a flight direct to Gatwick for another three weeks, so I have to go via Amsterdam.'

What the fuck? Why did I just say that? I remember wanting to yell at myself for being such an idiot. Admitting that I was travelling to the only city in Europe where cannabis smoking is tolerated wasn't the cleverest thing I'd done in my life.

'Walk through again, please, miss.'

Shit. I stopped thinking and started talking. 'Have you ever been to London?' I asked the guard, who was now brandishing a hand-held electronic scanning device. The alarm went off again and my mind was numb and my body froze.

'No, I've never been.'

'You should visit. You'd like it.' I felt as though I was holding my breath and there was only the guard and myself in the entire universe – and not in a good way.

'Are you inviting me?'

'Yes. You should come and stay with me.' I laughed falsely, hoping it would be enough to steer attention away from the bleeping. I suddenly felt very alert and very focused. I was on trial for my life.

HOOKED

'Step back and walk through again.'

The alarm sounded again and I was convinced I'd been caught.

*

Two years earlier, in 2001, my life had been very different. I'd been strutting around London rubbing shoulders with trend-pots while carrying a purse full of money. I'd had a busy social life and a thriving career – and drug smuggling was not part of it.

At the time, I was already married to another bloke. His family were Gambian, although I'd met and married him in London. Two weeks after the wedding, I left him. I couldn't reconcile myself to the ridiculousness of the marriage. I'd made an idiotic mistake, but thankfully no one, not even my closest friends, knew about the wedding, so all I needed to do was to try to forget it myself – by any means necessary.

My boss at that time, in what I later thought of (ironically) as my heyday, was a huge hulk called Dean, who ran an agency. I'd met him through an advert in a local Surrey paper. He called me two days after I'd registered to tell me that my client that evening was a teacher. Apparently, the guy was shy, and I wasn't to speak to him when he answered the door. I had to wear red lipstick and be prepared to smoke – a lot.

Within minutes of my arrival at his flat, he walked into the living room wearing a red lace thong and a black suspender belt with fishnet stockings. I'd read the instructions that he'd handed me, so when he gave me a sliver of nylon I presumed he wanted me to use it to tie his hands together. I stood up, took a deep drag on my fag, blew smoke directly into his face and called him a 'stupid cunt' and a 'cocksucker'.

That was what he'd requested and that was what he was paying me for. I sat back down and ordered him to plonk his arse on the stool in front of me. He looked like a joke. Regardless, it felt very weird calling someone names to their face. But as I watched him contort with demented appreciation, I realised I was giving him exactly what he wanted. I barked every name, every combination of profanities I could muster as I blew thick smoke from my pursed lips directly into his eyes. A little over 20 minutes after we'd begun, he stood up and muttered something.

'Who gave you permission to stand up, you fuckwit? Speak up, shithead, I can't hear you,' I snapped, starting to enjoy myself.

'I've just come, thank you.'

I was flummoxed. I couldn't believe it. I hadn't touched him and he certainly hadn't had an opportunity to touch himself, and what? He'd ejaculated?

'I'll just get dressed, then I'll make you a cup of tea, if you like.' He smiled timidly before turning round, inviting me to untie his hands.

'Oh, right . . . er . . . OK.' I was confused as I freed him. I'd never seen someone come without physical contact. I was quietly giggling to myself when he came back into the room dressed in respectable chinos and a polo shirt, reminding me that he was just a regular guy, despite his fetish.

'It's been nice meeting you, sir,' I teased him. He looked authoritative with his glasses perched on his snout. 'By the way, have you got the money?' I'd forgotten to collect it when I'd arrived, since I'd been instructed by the agency not to talk to him. Call girls will tell you that rule number one is always collect the cash before you start. Yeah, we all like to think we're professional at our jobs 100 per cent of the time, but sometimes rules must be bent. He handed me a wad of 20s. I felt too awkward to count it in front of him. He seemed like a gentleman. 'Thanks. Three hundred, right?' I grinned and added, 'Anyway, I know where you live.'

Outside, I flagged down a cab, feeling very smug. I'd been right to trust him. Every penny of the money was there, 300 of the Queen's finest. And the bonus? He hadn't even touched me.

Hell, I was on fire. And so, it seemed, was my friend Petra, who was working for another agency. We were both raking in the cash. I was on my way to meet her for another job. This was going to be my year, I could feel it, although my smugness quickly evaporated as the cab bombed towards my next appointment. It was rare to have two in such quick succession. Usually I'd get at least an hour between them. Fifteen minutes after I'd left the teacher's flat, the taxi approached a gate leading to a row of huge terraced houses in Holland Park. My heart was racing.

I felt anxious peering out of the window looking for my friend, and then I spotted her beside some bushes. I paid the driver 30 quid and jumped out of the car.

'What are you standing there for? I couldn't see you!' I snapped at Petra.

'Where should I have been standing, dressed like this? Look at me! And don't call me Petra. It's Petronella, OK?' she said snootily as I walked towards her. We hugged.

'P, you always dress like that. What are you on about?' I tittered. 'And listen, babe, don't start with that Petronella bullshit. Not tonight. I'm gonna call you whatever I want!'

'Stop swearing, Katie!'

'God, here we go! I've only just got here and you're already having a go at me. Don't be an arsehole, P, not tonight. Listen, I'm *me*, and I swear. And don't forget you swear too when it suits. Anyway, you look nice,' I said, just being polite.

'You do too,' Petra said, without a glance at me. 'I'm sorry for snapping. I've just come on my period. Please let's not argue.'

'It's all right, I'm used to you. Just forget it. Aw, poor you,' I cooed. 'You've just come on? I friggin' hate that when I'm working.'

'I got the cab to stop at a garage on the way here so I could get a sponge. You know, stop the bleeding and all that. But, Katie, I'm worried . . .'

'About what?' I asked as we tottered along the street, staring at each house in turn.

'Well, what if the guy wants to go down on me? He'll get

more than he was expecting.' We both laughed and grimaced at the same time.

While Petra was sashaying confidently in her four-inchers, her pert bottom jiggling, I was uncomfortable. Heels were not my forte. I focused on my shoes in an attempt to distract my thoughts from the night ahead.

'Anyway, do you like my new T-shirt?' Petra asked.

'"Bored of the Beckhams". Nice!' I laughed.

'Of course, I customised it – slashed the back and lowered the front – but you'll see that when we get in the house. I think this is it here.' She always spoke so fast. 'Let's get in there.'

The anticipation was nerve-racking. It was past midnight and we were wearing skirts that would have been short even for a hot summer's day. Petra had passed on the dress code when she'd asked me to join her at the party. We rang the doorbell and smiled nervously at each other.

'OK, don't forget to call me Isabella,' Petra grinned at me.

'Yeah, and I'm Jasmine.' I'd done this many times before. But the truth was, making contact with a stranger who would use your gash for cash never ever got any easier. I never knew what to expect – how the guy would look, what he'd want from me or how his cock would smell. It all added up to making me feel anxious as hell.

'Fuck, I'm cold!' I complained. Petra glared at me. She was a snob, Petra; I, on the other hand, spoke my mind and found my friend's conceitedness funny but often annoying.

'Are you here for the party?' asked the weary-looking, tuxedo-clad butler, his eyes focused on the space between us as he opened the door.

'That's right,' Petra replied in her poshest English accent. She would often try to hide the dulcet tones of her native Ireland. I've no idea why. When she was talking about home and she was relaxed, her real voice was a pleasure to listen to. I half grimaced, partly at my friend's overpronounced words, but mainly because I was anxious about what was to come. We edged past Jeeves, with his shock of white hair; his expression remained indifferent. The poor guy looked as though he'd never had a day off. Hell, at times I felt like that myself.

As the door closed behind us, a young, good-looking Middle Eastern guy ran down the staircase and greeted us, smiling. 'Hi, girls, come up.' Petra led the way – she usually did. She turned to look at me, eyes questioning. She was excited as well as apprehensive, I could tell. We climbed the staircase to the entrance of a large sitting room in silence, which was broken only when the guy asked if we'd found his place without hassle. We both answered at the same time and giggled as the bloke extended his hand. He was friendly and he smelled fresh. Thank you, God. Yep, not too bad at all.

'I'm Sahid,' he told Petra as he leaned forward to kiss her bronzed cheeks.

Does he like Petra more than me? He approached her first.

'I'm Isabella,' she replied. 'Nice to meet you.' She pouted as he stared at her lewdly. Self-consciously, she moved an imaginary strand of her raven hair off her face.

'Lovely,' he said, as if judging a show pony.

'You look like a singer. Are you a singer?' he asked me.

'No, no, I'm not.' I was bewildered at his line of questioning.

'Where are you from?'

'By that do you mean where's my accent from?'

'No, your heritage, your parents . . . you look . . .'

'My mum's African and my dad's English.' I wondered where this was going.

'Interesting. You look Iranian.'

Do I? I wanted to ask him if he was, but it's an unwritten protocol that a hooker doesn't ask the client personal questions.

'So where's your accent from, then?'

'Yorkshire.'

'It's barely recognisable.' He stared at me. I couldn't be certain, especially after he'd introduced himself to Petra first, but I was pretty sure he fancied me. He took my hand, pulled me towards him and planted a firm kiss on each cheek.

'What would you like to drink?' he purred. 'Champagne?' Without waiting for a reply, he told us that he would send the butler up with a bottle. We thanked him and he excused himself as he left the room.

'Fucking hell! Look at us! Look at this!' I giggled. Petra looked annoyed, as if she thought I was a country bumpkin for being wowed by lavish surroundings, which she considered to be her birthright. Beautiful frescoes adorned the walls and two huge plum-coloured velvet sofas, each the size of at least a couple of ordinary ones, took up much of the space. Three large chandeliers hung from the ceiling of the L-shaped room and there were a couple of distressed cream antique cabinets and a large matching writing desk with upright upholstered chairs that had trimming the same colour as the sofas. The room was over the top and looked expensive; clearly money had been thrown at everything. The gold leaf on the mirror frames made it feel like a museum. It was vulgar, but who were we to complain?

'I wonder where the other girls are?' Petra mused.

'That guy seemed all right, thank God!' I said.

'Are you listening?' snapped Petra.

'To what?'

'To me, stupid. The other girls – where do you think they are?' She was terrified of competition. But at that moment I couldn't have cared less where they were; my only thought was how rude it was of her to refer to me as 'stupid'. It was passive aggression, anger wrapped in a shroud of humour. No one was laughing.

'I wonder if I can smoke,' I said, ignoring Petra's question.

'Don't you dare!'

'I wasn't going to, Mummy! I was just wondering if I *could*. You know, is it allowed? I wouldn't just light up, for God's sake!' I was fed up with Petra implying I had no manners.

Another girl came into the room. Finally – life. 'Hey, how's it going?' she said in a friendly Australian accent. 'I'm Charlie.' She had one hand up in a type of Native American salute and the other in a pocket of her tiny denim skirt, which showed off her slinky legs perfectly.

'I'm Isabella, or Isabelle, whatever you want to call me,' Petra laughed. 'And this is Jasmine.'

I was staring at Charlie's slender figure and long, thick, wavy auburn hair. She was sexy, very sexy. She told us that she'd already been in the house for a while, in the bathroom, and she was relieved that other people were here.

The butler walked into the room holding a bottle of Veuve Clicquot, the bottom half wrapped in a white cloth. His face sullen, he poured champagne into three glasses and handed one to each of us before leaving again.

'Well, cheers!' laughed Charlie.

'Chin-chin,' I said, taking a large gulp. It seemed as though the three of us had been accepted into the inner sanctum. I looked at Petra, who was taking a tiny, delicate sip, holding her glass at the bottom of its stem.

Four more girls appeared, all of them tall with midriffs, boobs and spindly legs on display. We all introduced ourselves. There was one girl in particular who stood out, an English rose. She was striking, stick thin and carried herself elegantly. Her skin looked as though it had been drained of sunlight for the whole of her adult life. She appeared fragile, with a haunted look that oozed melancholy. She barely spoke, communicating largely with her brown eyes, which seemed lifeless.

All of us, with the exception of one girl, Helena, who looked a bit younger, appeared to be about the same age, 24 or 25. The new arrivals took champagne from Jeeves, who had silently re-entered the room, and then all that could be heard was the clinking of crystal and muted conversation, until, that is, Sahid and another man walked into the room.

The new guy, older and shorter, with excess stubble on

his face, interrupted our bonding, saying, 'Hello, ladies,' in a gravelly voice with a heavy foreign accent.

'This is my brother,' Sahid said, but didn't name him.

'Hello,' we all replied in unison, preening ourselves. I knew that this was the moment when the party would begin.

CHAPTER 2

Sahid walked purposefully towards a cabinet and turned on the stereo. At last, music to break the tension and inject some life into the proceedings.

'Hey, girls,' he called out, 'who wants some of this?'

I went over, never one to miss out on an opportunity. I'd guessed what he was talking about – don't ask how, I just did – and I wasn't wrong. In front of him on the table was a sugar bowl full to the brim with cocaine.

He thrust his arm around my hips, pulled me onto his knee, handed me a rolled-up £20 note and ordered me to do one of the lines he'd racked up. He didn't need to offer twice. I sniffed hard and the powder whizzed up my nostril. I pinched my nose to ensure that none was about to fall out. It wasn't stinging; it was good stuff.

I grinned at him, handed back the note and kissed his lips, to which he responded by sticking his tongue in my mouth. I reciprocated and thanked him. This guy was far more attractive than his chubby brother and since it seemed there were only these two men to entertain, I wanted to secure Sahid, although it flitted through my mind more than once what the heck these two guys were going to do with seven women. I mean, there wasn't even a balanced number of us.

I hated the taste of cocaine and needed a drink to mask the disgusting flavour that was trickling down my throat, so I told Sahid I was going to get my glass, which I'd left near the hairy brother who was holding court with the English rose, clinging on to her for fear she might run away. I could feel my nose running. It always did when I was sniffing charlie. I pretended to cough and wiped my nose discreetly with my hand. 'What's your name?' Sahid's brother asked aggressively. I instantly sensed he didn't like me. I often thought that men didn't like me because I wasn't quite as polished as other girls. And even though he was far from being God's gift to women, I still cared what he thought of me.

'Kiss me. I want you to kiss me,' he demanded. *What a creep.* He gripped my arm and pulled me towards him while still holding on to the other girl, who seemed totally apathetic. So I kissed him. After all, that's what I was there for.

Call girls kiss wealthy punters. You want them to like you. There's always the possibility that they could become a regular, which is a prostitute's ideal scenario, since it's easier to screw someone you kind of know than a man whose cock you've never ridden before. And when you're screwing a guy who's wealthy enough to give you more than just a fuck, you'll do virtually whatever the client wants. Poorer clients, on the other hand, don't always get kisses, unless they're good-looking. They're two a penny. Who cares if they want to see you again or not? They're hardly going to take you to an exotic location, rent you a flat or buy you gifts.

When he released me, I grabbed my champagne glass, turned my back, wiped my mouth and returned to the other girls, who were at the table. Helena had perched herself on Sahid's knee. 'Could I have another drink, please?' I asked him.

'Sweetie, you can have whatever you want,' he responded. 'Come, give me your glass.'

'Do you have any vodka instead of champagne?' I asked in a girly voice, uncertain if he'd think I was rude for dismissing the bubbly – or if he'd think I was a shameless alcoholic.

'Of course!' he replied, getting up, turfing Helena off her pew. 'That's a fantastic idea! I like your style.' *Brownie points for me, then* . . . I could feel the coke kicking in; a rush rippled through my body. Excitement? Anxiety? It was hard to differentiate. Sahid poured nine shots of Stolly, Stolichnaya vodka, and called over his brother and his companion. Petra and I grinned at each other. We were thinking the same thing: it's vodka that makes things happen; that's when the naughtiness usually begins.

'You OK?' Petra asked me.

'Yeah, I'm good. Are you?' I winked at her. She nodded back. She'd clearly had a sniff too.

I searched my bag for cigarettes. The predictable R&B that people with no musical taste play when they're trying to appear hip and worldly was blasting through the unseen speakers. Regardless, I was feeling elated, in the first flush of the cocaine high.

I'd already spotted the older brother smoking a cigarette, so I politely asked him if it was OK for me to light up.

'No,' he barked. 'Only I can smoke in this house.'

Oh my God! 'OK,' I said awkwardly, not knowing if he was joking. I was furious.

'Of course you can smoke,' he bellowed, eyes scanning the room to see who'd heard his comment, as if he was trying to embarrass me. It worked.

Tosser. I gave him a reserved smile, humouring his pathetic attempt at a joke. He was an arrogant arsehole, ugly, rude and he clearly thought he was a demi-god, which really grated on me. Under any other circumstances, there would have been no chance I'd have fucked him, ever. Neither would the other girls, if they had any sense. But money and the power it affords are a huge aphrodisiac for many women, elevating a short, scruffy, weasely excuse for a man into the equivalent of Michelangelo's David.

I lit a fag and took a deep drag. It went down so well with powder. 'Oh, would you like one?' I asked him as an afterthought, reluctantly smiling. I wanted to spit in his face. He helped himself, staring straight at me, saying nothing.

I turned away, needing to take a dump. I went over to Charlie, who was comparing shoes with Petra, and asked her to direct me to the loo. Coke is a stimulant and my first line always made me need to empty my bowels.

'I'll come with you,' Petra piped up.

'At your own risk – it'll be smelly,' I chuckled.

Waves of alertness gripped me and rushes of excitement consumed my body as I followed the directions to the bathroom, alone. The cocaine was doing its job. Along the hall, I opened a door, straight into a dimly lit bedroom that had a gold taffeta throw draped over the bed. I took a couple of steps inside to have a look.

'Are you looking for something, miss?'

Shit. 'Yes, the toilet,' I stuttered, turning my head to look at the butler. 'Can you, er, tell me how to get to the bathroom, please?' I desperately tried to lose my Northern accent and wished, in my heightened state of awareness, that I hadn't used the word 'toilet'; 'loo' would have sounded much nicer.

'It's just there on the right, miss.' His eyes directed me to another door. The guy talked in such a clipped voice you could easily believe he was faking it.

Pulling down my skimpy thong, I did what I had to do with ease; it slithered out quickly, as it always did after a line. I headed back past the bedroom towards the room where Sahid was still sitting surrounded by his harem of girls. The older brother was now hanging on to a svelte Nubian beauty's tight arse.

'Where's your drink?' Sahid shouted as I walked towards him 'Go! Get a drink!'

'I was wondering when you were going to offer me one,' I grinned. Petra followed me to the cabinet, as did the English rose, who was still very unchatty. I grabbed the Stolly and poured it into three tumblers. I handed an excessive amount of vodka to the rose, who took the glass and giggled nervously. She looked like a bird that hadn't eaten for days and didn't quite know what to do with itself when presented with a worm. Petra passed me some cranberry juice after topping up her own, and I offered the troops in Sahid's direction a top-up. They didn't hear me.

'Babe, do you want a drink?' I asked the host as I approached him in a servile manner. My use of the word 'babe' made me realise that I was starting to relax. The girly girl perched on his knee passed me the glass that was on the table right in front of him. God forbid he should lift a finger.

'Here, have a line,' he said. 'You didn't do your line!' He was clearly excited. I whiffed another, deeply, then sparked another cigarette; putting my head back, I watched the smoke rise as I exhaled. I smoked like a man who had been read his last rites when I sniffed and drank.

Petra had taken off her shoes as, not surprisingly, her feet were hurting. She was wearing Perspex-heeled 'stripper shoes', as I called them, much to her annoyance. She always reminded me that they were Pucci but I didn't care who had designed them: Pucci, Gucci, whatever, they were hideous. 'The gear's fuckin' strong,' she said, staring at me, searching for a response as she tried to compose herself.

'Yeah, I know. Good, innit?' I grinned. I was feeling sexy and embracing the sensations that were flooding my veins. 'You should have a neat brandy. That'll level you out,' I said, the voice of experience.

Stress was written on Petra's face as the cocaine took hold; she often showed it with a slight frown between her eyes. She'd soon be all right. I wasn't worried; my own high was coming on nicely and I was feeling sociable and confident. One of the girls turned up the music, encouraging Charlie to start dancing with a girl whose name I simply couldn't remember. The nameless girl was up herself and was clearly one of those hard-nosed bitches, full of attitude, which quite honestly I found intimidating, so I avoided her.

The two girls looked sensuous and graceful as they danced like pieces of ribbon entwining in a warm, tropical breeze. I was captivated.

HOOKED

As I watched them, I felt a hot hand on my behind, up my layered black high-street skirt, firmly rubbing my squidgy brown bottom.

CHAPTER 3

'Come. Sit. Talk to me,' the ugly brother breathed in my ear. *Shit, here we go.* 'You don't have panties on, huh?'

Panties? What an awful word. I cringed, but turned to face him, putting my French-polished, nail-extensioned hand on his face. 'Of course I do.'

'I don't feel anything. Let me see.'

There he was, wanting me to prove that I had knickers on. *Fuck*. Not showing him anything, holding a vodka cranberry in one hand and the oaf in the other, I led him to one of the velvet sofas that I'd eyed up on arriving at the house. We sat down. I sat forward, with one hand on his tracksuit bottoms. On his feet he had a pair of bizarre white leather pointy slippers, which looked ridiculous.

I tried to put some space between us, smiling through gritted teeth, reminding myself of the cash I'd be getting at the end of this ordeal – the 'gift' as many punters liked to call it. Some guys preferred to describe the exchange in a way that made it more palatable for them; it was easier for their pride to pretend that they were doling out favours rather than admit they were simply paying for sex.

'So, tell me about yourself,' sleazed the brother.

Oh, fuckin' great . . . why do these guys always ask this? They didn't care, plus it was none of their business. It wasn't as though I was going to tell him the truth: 'Well, since you ask, I've actually got a cocaine habit. I'm an alcoholic. I left my husband and I've got a boyfriend. Oh, and, by the way, I'm prone to bouts of depression. Over to you now, sweetheart. What's the story with you and your stinking attitude, and, tell me, why are you dressed as though your clothes were found sitting outside a charity shop? And can you *please* explain why you have those hideous things on your feet?'

Instead, I smiled sweetly, avoiding his gaze, and, nursing my drink with both hands, asked him what exactly he wanted to know.

'How old are you?'

'Twenty-one.'

I was 24. I knew he'd want to think that I was very young and naive and that I'd stumbled into this line of work by accident, to pay for a degree in something pretty like jewellery or bag design, that I was a lowly student just trying to get by. He wouldn't want to know that I was a cynical and experienced, albeit young, woman who'd had this same conversation with the likes of him more times than I wished to remember.

I could say anything to him; he wouldn't be listening anyway. We both understood the reason I was there, so instead of attempting to airbrush 'normality' into the situation, it would have been easier and more honest just to fuck.

'Are you turned on? Sweetie, are you going to show me those panties?' he asked me, rubbing my thigh. I could feel his glare burning into the side of my face. My mind was racing and I just wanted to be away from him. *Am I turned on? Am I turned on? What a loser!* 'Take a look in the mirror, mate, and ask me that again,' is what I'd have liked to have said, but instead I kissed his hairy top lip and said in a seductive voice, 'Darling, of course I'm turned on. You turn me on.' I smiled to myself, wondering how I'd managed to say the words without laughing or slapping him or both – but this was my job.

I manoeuvred my head away from his face and suggested that I get him a drink, just so I could fill up my own.

'Yes, but hurry!' he responded.

'Two minutes!' I said, with no intention of hurrying.

'You all right, babe? How're you feeling?' I asked Petra, who'd come over for a catch-up.

'Yeah, levelling out a bit now, bunny.'

'That's good. I'm trying to find the Rémy Martin for fuckface over there. God, I feel wasted. Am I not looking properly or is it not here?'

I was lost in a cocaine haze. 'It's there,' Petra chuckled, pointing to it right under my nose.

I started watching Charlie and the other girl grinding against each other; they looked sexy and clearly felt so, as their lips were locked and their hands were fondling each other's breasts. The Aussie girl was wearing a chiffon top and her prominent nipples, perched on a pair of tiny boobs, were jutting out waiting to be sucked. Her dance partner dutifully obliged. Sahid noticed the girls smooching and he went over and put a hand on each of their lower backs, an unspoken signal for one of them to start kissing him.

I bent down and, without asking, helped myself to a line that was already racked up on the table. I poked Petra, who was reapplying her Juicy Tubes lip gloss, in the back. She sniffed and left to go to the loo.

Sahid was in an embrace with Charlie, while also touching up the girl with no name. The two girls were now dancing in their underwear and he called me to join them. The arrogant girl I was wary of walked past me as I went expectantly towards the others. I'd forgotten all about getting the brother a drink. Sahid told me to take my top off, which I did, and he told Charlie to kiss me, which she did. I was nervous despite being wasted. Kissing girls and licking snatch weren't top of my list of things to do before I turned 30. I had only ever attempted to be with a woman once before, during a job, and that was a memory I preferred to forget. Charlie started nuzzling my neck, while I self-consciously put my hand in her hair and started stroking her head. Feeling awkward, I threw my head back, pretending that I was fully engaged in the performance.

My heart was racing and after a few long moments I became aware that only Charlie, Sahid and I were left in the room. I didn't want to be there. The build-up to paid sex was usually worse than the actual fucking because I didn't know what to expect from the guy, and, in this case, the girl. I never felt the same anxiety about free sex; usually drunkenness prevented nerves. Once a punter began touching me, I would be able to assess what kind of sex it would be, then I'd know if I would be able to allow myself to enjoy it or if it was going to be a horrible effort. It wouldn't be too bad with a guy like Sahid, even if his technique was rubbish, because he was young and good-looking, but even if he was a good fuck, I was determined not to be seen to be genuinely getting off on it, not in front of another woman. I'd feel too ashamed. But if I'd been with the brother, hell, it would've been an uphill struggle – he resembled a bulldog licking a thistle.

'I don't do women,' I'd say to the agency boss whenever it was suggested, but this job had come through one of Petra's contacts. However much I'd admired Charlie's pretty face and fit physique, the thought of burying my head between her legs did absolutely nothing for me. In fact, it did just the opposite: it made me feel ill.

'You OK?' she asked me quietly as Sahid dimmed the lights further.

I was unable to hide the crinkle in my nose.

'Do you do girls?'

'Er, no. Not really. I'm not used to it, you know.'

'No probs, sweetie, I'm just going to pretend, and you do the same, OK?'

This was going to be difficult. Charlie squeezed my hand. We smiled at each other. Her humanity touched me; she suddenly became more than just a hooker. The girl was all right, clearly sensitive and empathic. Whores judge whores too, you know – and usually pretty harshly. But Charlie had proved herself to be just like me: an ordinary woman with an unconventional job.

Sahid had already checked out. His eyes were raging: show time. High and horny, all he wanted was to fuck. I dropped my skirt and got into character. Jasmine came to life as I took the guy's shirt from out of his trousers while standing behind him. Charlie was kissing him and rubbing his crotch over his jeans. Without a word, we both swapped positions and enveloped him with the movement of four exploratory hands.

His jeans were off and he lay on the carpet, where we joined him. My ears were ringing and my head was buzzing. 'Do you like that?' Charlie asked him. 'Do you like sucking on my titties?' She was genuinely getting off on the power trip of seeing him out of his mind with excitement, with her boobs shoved in his face. She swung her body off Sahid's chest, turned around, moved up to his head and started kissing him upside down.

I looked towards his mound of pubic hair, to see the state of his cock, and a sly, relieved smile crept across my face. He couldn't get it up! *Perfect*. The cocaine had worked its magic. I sighed with relief, then suddenly I remembered that we hadn't yet done the girly thing. *Shit*. My anxiety levels rocketed again. There was no way Sahid was going to let us off that easily; it would probably be the highlight of his evening.

I rubbed his limp cock and his balls, which were far too big for the size of his penis, even if it had been erect, but I knew that there was no way this little beauty was coming to life. I could just faff around and make some 'mmm' sounds, make him think I was involved. But what exactly was the point? It wasn't my fault his knob was flaccid. I sneaked a look at my watch; 40 minutes to go until I could take my cash and run. *I can get through this. Easy.*

Charlie asked limp dick to repeat what he had just mumbled. She then raised herself onto her knees. She was wearing full white knickers, which I remember I found understated yet raunchy. She pulled them to one side as she sat on Sahid's face, feeding him her cunt. Despite being high, I was embarrassed, but Charlie was not remotely self-conscious. We grinned at each other. I didn't know what to do with myself. I took his penis in both hands, eager to appear as though I was actually contributing to our charade. The moans and sighs Charlie was emitting sounded convincing and within a couple of minutes she let out a loud groan. For a few seconds, she wavered on and off Sahid's mouth, giving the impression that her clitoris was too sensitive to be touched after her intense climax. Acting or not, she did it well.

She told him that it had been 'amazing', then stood up, smirking. Sahid sat bolt upright as if coming out of a trance. I stopped toying with his bits and that was that.

'I'm going to have a line! Come on! Let's have a line! Let's have two! Come on, come on!' he said frantically, as he headed towards his comfort zone: the table and chairs. Sahid and I sniffed and drank, then sniffed again. I noticed, even in my state of inebriation, that Charlie wasn't doing either, which I found really odd.

I went to the loo to call a cab. Thirty minutes. Rubbing my nose, which was stinging now, I went back into the sitting room, where round two was about to commence.

'Where have you been?' Sahid asked. I was surprised he'd even noticed that I'd disappeared. 'I want you to kiss and I'll watch.' He was wagging his finger between the two of us. My heart sank. He said he wanted to watch Charlie go down on me. Poor girl was doing all the work, but I wasn't complaining. I lay down, Charlie followed and Sahid slumped into his chair, legs splayed. He looked out of it. He was fucked. That was good. He wouldn't know exactly what was going on, allowing Charlie and me more scope to act during our two-minute porn scene.

She obviously knew what she was doing as she moved towards my face as if to kiss me, her hair obscuring Sahid's view. She used the same trick when she put her head between my legs, so the guy didn't have a clue that nothing was happening. I made a few moans and that was it. I didn't even think he warranted some faked orgasmic convulsions since he was visibly wasted. I looked at him as he clung pitifully to his tiny cock. Show over.

HOOKED

My heart rate started to decrease as Charlie and I stood. I got dressed, telling them that I had to leave because I had a taxi booked. When Charlie chose to go was her business. I'd done my time. Once it's over, it's over. However rude it might have looked, right then I didn't care. The four hours were up and I was off.

I took my envelope from Sahid and dropped it into my handbag. It would seem ungracious to count the money in front of the host; it wasn't the done thing with seriously rich clients. Any discrepancy and Petra's contact would sort it out. I suddenly felt desperate to leave the house. I would stop all this very soon; it was only for now. But already 'for now' had lasted too long.

Inside the taxi, I peered at the cash; new £50 notes. I was heading home more than a grand richer. 'How was your evening?' the taxi driver asked me.

'Not bad. Not bad at all,' I replied, grinning, clutching my bag as if my life depended on it. I'd managed to get through two jobs in one night without having full sex. But, believe me, I certainly made up for that on other occasions.

CHAPTER 4

I had no idea, on the morning of 28 May 1982, that my mother's glistening, tear-soaked, black skin would be my last memory of her. I turned around to wave, and she waved back as an air hostess gripped my wrist and led me away.

That was the last time I ever saw my mum.

The stewardess marched me through Lusaka airport in silence and eventually she popped me onto the plane and into a seat, alone. I didn't understand what the hell was going on around me. I was frightened, but I didn't cry. *Where is my mummy? Who are these people? What is this thing I'm sitting inside?* I came from a tiny African village, so aeroplanes and air hostesses didn't feature heavily in my vocabulary and certainly not at all in my experience.

That day, one week after my fifth birthday, was a turning point in my life. The last words I heard from Mummy were 'Be good for Daddy', spoken in Lozi, our tribe's language. I spoke no English at the time.

*

My mother, who worked as a teacher, met my white, English father when she took a job at the same school where he worked. By the time they met, my father had already been living in Zambia for a number of years, teaching in a town in the middle of nowhere. The way I've understood it, it all sounds a little Mills & Boon, but that's the story Daddy tells, and if it is invented, it really doesn't matter.

My mother and my father married quickly and were divorced within a year. Daddy was 49 years old, Mummy, I'm guessing, around 24 when their 12-month marriage failed.

Constance left her English teacher and married a Zambian lorry driver. She and my father had not had a baby, and she needed a child to gain respect as an adult within her community. Now her hopes lay with her second husband. Very little time had passed when my mother's family heard the news that Constance was pregnant. Finally, the whispers surrounding my mum's fertility and the fears that she'd been cursed by spirits were silenced.

Of course, it was cause for celebration: my grandmother's youngest daughter, my mother, was about to have a baby, the baby she'd waited so long to produce. No doubt no one felt anything other than joy when a healthy baby girl was finally born. Now that my mother and her husband were regarded as mature, they finally moved into their own space within her family's compound. No one, including my mother, it seems, suspected anything unusual about the baby's caramel skin tone. It would only be a matter of time until my skin darkened to a rich dark brown colour that matched my mum's and her husband's complexion.

Let's face it, what woman would question the paternity of her baby because she'd had just one indiscretion with her ex-husband? And, come on, if Mummy did question who the father of her child was, she probably dismissed the thought. After one night of lust? Surely not.

Time ticked by and my skin did not darken; eyebrows were raised. Village gossip spread and my mother's fidelity was questioned. Everyone knew she had been married to a white man who had moved far away to start a new life after she divorced him.

'The child's colour will change soon enough,' she said. Fifteen months passed and I still did not match my mother's skin tone. She'd been caught red-handed. The baby was mixed race. Nothing could hide that. One of my parents was obviously white, and it certainly wasn't my mum. It was obvious to everyone that she'd had a liaison with a white man, and more than likely it had been her ex-husband. Now, there's being caught, you know, snooping through your partner's pockets – and there's being *caught*. There was no denying her situation.

It took Mother more than a year to accept that I wasn't her husband's child. Of course, he left her, but still she was desperate to salvage her marriage. Her only option was to get rid of the evidence. Her marriage was in tatters, as was her standing within her community. Something had to be done, so she sent me to live with my dad, who didn't know I existed until I arrived at his front door.

People talk, as we all know, and especially when there is little else to do for entertainment except gossip. The poor girl was left with little choice but to leave town, despite her sending me away. In 1970s Zambia, a male-dominated country, a woman known to have cheated on her husband was rewarded with instant excommunication from polite society. My mother's family were country folk; the shame heaped on them as a result of my birth would have been more than they or Mummy could have borne if she and I had stayed. Such things mattered greatly. So began the back and forth between my father's colonial home and my mother's poverty-stricken residence. God only knows how she explained the little girl who made the occasional visit. I was too young to know what she told the locals.

Mother and Father lived roughly 250 miles apart. Whenever I went to visit her home in the Western Province, Dad would drive me halfway and Mum would take a bus to a meeting point, pick me up and take me back to her place.

Mum had one room within a compound, a communal living area in a square formation with each room facing inwards. People cooked outside, there was no electricity and no running water, except for one outdoor pump, and our only furniture was one bed. A family lived in each of the rooms, and in the dusty centre of the square was one shower, which was shared by everyone.

HOOKED

My very first memory is of sitting as a toddler in the slime watching my mum take a shower. I remember staring at the bush that grew between her legs and looking at her large breasts. She had a strong, muscular frame and was a handsome woman with dark, mahogany skin, big hips and a short afro; she was 5 ft 8 in., a little shorter than I am.

I remember her clearly, moments suspended in the abyss of time. She was distant and unaffectionate. She made me sleep on the stone floor while she slept in what appeared to me to be a huge bed, her head propped up on a stack of pillows, and I hated her for that, especially when my half-sister was born and was allowed to sleep in the bed with her.

I craved to be at Daddy's house, where we had electricity, running water, a cook and a maid, who also doubled as my nanny, where I had friends and there were monkeys swinging around in mulberry bushes in our garden. There, at Daddy's, I got cuddles, lots of cuddles, tickling, kisses, laughter, ice cream and Coca-Cola in glass bottles. There, I'm sure I felt loved. My father and I didn't speak the same language, but the maid and the cook, who were at our house every day, both spoke Lozi. They also spoke English, so they would interpret for us, but Daddy and I usually used gestures.

Dad's house had all the usual amenities that we take for granted in Britain, except a television; my father always preferred to read or listen to music. He was an academic whose entire life was dedicated to learning and, until I took a major life detour, he tried to instil many of his values in me.

My father returned to England after 27 years teaching in Africa, aged 54. He was ready to hang up his mortarboard. He wanted to enjoy life, find himself a partner, travel, go to art galleries and discuss the latest offerings from Opera North. Instead, he had to look after a mop-haired, brown-skinned five-year-old daughter, straight out of the African bush. I was cold when I arrived in London wearing just a cotton summer dress and with no luggage. Mum had put me on the plane ten hours earlier as Kumba, and the air hostess handed me over to Daddy as Kate, the name he'd chosen for me before leaving Zambia. Armed with an English name but not yet a British passport, I was about to begin my new life.

I had no idea what was going on. I had no concept of where I was and, since my father was unable to speak Lozi, explaining proved impossible. We communicated using drawings and our own sign language until I started school and, with the help of a private tutor, learned English.

For the first four weeks after I landed in May 1982, Dad and I stayed at the house of a lifelong friend of his. She was to become my Auntie Flo. He'd been staying with her for a few months before my arrival. Eventually, he bought our first house, on a leafy, suburban road in a seaside town in North Yorkshire.

Auntie Flo was an old-fashioned former schoolmistress who had never married or had children. Although my friends were terrified of her, she was immensely kind and she loved me. I never regarded her as a surrogate mother (which I think she would have liked), but we were very close nevertheless. The thing is, I never lost sight of the fact that I already had a mum; no one talked about her, there were no photos on display, but still I never forgot her. Constance became my secret, to be shared with no one. I had no idea where she was, but in my mind she was with me every day of every month of every year.

CHAPTER 5

In February 2001, Petra and I had placed adverts in the local rag. Mine read: 'New girl in town. Cleo, an exotic temptress that will make all your desires come true.' Classy.

I suspected Petra had done some whoring, in between stripping, while she was supposed to be working for her uncle, doing paperwork at his antiques warehouse. She'd never confirmed it, though, and I didn't want to embarrass myself or her by asking. One thing was for sure: if she had already worked as a hooker, she'd probably never really given it up. The money is addictive and Petra valued possessions. In retrospect, she was living a fantastic lifestyle, with a nice flat in Westbourne Park, a sports car and a Dolce & Gabbana wardrobe.

When we decided to start escorting, Petra and I had been hanging out together for less than a year, after meeting in a bar in Putney. We'd started chatting in the toilets, as drunk people do. She complained to me that she wanted to stay out and go to a club but the guy she was with didn't. I was in the bar alone, doing my usual trick, pretending that I'd gone in there looking for someone, then tagging along with a couple of random guys for company. Staying in the house alone with just my mind for company was unbearable for me. Once Petra and I started talking, we quickly established a mutual love of a good time and stayed out together for the whole night, and quickly became friends.

The same night my advert went into the paper, I was knocking on my first punter's door. I was very drunk. I don't remember having sniffed coke, but I do remember Petra's advice: 'Pretend it's a one-night stand. It'll be easy that way.' Like I said, I never asked her if she'd previously fucked for money, not before we had the giggly conversation agreeing to try our luck at hooking, but it was pretty evident that she'd tried it *at least* once.

I'd slept around a lot, so what could be so difficult about having a one-night stand with a bit of cash thrown in? It would be 'easy', apparently. The main difference between a one-night stand for free and sex for money was that the prospect of random sex had never left me quaking with anxiety as I was that evening. I was overwhelmed with fear, even though I was tanked up. It didn't seem fun, as I'd thought it would be when Petra and I were plotting it; even when she'd answered the phone to the punters in an over-the-top seductive voice, I was in nervous hysterics. I had not been brought up to believe that sex was bad or wrong, and I certainly hadn't received any religious indoctrination about prostitution being wicked or sinful. Daddy and I had never really talked about sex – apart from when I was 16 years old and he warned me that if I ever got pregnant, I couldn't expect him to bring up another child at his age.

So why the acute fear, just because I was going to get paid for use of my vagina? Perhaps it was because I didn't have any idea who the guy who would answer the door was. Maybe it was because society's belief that I was about to do something unutterable had managed to filter through to me. Or maybe somewhere inside I felt that my choice had been taken from me. Whatever the reasons, I was overwhelmed with jitters. But desperation forced me on. After I left my first husband, I had nada, zilch, nothing. I was totally broke. I had no savings, no bank account; I hadn't had one of those since I'd taken a loan that I hadn't repaid. I had no cash stashed under my bed or hidden in my purse. Even the cigarettes I'd been smoking had been bought using Petra's money.

When I'd been with my husband, before running off two weeks after our wedding, it hadn't been like this. But I'd felt compelled to leave him because the notion of being married to him was just silly. Our union had been about not love and respect but insecurity and my fear of being alone. Although he was kind and he cared about me, I'd always known we would never be together in a long relationship, never mind marriage; he was about three inches shorter than me for a start. I had left our flat and moved into a grotty bedsit with nothing except clothes and an obsession with cocaine and alcohol. These were the consequences. I had no time to find a legitimate job; besides, I had so little confidence that it didn't even cross my mind to try. I had zero pounds and an equal amount of pence, and I had to act fast.

I told the punter he was my first. I don't remember his response; his focus was on wrapping my pussy around his face as quickly as possible. He seemed frantic. It was surreal, not frightening, although I felt I was holding my breath the whole time, waiting for it to be over. That was my first lesson about hooking. When the client calls, he wants you with him as quickly as possible, because – yep, you guessed it – he's got the horn. They call because they want to screw someone, and straight away.

I left my first client elated – 80 quid richer just for that. Petra had been right.

The next morning, 'just for that' didn't seem so simple. I awoke to the horror of what I'd allowed myself to do. The shame was immeasurable. Between that and one of my typically relentless hangovers, I was just about ready to top myself. Sharp pains pulsated through my head. That was usual for me the morning after, but this time, strangely, I was convinced I could hear an internal voice screaming at me, berating me for allowing myself to fuck someone for cash. My heart was booming. I could barely move. I was certain I could hear a voice. I sat on the sofa and gripped my head. The voice seemed to get louder and I started to hum out loud. I was aware that it wasn't coming from outside. It was definitely inside my skull. I felt I was suffocating. The voice was female. I pleaded out loud for it to stop. Within moments, the noise in my head subsided. I was petrified. It wasn't a panic attack; I was versed in dealing with those. This was something new to me, an event that I've never forgotten and, thankfully, have never experienced again. I remember worrying for months afterwards that the voice would reappear. I also remember questioning whether it was a symptom of schizophrenia, although I don't believe now that it was.

After that, I had to drink. I had to have something, anything, to calm my anxiety. It was then that I understood that it had not just been my body that had been fucked. My mind had been too.

I wanted to speak to my dad or my close friend Jim, but Jim was a nightmare to get hold of because he refused to get a mobile phone. I desperately needed to hear a familiar voice. I felt isolated and frightened about my actions and my sanity.

I dialled my dad's number – big mistake. I got my stepmother, Elaine.

'Elaine, how are you? Are you OK?' Although she couldn't see me, I faked a smile, desperately trying to sound upbeat. My heart was still racing. I just wanted to feel loved.

'Hello, Kate.' *Fuck*. She sounded serious. 'We haven't heard from you for a while. How are you?' she asked with a sense of urgency that put me on the defensive. Why I'd thought they'd be anything other than edgy with me was a mystery. Every week they rang me and more often than not I didn't answer. I couldn't. Usually I felt too ropey or high to be dealing with my folks, so whenever I rang them, they always, without fail, suspected the worst.

'I'm OK,' I sighed. I shouldn't have called them. Now I was waiting for the inevitable conversation to begin.

'Are you still working?'

Here we go. All I could think of was the punter from the night before. I hesitated. For a moment, I wanted to bleat on about some fake office job, but I said, 'No, I'm not working right now.' I cringed. I knew Elaine wouldn't let me leave it at that. I was stressed and wanted a frivolous chat – you know, to talk about the weather or something.

'Oh dear, I thought you were working as a receptionist in the City. What happened to that job?'

'It just didn't work out . . . er . . . it was a temp job. I thought I told you that?' I'd forgotten that I was supposed to be working in the City. This was exactly why I didn't speak to them when I felt fuzzy, which was most of the time – I hated being caught out.

'No, you didn't say anything about that.' Elaine sounded despondent.

'Please stop worrying. I can hear it in your voice, Elaine.' I wanted to cut the call short now.

'What do you expect, Kate? Eh? When are you going to sort yourself out?' She sounded as if she was on the brink of tears.

I hated that question. 'Elaine, stop it! You're always asking me that.' I felt shaky. The previous night's escapades, now this . . .

'I don't know how you expect me to feel.' There was never any chit-chat between us; it was always so serious.

'Oh God, please don't make a fuss!'

'Kate, you've got to stop phoning us and upsetting Elaine.' The angry voice was my dad, who'd taken the phone from his wife. 'It's not fair. Whatever you want to do with your life is your concern, but you're not going to upset us like this. You clearly don't want our help. You go ahead and live how you want.' His voice was quivering and I pictured him looking at me sternly. I kept quiet. 'We'll stop picking the phone up to you if this continues. Do you hear me? It's gone on for too long.' I'd heard this over and over again, and there had been times when, for months, they'd exercised the threat.

'But, Dad . . .' I sniffed.

'This is going to have to stop, Kate! I'm sick of it. I've had enough!'

'I'm fucking bored of you shouting at me all the time!' I screamed back at him.

He slammed the phone down. Their defence mechanism was always to put the phone down on me, and mine was usually to lie to them, although on this occasion I hadn't. Maybe it would have been better for all involved if I had.

I was trembling as I tried to call back. They'd taken the phone off the hook. They always did that as well, and it never failed to make me feel completely isolated. My dad was my only family.

I spent most of the cash I'd earned from fucking a stranger on a gram of coke, and the rest on fags and booze. The chemicals fuelled my anger, but I was convinced I wasn't feeling anything. Then, of course, I was skint again. Once I was out of my head, and fuelled by resentment towards everyone who crossed my path, selling my snatch to another bloke who wanted to use me instead of his hand seemed almost palatable.

The problem was with the mornings. Daylight represented hell. Another day and I'd be doing it all again. I knew I would. I didn't know how not to. What else did I have? Nothing. I was lying in the bed I'd made, paralysed with anxiety from the second I opened my eyes, and as before I would *have to* drink or sniff to soften my crippling unease.

And just like that the cycle began.

*

In June that year, I moved out of the bedsit, which despite being horrible was much too expensive, and into a room in a shared flat in Putney. By now, I was managing quite well to put my marriage behind me. More money meant more booze, and more alcohol meant more charlie.

I continued hooking and, after a time, I became consumed with paranoia, usually in the depths of the night, about the safety aspects, or lack of them, that went with my job. Sometimes I'd be rigid with fear and the dangers of my reality would torment me, constantly tap, tap, tapping in my head. So

HOOKED

I decided, like an old pro, that my destiny lay with an agency and not in independent prostitution. Besides, I'd make more cash as well as being safer – or so I thought.

When I first joined the agency, I went to their offices in Earls Court and met Dean, the pimp. 'Big Daddy' was how he liked to be known; 'wanker' was how he was usually referred to. He took me to a grotty hotel by the side of a dual carriageway, near Hammersmith. The whole set-up was seedier than a third-rate B-movie. It was a place where dirty old men, like him, took drug-addled girls, like me, to have sex with them in cold, sparsely furnished, damp rooms, like this one.

I lay on my back; he pulled down my knickers and gave me head. I moaned in an attempt to speed it up. I hated punters eating me out, unless they were fit – it felt more personal than penetrative sex. I could handle jumping on a client's cock and bouncing up and down at a rate of knots, but guys I didn't fancy licking my pussy always gave me the creeps. But when masturbating, the more a guy repulsed me the more I got off on it – a little self-loathing sneaking out.

The over-eager, overweight pimp unwrapped a condom. He handed it to me to roll onto his small dick, which I remember had a grotesque amount of foreskin. I presumed this was a test to evaluate my competence. I slipped it onto his cock. He entered me. A few deep thrusts, a grunt, and it was over. I didn't climax on that occasion – but the second and last time I had sex with him, months later, I did. He lay down as I got up. Not knowing what to do, I lit a cigarette and told him that I needed to go.

'Give me a minute. I'm fucked,' he panted. His skin was glistening with sweat. He wasn't the only one that was fucked. I was fucked *off* and wanted to get out of there. I felt disgusted. I stared at him and his wobbly belly; he was gasping for air as he lay in front of me. I was convinced I could see a well of sweat sitting in his belly button. This was all so wrong.

HOOKED

'I need the money, Dean. Have you got the money?'

'Yeah, babe, give me a minute,' he answered, with his eyes closed.

Hurry up, you fucking idiot. I hated him. I'd let him use my body and now I had to hang around until he'd composed himself enough to roll off his arse and give me the money I'd earned. Agitated, I went into the bathroom and stared in the mirror, repulsed. My eye make-up had smudged. I ran water over some tissues and tried to wipe it away. I touched the skin on my chest. *Foul.* It had his sweat on it. I grimaced and called myself names under my breath. I reached for the towel to wipe myself dry, desperate to get the hell out of there.

I heard him move. Finally, he'd sat up. I went back into the bedroom. 'That was fuckin' great. I needed that,' he said. *Loser.* I hadn't done anything and he was telling me it was 'great'. I barely managed to humour him with a grin, focusing only on the cash he'd pulled out of his back pocket. He counted it, handed me £300 plus a £50 tip and asked if I wanted a lift home.

'I'll get a taxi,' I replied as I reached for the money. For a brief moment, we both held on to it, making eye contact. He started laughing, patronisingly, then let go. *Cunt.* I felt humiliated. *Fuck him.* It was time for me to go. I grabbed my coat, put my feet into my shoes and scurried towards the door.

During this time, the only thing keeping me attached to any semblance of normal life was Jim. My Jimmy. The only supportive constant I'd known during my adult life, my 'Mr Big'. Jim and I had met when I was 19 years old and he was 27. For years after we met, he called me virtually every day. He always brought an exuberant energy to life's problems and he was, without a doubt, fiercely on my side. I needed that. Someone I could rely on, someone who never turned his back on me. He was probably the only person I trusted enough to expose my real pain to.

*

44

'Jim?'

'Ooh, bloody 'ell, this is a surprise. You callin' me for a change, pet. Are you OK?'

'Well, I thought I'd balance things out a bit by calling you.'

'It'll take more than that, kidder.'

'Very funny. No, I'm not OK, actually.'

'Oh, sweetheart. What is it, eh?' He was used to these phone calls.

'I'm really unhappy, Jim.'

'Have you spoken to your dad or something? What's happened?'

I winced at his first question. It made me sad that he was so quick to link my unhappiness with my having spoken to my father. The breakdown of communication between my dad and me was a constant source of pain. 'No, nothing's really happened. You know, just the usual stuff. And yeah, course, my dad's upset. He's always pissed off with me, you know that.'

'Fuckin' hell, Katie, you should save yourself the heartache of seeking their approval all the time and accept that they don't like how you live.'

'Jim, please, not now . . . Who said I was seeking their approval?'

'You always are, darling, and he always disapproves of what you do. They'll never agree with how you live your life.'

'What do you mean how I live my life?'

'Katie, you know what I mean. Your dad will never be happy till you get a job and stop drinking and whatever else you do down there in Shitsville.' That made me laugh; Jim hated London. He was one of those people proud to be Yorkshire. Some of that pride was genuine, some was manufactured to get up my nose. Jim's whole family had been born and had grown up in the North, and they'd 'worked in the fields till their hands bled', according to him. That was something he relished telling people in an exaggerated Yorkshire accent.

'Look, sweetheart, I know it's difficult for a little Pushkin like you, isn't it, eh?' He often talked to me as if I were a five year old and I liked it, when it suited me. 'Pushkin' was a name that he'd made up. He'd always called me either 'pet' or 'Pushkin'. 'C'mon, wipe your tears away. You're too pretty to be crying.'

'I don't know what to do . . . I don't know how to make my life OK and make Dad happy.'

'Well, maybe you can't make him happy at the moment. Maybe they have to realise that you have to do the things that you feel compelled to do, even if they don't like it. I mean—'

'Oh, please, Jim, don't go on.'

'Look, I don't like the things that you do to yourself, but I realise that there's nothing I can do to stop you from doing them.'

'Oh, shut up, you big drama queen.'

'The least you can do is let me speak, for fuck's sake.'

I was feeling anxious and queasy. Arguing with my only ally wasn't too clever – but somehow I always knew Jim was on my side. He'd never shown me otherwise, even after I'd broken his heart when I left him all those years previously.

'You have to find your own way.'

'God, you sound like my father.'

He ignored me. 'But, Kate, don't impose yourself on your dad, eh? He's getting old now. He doesn't need the hassle.'

'I know he doesn't!'

'And something else . . .'

'What now? Oh, and, by the way, before you carry on, I don't impose myself on them. They don't give me a fucking chance to.'

'I know, pet. They don't know how lucky they are. I take the brunt of your bloody shenanigans now, eh?' he said, trying to be light-hearted.

'Oh, piss off, will you?' I felt tearful, but anger prevented me showing it.

'I'm joking. Fucking lighten up, you miserable cow! Listen, I'm at work, so I'll talk to you tomorrow.'

'Don't bother,' I snapped.

'Shut up, Kate. I'm calling you tomorrow whether you like it or not. Dry your eyes and——'

'I'm not crying,' I croaked, my voice cracking with emotion. I was all over the place. I felt so damned lonely.

Jim's tone completely changed. 'Come on. Everything'll be all right. I still have faith in you, sweetheart. I don't know why,' he laughed, 'but I do, and that counts for something, eh?' I couldn't hold the tears back any longer. 'Look, if a genius like me can still love you like I do, throughout all the drama and traumas you've been through, you must have something special, eh? Because it's no secret that I'm an artistic genius, our kid. There's no denying it.' He sighed theatrically and then started laughing at himself. I tried to smile through the tears and managed a pretend snore. I'd heard this so many times before. 'You know I'm many things, pet, but——'

'Stupid isn't one of 'em,' I said, finishing his sentence, mimicking him. I wished he was there with me. I wanted a cuddle.

'Oi! You cheeky sod!' he said, laughing. I chuckled half-heartedly, but my mind was on my dad. 'Go buy yourself something nice to eat, eh? And get yourself a magazine or read a book and put your feet up. Try and relax.'

'When do I ever read books?' I sniffled.

'Aye, you've got a point there, Pushkin . . . with the attention span of a goldfish, it might be difficult for you, eh?' I loved hearing his almost childlike giggle. 'Anyways, I gotta go. Listen, don't worry about things. Everything'll be all right.'

'Are you sure?' I didn't want him to put the phone down. I didn't want to feel alone again.

'Course I'm bloody sure! I love you. Never forget that, Katie, I love you. And anyway, have you murdered anyone?' Classic Jim.

'No, course I haven't.'

HOOKED

'Well, you'll be all right then. Just stop bloody worrying. I'm here for you. You should know that by now.' After all these years, his openness continued to surprise me, an emotional jolt that reminded me that I was loved. 'You'll be OK, Kate. You'll see.'

Somehow, I didn't believe that.

CHAPTER 6

When I was 19, I'd gone into rehab in Weston-super-Mare on orders from the Probation Service. I'd been living alone in Yorkshire and they'd been instructed to keep an eye on me after I'd managed to get arrested numerous times for shoplifting, which I'd been doing to supply my drug habit. In my teens, I attempted to subdue my ragged emotions using black-market prescription sedatives and sleeping pills, occasionally heroin and, of course, alcohol. These were expensive.

Heroin is not physically addictive if used sporadically, despite what some folklore will have you believe. I soon found out, though, that if you use it for two or three days consecutively, the body begins to need it. Before it rapes you of your freedom, there are warnings: vomiting, itching, an inability to be productive. But even if you avoid physical addiction, the dreamlike state it induces can be too bewitching for a person who seeks total freedom from reality, causing psychological dependency. Let there be no doubt: this shit will wipe the floor with you and take you hostage. People call it smack for a reason.

After rehab, I was advised to go and live near Dad and Elaine, in Yorkshire, which I did. That was when I met Jim.

It was August 1997 when I returned from my stint in rehab, and Dad and Elaine were apprehensive. During the years leading to my institutionalisation, I had turned into a renegade and destructive teenager, but still, after I graduated from the treatment centre they allowed me to stay in their house. Elaine announced within a few weeks that she had found me a place of my own; they'd pay the bills and help me financially for the first year. Luckily for them, Elaine had the keys, so I could move in immediately. I was crapping myself and so were they. The thought of me living nearby, permanently, unnerved them.

I moved into the modern, clean but cold room and tried to make the most of an oppressive environment. Drying my clothes after Elaine had washed them proved to be a depressing task. We had a system: Saturday morning, approximately 10 a.m., I'd leave a hold-all outside my flat door for them to pick up. They'd wash the stuff, and return it for me to dry, which was difficult in one room with no radiators. I was afraid to complain, worried that if I did, they would refuse to assist me further and stop bringing round the occasional bag of Netto food. I had to keep quiet and praise the generosity they lavished on me. I understood well that their fears about my stability would make them close ranks at any sniff of 'bad attitude'. I knew the consequences if I didn't behave according to their rules: silence.

The treatment centre I'd been in was based on the 12 Steps of Alcoholics Anonymous, so I was advised to go to AA or NA meetings as follow-up after rehab, which I did, although I was unclear about what was going on. I wasn't happy and I still felt completely alone. The main cause of my self-medicating – my mum and my feelings of loss in relation to her – had never been broached while I'd been in rehab.

Not long after I moved into my new flat, the inevitable relapse happened. I was going to the meetings, and I thought I'd asked for help from people who were willing to support me from the fellowship, but after six months of rehab, the only thing that was really different was that I wasn't drinking or popping sleeping pills. So what? 'Any idiot can stop taking drugs and drinking. Staying stopped is the problem,' the therapists had barked in my treatment centre. They followed that philosophy and also taught: 'Drinking and drugging are a symptom of a greater problem. To start recovering from addiction problems, be they physical or psychological, the root of the problem must be dealt with.' Which meant I had a long way to go.

Shortly after leaving treatment, I blew my flimsy sobriety during a solitary wine binge at home. The guilt was horrific.

I began again to court the demons that had thrived on my unhappiness. Initially, however much I drank, I didn't get drunk. I drank with gusto, consuming every type of alcohol. I convinced myself that I would only indulge for a short time, and therefore I wanted to taste everything that I'd been missing. I couldn't stop mentally beating myself up for letting myself – and of course Daddy – down. But gone were the days of perfect daughter-dom; by that stage, disappointing my father was something I was accustomed to. He'd known about the booze and the pills. He knew everything, but he couldn't know about this relapse. Everything would be all right, I decided, if I avoided drugs.

My fall from grace had to be kept secret. As for rehab and the counsellor who made regular contact with me, I'd just lie or, better still, avoid speaking to her. I continued drinking alone and cursing my life, until I'd justified to myself my violation of the 12 Steps. It didn't take long for me to raise myself out of solitary confinement and become reborn, angrier, more bitter and feeling more of a failure. I hated myself.

*

By the time I reached my teens, my relationship with my father was already in tatters, and it fragmented further when I was 14. We'd struggled to understand one another for at least a year as a result of my acute mood swings, virtual inability to stay awake due to depression and refusal to do schoolwork. I began to see my school's psychologist, who referred me to a psychiatrist. There had been a sudden shift in my temperament and my attitude was dismissive. I didn't see the point in anything, including living. I questioned everything. I disliked everything. I felt a growing anger towards my father, whose approval I continually strove for. I could no longer cope with attempting to be a perfect and obedient daughter. My obsession with making Daddy happy was driven by my fear that he would leave me if I wasn't everything I believed he wanted me to be. My covert hatred towards my mother had also begun to bleed into my behaviour and I began to drink alcohol when I was alone.

It had become apparent to everyone who knew me that something was amiss, but little or nothing was resolved through my consultations with the psychiatrist because I felt unable to be honest and was confused about my feelings. I was eventually signed off school and my father was broken. I don't remember being prescribed anything then. That came later. I was aged 16 when my doctor prescribed Valium for anxiety. Of course, I abused it, along with street drugs such as speed and ecstasy. These drugs didn't induce what I was searching for. Uppers weren't my thing at the time. I needed my mind to be quietened; I wanted peace, not energy. My mind was too busy even without stimulants. So when I was introduced to prescription drugs, courtesy of my doctor, I settled down to a committed relationship with sleeping pills. My desire to remove myself from my feelings had become a compulsion and I had no choice but to nourish it.

At home, my father was witless with worry. The two of us rarely talked. I preferred my own company. In my isolation, the brooding resentment towards my mother ripened. Dad and I never talked about her, ever. I only knew her name. As I grew up, it had been made clear to me that the subjects of Zambia and Mum were out of bounds. Daddy didn't instil this in me maliciously – but the silence and awkwardness that cast its shadow if ever I broached the subject gave me a clear sign that this was a no-go area. I adhered to this unspoken rule, fearing that Daddy would leave me if I did or said anything that displeased him. So Mummy became my dirty secret.

Once I'd begun drinking again after rehab, I got friendly

with my neighbour, Aaron. He was in his late 20s. Our bond was based on booze and uncompromising opinions on everything. He drank every night around the locals and I joined him. He knew everyone and he talked a lot, so he was good company for a lone star gliding through unknown territory.

There were seven pubs for approximately three thousand residents. It was a North Yorkshire town with few jobs and no other entertainment, so there was no shortage of folk getting pissed, arguing, fighting and causing mayhem. A lot of young people lived there. So I never felt as though I didn't have anything to do – a pub visit was the solution to everything. It made a change from drinking alone. It was while I was in one of these pubs, sitting in the window drinking with a girl I'd just met, that Dad and Elaine drove past and spotted me. Thankfully, I'd also spotted them. I'd been half keeping an eye out in the same way that they were clearly looking out for me. I watched the car slow down and hid my drink on a window ledge. Elaine came to give me a message from the shop where I was working, before getting back into the car. I didn't have a mobile phone. Apparently, my father, who was astute when it came to my attempts at being sneaky, asked her if I had a drink in front of me. Elaine told him that I hadn't – and that was how Daddy's suspicions were confirmed: his girl had fallen off the wagon. He wasn't stupid. The idea of me sitting in a pub drinkless was like someone else sitting in a barber's shop and not having a haircut – unnecessary and a bit suspicious.

I avoided them for weeks and when eventually I did see them I was blasé about my relapse, explaining that I'd be all right as long as I stayed away from drugs.

'But alcohol is a drug, Kate.'

I couldn't say anything and I certainly didn't admit that I was drunk at the end of each day. Dad and Elaine had been hugely influenced by the treatment centre and the counsellors whom they'd both seen because of their anxieties about my behaviour, but I don't remember them giving me a particularly hard time about relapsing. I wouldn't have noticed anyway; I was off again, riding my own wave.

*

When out on the razz, dressed in short skirts and wedge heels, guzzling cheap wine from chipped glasses, I'd constantly hear whispers about a bloke called Jim. I didn't know him, but the more I heard that he was a 'rogue' and should be avoided, the more intrigued I became. I heard reports that he had tight curly hair and a nose that'd been broken so many times it looked like a crooked beak. 'Stay well clear of 'im, Katie,' Aaron warned – and so did the barmaids at the Frog and at the Forresters and the cashier at the local Co-op. At the mere mention of his name in the Mucky Duck, threats of expulsion permeated the air. He was barred for life, apparently.

'He's a wrong 'un,' they'd say.

'Wrong 'un, you say? Interesting,' I'd think.

I was in the Granville Arms, or 'the Grannies' as the locals called it but I never did. I despised those awful, shortened, overfamiliar names that people adopt to claim something as their own. Besides, I'd gone to this town, which was Elaine's home, not to fit in with the local traditions but merely to be nearer to my dad, who'd moved there after he'd married Elaine. Despite being raised in Yorkshire, I never felt an affinity with the place or its country folk and refused to use Yorkshireisms. My father didn't either, and that was one aspect of my upbringing that I hung on to.

That evening in the Granville was a night I will never forget. I finally came face to face with Jim . . . a thickset, mean-looking, foul-mouthed, smart-arsed white 27 year old who chastised everyone (and by 'everyone' I mean exactly that) with his sharp wit and animated gestures. No one was spared Jim's eloquent use of language. He could be (and often was) ferocious with it. He enjoyed riling people and loved to get a reaction, even a negative one. None of the usual rules of social etiquette seemed to apply to him. He was clearly clever and well read, and he outsmarted everyone. He stood firm when faced with furious revellers who were exasperated with him (and themselves) because they'd fallen victim to his merciless teasing. Although half the pub-goers enjoyed his wit, the other half hated him for it.

My first thought was that he looked too trendy to be living in that small town, my next that he was an arrogant twit but he was clearly devilishly intelligent. I'd never met anyone like Jim. He exuded contradictions and, at 19 years old, I'd already read enough to see similarities with how I imagined Oscar Wilde might have been received in his day – with both love and utter disdain.

That November evening, I had asked scores of people to my flat for a party. In a very small town, the prospect of a gathering that included booze was enticing, especially to those wanting to drink after the lock-ins had finished. Aaron assured me that there'd be heaps of people, no doubt coming to grab whatever was on offer.

Later that evening, I panicked and rushed home alone, realising that a party in my single-person bedsit was not a brilliant idea. I drew the curtains and lay on the sofa in silence, waiting for a barrage of people to knock on the door. I remember lying in complete darkness, barely daring to breathe. I braced myself for mayhem. Nothing. Not a sound. I continued to lie still, waiting for the onslaught of revellers. Still no one came bashing on my door. I was getting pissed off. Had they forgotten me? Why hadn't hordes of people wanted to come to my party? Didn't they like me? I started to feel miserable as the effects of the night's drinking began to wear off. And then, finally, I heard something. I sat up and again: *thud*. Someone outside the window was throwing stones. I sneaked over to the curtain and peeked through a gap and there stood one person: Jim. One thing was for certain, I decided: he wasn't coming in. No chance. After my encounter with him earlier that evening, I rejoiced in having the opportunity to clip his wings and tell him to go away.

'If you're here for the party, it's not happening. I'm going to bed,' I snapped out of the window.

'Open the door,' he slurred.

'Who do you think you're talking to? Go home,' I slurred back.

'I thought you were having a party?'

'No, I'm not. I just told you that.'

'Just open the door and bloody shut up, will ya? I know you want me to come in.' He laughed.

I was pissed off yet excited by his cockiness. Jim was a good-looking guy, and his wit, even though he'd been using it against people, had been noted earlier in the evening. I stumbled down the stairs to hurl abuse in his face. I don't remember the content of our exchange, but within moments he came inside. We talked through the night and the next day he took me out – to a local pub, of course. I was in awe of Jim. He was fascinating. He talked to me about life, about family, trust and friendship. He explained how he believed that nothing in life mattered except people, and that lessons could be learned from everything. He'd been travelling around southern Spain for three months, painting along the way. He told me about his plans to travel to Cameroon, just four weeks later, to draw – which he decided against once we'd met. We talked about the meaning of integrity and how, he believed, most people didn't understand the concept. He was vocal, passionate, eccentric. He told me fantastical stories about experiences I longed to be part of. For the days that followed, we talked. There was no kissing, no touching, just talking.

From that evening, our spirits were joined. I was in love with him. From that first meeting, he became my biggest influence. He helped me to appreciate that shapes could be viewed from different angles. He opened my eyes to beauty that I had never previously noticed. He offered me something that I had forgotten existed: loyalty.

Still, despite all Jim's panache, nothing and no one could subdue my hunger for excess. Surely, had we stayed together as a couple (which Jim wanted more than anything) the course of my life would have been drastically altered. Years later, I would not have become a bigamist and a drug smuggler, that was certain.

CHAPTER 7

I charged £300 per hour for use of my snatch. Dean et al. took 50 per cent. His commission was for nothing, considering I gave a driver money to sit outside the client's place as my 'security'. Let's face it, what the hell would he have done if a client had set about me with an axe the moment I was alone with him? It's not as though he'd have heard me scream from the car.

In the autumn of 2001, I was 24 years old and my luck seemed to change. I was walking along the South Bank, minding my own business, when I was attacked by a wasp that was intent on sharing my can of Diet Coke. The bloody thing wouldn't leave me alone. Panic rose, I flapped my arms around, slipped on an empty crisp packet, then started to squeal. There was no time for pride. I ran into a cafe that was by the side of the walkway, ignoring some clapping from passers-by. Inside, puffing for breath, I realised how I must have looked and rushed into the toilets to take a breather. As I left the bathroom determined to walk straight out of the door, head held high, someone called, 'Excuse me, miss.' It was Joel. I stopped. He offered to buy me a drink to help 'soothe my nerves' and we both laughed about Waspgate. I sat down, we chatted and that was the beginning of our *thing*.

He was full of himself, a handsome, permatanned, rich-looking bloke who was self-assured and mischievous. I liked that. He boasted about the success of his textile companies, the size of his dick and his luxurious lifestyle. He had qualifications in everything except cake-baking, it seemed. Although he was a show-off, his cheeky humour and boyish grin made him inoffensive. I gave him my number. Yeah, he seemed to have some dosh – but money alone wasn't enough to persuade me to dish my number out to a married man who was clearly 20-odd years older than me, not without a definite proposal of money for sex. When I was with a client, I was not the same girl as I was in my civvies, and despite my father being old enough to be my grandpa, I didn't have a thing for older men. Joel waited two weeks before arranging a date, which took place in a hotel in Knightsbridge.

Lots of flirting, too much champagne and more cocaine than was necessary later, Joel and I started thrashing out the possibilities of our having an affair. I loved his spirit, and his bond with drugs and booze was obvious, so when he suggested that I leave the room I rented and find a bigger, 'more comfortable' place to live and said he'd pay the rent – *he'd pay the rent!* – I couldn't believe it. We hadn't even had sex and he wasn't a punter – he thought I was a receptionist – so I was suspicious of his motives for all of two minutes. His justification – if he was to pay weekly hotel bills, he might as well rent me a flat – made sense. It would have been rude of me to argue and who the hell would let this opportunity pass them by? Not me, that was for certain. It felt like a business transaction, but so what? At least we both understood the parameters.

Five days after our date, I moved into a swanky one-bedroom flat in Putney, which, at £1,200 per month, cost maybe a tad more than he had originally anticipated paying – but since he'd led me to believe that he was so damned wealthy, I thought I'd try my luck. I cringed when I confessed the amount over the telephone. He didn't flinch. After his constant bragging about his wealth, his pride wouldn't have allowed him to refuse the request. He'd have looked all mouth and no trousers, and this coming from a man who kept saying, 'You'll never forget me, Katie. I'm going to change your life.' He had to come up with something big.

He paid the fees over the phone, gave his details for the

relevant credit checks and I moved in, unable to believe what was happening. The place was sexy and minimalist: a raised kitchen off the back of a spacious living area, wooden parquet flooring and everything sparkling new. There was no way that I could ever have afforded it without Joel. Well, actually, I could have afforded it, but getting my shit together to have the opportunity to move in would have been impossible. I'd have had to save months of rent to pay up front, since I had more chance of passing a kidney stone than a credit check. Considering all my money went on intoxicants, I didn't have a hope of getting my arse into gear to save what I'd have needed to move into a decent place. God knows I wouldn't even spend 20 quid on a designer foundation or perfume for myself, never mind thousands of pounds in one swoop on rent. Luckily for me, the scratty room I'd rented before hadn't required bank checks – the landlords were just pleased that some mug was paying the mortgage.

About three months after I moved into my new premises, in which I vowed never to screw punters, I got involved in the most serious relationship I had during my hooking career. It wasn't until that relationship began that my dad and Elaine started to take second place in my world.

Faye, a friend of five years, and I had just arrived back from two weeks in Gambia over Christmas and New Year. We'd spent the holiday drinking, lying in the sun and dodging my first husband's family, who still lived there.

Faye was a drinker, no doubt about that. She could certainly give me a run for my money on that score, but she never took drugs. She was from Lancashire stock and had gone to London to study law. Our initial bond was based on our Northern-ness, and after frequent meets in local pubs, a close friendship developed. She was gregarious and sociable, a buxom girl with bright-red hair and a womanly figure. She looked like a burlesque performer.

The night after we'd arrived back from holiday, Faye and I went out and got chatting to two drunken guys who insisted that we join them at a birthday party in a nearby bar.

'Jesus Christ!' Faye giggled, sipping white wine.

'What's wrong?'

'You know I'm not into men as a rule, right?'

'Yeah . . .'

'But have you seen that guy over there?'

He was tall, about 6 ft 4 in. with an athletic build; he clearly worked out. He was good-looking enough to be intimidating, with a well-defined jaw, a prominent Roman nose and longish, shaggy golden hair – a typical surfer type. He had a number of tattoos, which only added to his hotness. But the jewellery? That would have to go! He was exactly the type of bloke I thought would never look twice at me cos I didn't match his style. He kept looking at Faye and me, and I kept looking back. I liked that he wasn't afraid to hold eye contact when he caught my gaze. But how do you know for certain who the guy is interested in when you're with a mate? From a distance, I could cope with the glances, but instigate chat? You've got to be kidding. In spite of my line of work, I was shy about approaching men. I couldn't do it, not when I fancied them.

Within minutes, he was standing in front of me, big grin, his hand sticking out. 'I'm Alex.' His openness caught me off guard and I could only smile self-consciously in return. *He's fit. A nice mouth, good teeth . . .*

I watched his lips move as he talked. I could tell that he knew he was good-looking, but that was OK. I liked confident men and I guessed he'd be a good fuck. He clearly liked women – a lot – and that's obviously a good thing when it comes to sex.

That night, Alex came to my place, and he stayed for weeks. Good – very good – but inconvenient: a girl still had to earn a living. He didn't have a clue that I was a hooker or that sugar pops Joel was paying my rent. It was better that way – healthy, in fact. It would have been completely selfish and stupid to spell the details of my life out or to use the P word in relation to myself to a boyfriend. It's plainly disrespectful of a hooker to burden someone who cares about her with a statement about the nature of her employment. Expecting a man to ignore or accept the fact that the woman he is sleeping with is having sex with countless men for cash is, to say the least, naive and reckless. For the record, I don't regard my keeping shtum about my activities as dishonest, only sensible. And my decision not to tell Alex that I was married was purely down to fear – I didn't want him walking out on me. He was a young, good-looking guy; he could have chosen to be with any number of women who didn't have baggage such as a previous marriage.

I even tried to keep my disastrous relationship with my dad secret from him. I didn't want him to disapprove of any aspect of my life. He was very opinionated and my solution if anyone ever questioned me about anything that made me uncomfortable was deny, deny, deny.

In many respects, having Alex, having someone, helped ease my worries about how I was living. He was a luscious distraction. On the other hand, fucking strangers and then trying to connect emotionally with a boyfriend was massively difficult. I didn't want to continue sneaking around, but I didn't know how to change. When I met Alex, who wanted to stay with me for longer than an hour, I was determined to hold on to him.

*

I couldn't understand how people lived regular lives involving work, family, shopping, bills. The thought of having a legitimate job, paying my own rent, filled me with horror and the certainty that such a life was not possible for me. Add to that living without drugs and booze – well, that was for other people. I was an all-or-nothing girl and abstinence seemed impossible at that time.

When I'd been through rehab years before, having my safety blanket taken from me was more emotionally painful than anything I had ever been through. Did I want to volunteer myself for that again? No chance. At least not yet.

HOOKED

During the seven-day detox, my dreams were vivid: bright colours, sounds, clear visions transporting me to places and people from deep in my past that I hadn't recalled for years. My nightmares seemed more real. Night after night, horrors would scream at me and I would cry and shout back in my sleep. Then there were body jerks, muscle spasms, twitching and itching. God, the itching. My legs were covered in red marks after a few days of constant scratching. It was as though insects had crawled under my skin and were coursing through my veins. My nerves were shot to pieces. In the daytime, I experienced extremes of hot and cold. I battled to remain focused on what was happening in the groups as the drugs that had polluted my body for so many years were leaving my system.

The physical elements of withdrawal were enough to make someone either wonder what the hell they'd done to their body or to make them want to leave, to go and score, to relieve themselves of their symptoms. Usually if a patient left the centre early, they did so after they'd done their detox, when they were feeling physically well again. During detox, the Librium disorientated them enough so that they couldn't seriously consider going back out onto the streets to forage for narcotics. Generally, two or three weeks after starting treatment, people would express their desire to leave, to try to escape the worst torment of all: *themselves* and their emotions.

Imagine being tied to a lamp post naked and humiliated. Imagine people staring at you, laughing, throwing insults and occasionally poking you, just to make sure you feel as bad as you possibly can. But the reality is, the only person persecuting you is yourself and although you keep hearing a small voice telling you this, you don't believe it. How can you when you're convinced that everyone in the crowd is slinging rocks and dirt in your direction? Meanwhile, all your emotions – sadness, fear, anger, joy – are magnified by 50. There's nowhere to run. You are trapped. You feel vulnerable, confused, you question everything. The only means of eradicating your exaggerated emotions is to face the tyrant: yourself. Occasionally, something will tickle your naked skin and you will burst into hysterical laughter. You have no control of when the giggles will subside and when eventually they do you fall into a well of despair, because you're supposed to be experiencing a positive change here – not mania. And although there are glimpses of positivity, nothing is consistent. You feel clumsy. Everything you do is awkward. You berate yourself for being a fuck-up.

Imagine all this and you start to get a taste of what someone coming off drugs and booze is trying to deal with. In fact, there is no one staring at them, no one berating them, no one tickling them, no one poking them – only themselves. And when people around you are kind and supportive, it's virtually impossible to believe what they're saying. On top of that, there was guilt. Guilt about my treatment of my father, guilt about my sleeping around, guilt about my treatment of Elaine, whom I'd blamed for my dad's switch to a 'tough love' regime (which was very tough, by the way – I hate that expression now).

In the end, I relapsed shortly after completing Step 5 of the 12 Steps. Although at that time I wasn't a whore in the traditional sense, I still used men as they used me – for whatever I could get. Of course, if I went back into rehab, I would have the devastation of facing my more recent shenanigans, and I was in no hurry to do that. I was ashamed of my life and what I had turned into. I had been well educated and given fantastic opportunities, and here I was living the drug-addicted, stereotypical call-girl existence. No one who had known me when I was growing up would ever have imagined it.

Everything I did was overshadowed by the reality that I was a hooker. Who could I admit this to? I found the shame impossible to shake off. In many people's eyes, I was a loser who would never make anything of herself. Without drugs, drink, schemes, who would I be? If I could keep running and continue getting up in the morning to repeat the day before, that was my answer. My emotional experiences in rehab had been horrendous and my anxiety levels rocketed if I even thought about going back in there. Head-to-head combat with my buried feelings was not something I was ready to dive into.

I knew that simply stopping drinking, drugging and prostitution wouldn't be enough in the long term because I understood that my problems went deeper than that. Every aspect of my life was chaotic. My use of drugs and alcohol was a bid to try to deal with my feelings of inadequacy and anger about my mother leaving me and the constant anxiety I felt. Selling my body enabled me to pay for my emotional pain relief, but the physical act also subdued a desperate need for validation, despite the trauma I went through beforehand. I was sexy, I was worthwhile, I was wanted, even if it was for just one hour.

CHAPTER 8

One Friday afternoon a few weeks after Alex and I met, I went to the local M&S to pick up some of the fancy food that I knew he liked, including a bottle of bubbly, before the weekend began. At least I could make him happy, even if I made my parents miserable.

I wanted to be the dutiful girlfriend. I lived for the weekend, when I could spend two whole days with my boy. The sun was shining and the urge to get out of London gripped me as I walked quickly, head down, along the street. I desperately wanted to get away. Going on a holiday would be good for my new relationship. So what if I paid for it? It would bring us even closer together.

I wanted a drink badly but had held off. I'd already noticed that Alex had some old-fashioned, fixed ideas about women's behaviour, and boozing during the day was a big no-no. Not feminine, apparently.

Knowing he'd be at my flat (OK, Joel's flat) at any moment, I pottered around, unable to be still. I kept going into the bathroom, staring at my attempt to cover up my spots, picking the corners of my eyes and trying to decide whether the whites looked white enough. Under the bright lights, I noticed a dark shadow above my top lip. Pulling the skin taut, I decided I could manage by using a dab of concealer to mask the dark hairs growing through. I'd wax the next day.

My attention moved to my vibrant 6-ft flatmate, my yucca plant, Freddie. He'd been in my life for three years and I was proud that I'd managed to hang on to him and take good care of him during that time. I chatted to him daily and he kept all I told him secret. Freddie was fed and cleaned regularly. Regal and imposing, his presence was felt by anyone who met him – not that many people did. My home was my sanctuary. One client, who claimed to be a policeman, would come and do me from behind on my bed, and Faye would occasionally pop round. No one else, really.

Oh, actually, one other guy, with whom I'd had an endless paid coke-and-sex session that had continued at my place, had also come over. I ended our fuck-fest doing him for free – not very professional, but that was never something I concerned myself with too much. The guys were pounding my pussy – how professional can one be while getting rogered? I've no idea how someone would offer their body to be used in a professional manner. No contracts were signed and both parties were always at least partially naked.

I've always struggled with the idea of prostitution being regarded as a profession. I think it's a ridiculous concept. OK, I guess when a woman is having sex with a man she wouldn't normally bang (for free), or if she agrees to do something with a punter that she dislikes, then perhaps by a great stretch of the imagination that act might be classed as a 'professional service'. But that's only because many people go to jobs that they despise and get through them just for the money. Of course, there's a financial transaction that takes place, in the same way as there is when you're sitting in an office. But when I was ten years old and I washed my dad's car for a quid, just because I got paid didn't make me a professional car valet. And even if I were to do it now, as an adult, I wouldn't suddenly have to start filling out tax returns.

*

A light tap on the door and there he was – the man who would enable me to be free of my worries for the next 48 hours.

'You smell delicious,' he whispered as he kissed my neck. 'I want to taste you.' *No messing around with this lad.*

'Later.' We kissed hungrily and waves of pleasure pulsated between my legs.

HOOKED

'I'm feeling it. Are you, baby?' he asked me as I led him to the sofa. I nodded. He grabbed my ass and I purred. 'I'm feeling it' had become our way of saying 'I love you'. Our relationship was intense, but neither of us had said the words that hung over us expectantly.

'Let's both get in the shower,' Alex suggested. I'd already taken one shower before he arrived, but another one with my boy was not exactly an effort. Alex lathered himself from head to toe with a soapy sponge and he began massaging the bubbles onto my skin. He bent down, grabbed the shampoo, squeezed some into his hand and unhurriedly started to knead it into my hair.

'Lean back.' I did as I was told and closed my eyes as water trickled onto my face. Alex went down on his knees and without warning started to shave my snatch. He rubbed his hand in between my legs over my clitoris. It felt good, but I made no sound. He whispered to me to open my legs. I didn't argue.

I lifted my leg onto the side of the bathtub to help him as he slid two fingers inside my pussy; it was the least I could do. A little precision probing and he stood up. We snogged momentarily before he lowered his head to nibble one of my perky brown nipples. I gripped his hard, circumcised cock and started slowly tugging at it in a circular motion, my thumb brushing over the ridge of its engorged head. On my knees, a few firm sucks and without warning he ejaculated into my mouth.

Note: I don't like the taste of come. I understand that it can be a sexy thing to force yourself to swallow a bit here and there, but if I don't get warning that my guy is about to shoot his load into my mouth, in my opinion that's bad manners. I mean, that never happened with clients unless it was specifically requested beforehand, and if that happened, I gracefully declined, regardless of the extra money offered.

As I stood up, I spat his unwelcome deposit into my hand, not wanting to offend him by spitting it straight down the plug.

'Urrgh! Stop it. Don't do that,' Alex said as I tried to kiss him. 'I don't want to taste my own come.'

'Why not? You made *me* taste it.'

'That's horrible,' he spluttered, dramatically filling his mouth with water.

'I know it is,' I said.

A little later, I placed my hand on Alex's minimal chest hair while he stroked the side of my face as we lay on the sofa.

'What do you want to do tonight, babe?' I knew exactly what I wanted to do. I wanted to stay in, sniff coke, drink and exchange bodily fluids, but the suggestion couldn't come from me. Well, not the charlie bit. 'Let's go for a walk by the river and go for a drink, eh?'

Go for a walk? Bollocks! At least we're a step closer to getting some sniff if we're drinking . . . Drinks and powder went hand in hand. And I knew I wasn't the only one that thought this. Alex liked powder too. He liked it a lot, but he always played it down. Our mutual love of cocaine was the pink elephant that neither of us ever talked about.

It was a warm, bright evening, the sun glistening on the Thames behind us. Summer was round the corner. The pubs were busy, couples with their kids enjoying the breeze by the river.

'Give me a tenner, babe. What do you want? Wine?'

I nodded as I dipped my hand into the pocket of my denim skirt to give Alex the money. When he was out of sight, I called my parents. We'd had yet another row and it was time to make peace. I knew they'd never instigate it; it was always left to me. I found it virtually impossible to let go of our arguments without a follow-up conversation and since it was the start of my weekend with Alex, I wanted to smooth things over so I could get past it.

'Elaine, hi. It's me, Kate. Are you OK?' Without waiting for her reply, I continued, 'I'm really sorry about upsetting you last time.' I was pissed off. I was constantly apologising.

'I'm glad you've called us, love.' *Well, you wouldn't have called me.* 'I'm all right. Everything's OK at this end. Your father and I are going away in two weeks' time. I didn't get a chance to tell you before. It'll be good to get away.'

Away from me is what she means. 'Where're you off to?' I felt awkward but was trying hard to have a normal conversation with her.

'China. We're going to walk part of the Great Wall.'

I was jealous. 'Amazing. I'm really pleased to hear you're finally doing that. I know it's always been a dream of yours. When did you arrange it?' I tried to feign excitement.

'About two months ago.' *They never told me anything.*

There was a pause. The real topic of our talks was being avoided like a toxin. Me, my life, work . . .

'So are you definitely OK, Elaine?' I didn't know what else to say.

'I'm fine. It's your father. You know he finds all this very hard to cope with.' My heart sank.

'All *what*, exactly?' I asked harshly, knowing that 'all this' referred to me.

'Well, you know how he worries about you.'

'Yeah, I know. I'm a crap daughter, aren't I?' I tutted. 'Is he there, Elaine? Can I have a quick word, please? Alex is coming back in a minute with our dri– *coffees*, and I don't want to be chatting on the phone when he gets back.'

'Ooh, lovely! Are you out having afternoon coffee and cake?' Elaine asked enthusiastically.

'Hmmm.'

'Hello, Kate.' Dad had calmed down. Just days before, he'd been screaming down the phone that I should 'leave them alone' and that I was 'a bitter disappointment' to him. I'd been gutted.

'Hello, Daddy,' I said meekly.

'Hello, Kate . . .' He sighed. The tension was excruciating. For a moment we exchanged a silent understanding between us. Both of us were suffering, but neither of us had a clue how to restore our damaged relationship.

'Dad, I'm sorry—'

'Don't,' he interrupted me. 'Stop. I know. I know you are.' He knew that I was apologising for years of pain, not just for our last confrontation.

'Are you all right, Dad?'

'I'm fine.' Silence.

'OK, then. That's all I wanted to know.' What else could I say? 'Can I call you again sometime soon?'

'All right. Goodbye. And Kate . . .'

'Yes?' I asked expectantly.

'Look after yourself, will you?'

'Yeah . . . yes, I will.' I paused for a moment before ending the call. 'I love you.' I said the words and cringed before putting the phone down. He'd told me time and time again that he never believed it, and that wounded me. Neither my father nor Elaine had asked how I was. That was easier for everyone and, as always, more was said in our silences than in words.

Melancholy gripped me. 'What's wrong?' Alex asked, taking my hand. The kids round about us were squealing as they played. There, looking at me through long, pretty brown lashes was my man. How could I worry about anything? He was gorgeous. *Shallow? Me? Sue me.* Everything between Alex and me was good; for now, I didn't need to think about other things. *Sod it. What's the point of being down? It'll all be OK.* I wish it had truly been that easy to dismiss my sadness.

The sun was shining brilliantly through a scattering of clouds against a light blue sky. A troop of demure swans glided along the river, and occasionally a boat chuntered towards the bridge.

Alex's eyes flickered as he raised his sunglasses off his nose. I was feeling it, but 'it' on this occasion was aloneness. 'I love you.' He said it, just like that. I'm not sure how I expected it would happen the first time. I was caught off guard. 'You know that, don't you, baby?' I didn't want to hear it. Not then. I was too upset about my dad and my failings as a daughter. 'It's such a relief to finally be able to tell you how I've been feeling. I've been wanting to tell you for a while,' Alex whispered. I wished he'd be quiet.

'I love you,' I replied, fighting back tears. I didn't add 'too' – sounds cheesy, no? Tears dribbled down my cheeks. I knew that our relationship would inevitably fail; our liaison was based on lies of which only I was aware. 'Sorry, sorry,' I sniffed. 'I love you so much, it overwhelms me sometimes.' This was not the truth, the whole truth and nothing but the truth.

'Katie?' a loud, familiar voice shouted. Saved by a whisker.

Faye came bounding towards us, boobs jiggling, hair flowing, wearing a summer dress and a big smile, with her latest squeeze, Anna, draped over her. They sat down and although I was relieved to have escaped for a while the intense conversation I'd been about to have with Alex, I wasn't feeling sociable.

Faye looked radiant. Being in love was good for her. Anna was an attractive, articulate, slightly older woman with platinum blonde hair and a similar build to Faye. They looked good together.

'What do you want to drink, Anna?' I smiled after the introductions had been made. The last thing I wanted was to have to be upbeat and chatty, but for my friend's sake I had to try. I didn't want to be remembered as 'that grumpy, tall girl' by Faye's girlfriend.

Faye and Anna couldn't keep their hands off each other, which made me happy for Faye but envious that their romance seemed so simple and easy. I knew that they had just got together, but so had Alex and I, and somehow my liaison seemed far more complex. I longed to be able to have a stable relationship that wasn't based on secrets, but I knew I couldn't achieve that when I was living a secret life behind my boyfriend's back.

'I'm so tired, Faye,' I said after a while, with a fake yawn, laying the groundwork so that Alex and I could leave. Alex took my bait, relieved to be getting away from the girly chatter.

'You're going already?' Faye asked, feigning surprise, knowing that I wouldn't be there long when Alex was around.

'Yeah, I feel a bit ropey. We're going to get some food.'

I stood up and started swigging the remainder of my wine, for a moment forgetting that Police Constable Alex was there watching me. I wasn't supposed to do things like that.

'Hey, Katie, what you doing, girl?'

Oh, for fuck's sake. 'What? I'm finishing my wine before we go.' I looked at Faye and Anna, who politely tried to pretend that they hadn't noticed anything. Alex scowled and I tutted under my breath.

'Women don't drink like that, sweetheart. It looks horrible.'

'Please don't "sweetheart" me when you're pissed off, Alex . . . And, actually, women do drink like this in Yorkshire,' I grinned, glancing at Faye, looking for some camaraderie. She was still working hard on trying to ignore the argument.

'Well, you're not in Yorkshire now,' Alex said.

Whatever. He'd have to get over this.

'Come on, then. Let's go to Sainsbury's on the way back home and get some food. I'm going to cook tonight,' Alex said.

'I bought food earlier.' I felt proud that I had been organised for once.

'What did you do that for?'

'What do you mean? I thought it'd be nice if I planned ahead and got it all sorted out for us. You've been at work all day. I thought you'd want to relax and not think about it.'

I kissed Faye and Anna both goodbye.

'What food did you get?' Alex asked impatiently as we walked back to the flat.

'Stuff that's easy to cook. We don't need to fiddle about

with it. We can just bung it in the oven or the microwave. Not a big deal.'

'I wanted to choose the food.'

'What?' I scrunched up my face. 'Are you serious? Oh, sorry. I thought I was being helpful. Anyway, I've done it now. Listen, I've been thinking. Do you want to go out this evening?' I took his hand, trying to pacify him. 'Why don't we go for drinks in the West End for a change?'

'No, I can't be arsed,' came the sharp reply.

'Why not? We never go out together. C'mon, babe, let's go out. Let's get out of the flat.'

'You're always going out. What do you want to get out of the flat for? I just don't want to, not tonight. I'm going to stay in.'

'For God's sake, Alex, what's wrong? You're upset about something. It's the food thing, isn't it?' He looked at me blankly and didn't answer, which wound me up even more. 'Talk to me, for fuck's sake,' I snapped, raising my voice.

'Don't shout!'

'Well, *talk* to me then!' I didn't seem to be able to communicate with him. 'I can't do this bullshit, you know. I'm not into guessing games. They bore me. Tell me what you're in a strop about. I do everything I can to try to make you happy and you're still not happy.' I let go of his hand.

'So you're going to finish this relationship? Is that what you're saying?' He looked at me with eyes like slits. 'You're going to dump me so you can be with some dickhead that doesn't treat you right and who'll give you an apologetic fuck once in a while when you finally drag him out of his City office at nine o'clock at night?'

'What the hell are you talking about? I'm not sure if you're treating me right at the moment. And as for the "apologetic fuck"? What does that mean? I don't know what you're going on about.'

'I'm not treating you right? You've never been treated better. Tell me, who else has ever given you sex like I give you?'

HOOKED

I started laughing, dismayed. 'In case you hadn't realised, *honey*, there is actually more to life than good sex. I don't know where you get your fucking ego from Alex, but, believe me, I had great sex with other people before you came along. Don't deceive yourself into thinking that a decent rooting alone will keep a woman. That's so naive.'

'So you're saying you've had better sex with other fellas than you've had with me?'

When I thought about sex in this context, I thought about the men that I'd fucked for free. Punters never figured in my comparisons.

'Alex, I don't know why we're having this conversation. It's getting silly. This argument started with you getting arsey because I'd gone to buy us some food without consulting you first. It's even proper food. It's that microwavable cack that you usually like. What a joke.' I muttered. Even the ducks seemed to be laughing as they quacked beside the riverbank.

'No,' I said, flashing my eyes away from Alex as he tried to kiss me. He took my face in one hand and tried again. I was pissed off and feeling humiliated. *He starts a fight, then he tries to act as if nothing's happened. He's not getting away with it this time.*

CHAPTER 9

When we got back to the flat, I was still pissed off. I went over to the fridge and gave Alex a bottle of beer. 'It's the last one. Enjoy it.'

'Why didn't you buy more when you were at the supermarket?' I ignored him. 'So what did you get instead, then?' Alex asked as he rolled a spliff.

'Wine,' I said directly, not mentioning the champagne.

'I don't really drink wine, Kate. You should know that by now, babe.'

I wanted to claw his eyes out. 'Don't fucking start again, Alex!'

He started to laugh. 'That sounds like a warning.' He came over to the sofa where I was sitting.

'Yeah, it is.'

'Is my darling giving me a warning?' he asked condescendingly.

'Piss off.'

After a long silence, he suggested that we get some 'nosebag' – the word he always used for cocaine. It usually made me laugh, but not today. 'If you want . . . Whatever, really . . .' I was trying to sound as casual as possible. 'What about dinner? You don't want to eat first?'

'I'm not really hungry. Are you?'

I couldn't have given a monkey's about food. Not now drugs were on the menu. 'You're not hungry because I chose the food, right?' I said with an antagonistic grin.

'Don't start a fucking fight again, Katie. Please, not now. Just shut up, will you?' He sounded as if I was instigating rows every five minutes. Oh, and I hate anyone telling me to shut up.

'So you can say stuff but I can't, right?' I looked over at Alex, who had moved to the kitchen. 'What's that smell?' I'd smelled that burned plastic stench many times before. 'Hey, you! Have you got charlie in that spliff?'

'Yeah, do you want some?' he asked, casual as you like.

'You didn't say you had any sniff.' I jumped off the sofa.

'Well, I've only got a bit that I had left over from last night.'

'Last night? What do you mean? You had charlie when you went out with your mates? You said it was a quiet drink for that guy's leaving do.'

'It was, but I just got a gram and had a cheeky couple of lines,' Alex said, passing me the spliff. Who ever has a 'cheeky couple of lines' of cocaine? The only cheeky thing about it was him expecting me to believe what he was saying.

'When were you going to tell me that you had it?'

'Now.'

'*Now*? That's only cos I asked you.' I took a drag. The thick smoke went down my throat smoothly but tasted foul. 'You're a fucking dark horse, you know. I wonder about you sometimes, Alex. You're a bit of a sneaky one.' I was keeping a perfectly straight face. 'How much gear have you got?'

'Enough for a couple of lines, or one more spliff.'

'So much for only having a bit last night. Rack up, then.'

I was annoyed that he'd been sniffing without me, even though I'd been sniffing without him, although I hadn't said as much. Alex didn't like me drinking without him, or with him for that matter, it seemed, so admitting to doing cocaine when he wasn't there would not have been smart.

'Look, why do you want a line? You're smoking it right there.' Alex nodded towards the joint defensively.

'Yeah, but when I smoke coke, I may as well have necked a tranquilliser. It makes me so drowsy.' Smoking cocaine has the opposite effect to sniffing it.

'Well, if you don't like it, give it back to me, then. Anyway, what's wrong with feeling chilled out?'

'I suppose that's what heroin addicts say too, eh? Nope, it's just not me. I want to feel alert.' There was a time when I would have done anything to feel sedated. But that was long gone. 'Look, just get the gear out. Go on, I'll make it worth your while.'

'You're an animal with this stuff!'

'Says you! Hey, you're the one that has it on you and you're the one who was caning it last night – but it's *me* that's the fucking coke fiend? How does that work?'

He perched himself beside the glass table and I sat on his lap, my arms around his neck.

'I can't see what I'm doing,' Alex said impatiently.

'Stop fucking moaning, you. Just cut my line.'

'You're a terrorist, Katie.' He looked at me. I looked at him. For a moment, we exchanged saliva. 'This isn't going to last. Have you still got that guy's number so we can get more?'

'There you go again, you bloody cokehead! You whinge about me loving it, but, mate, you're worse than me.' I knew that comment would piss him off, but I found it quite amusing. 'You'll be firing blanks, the way you carry on, and then you won't be able to give me that baby we keep talking about.' I went to find my phone.

'Nothing's going to stop me making you my baby mama.' *Cringe.* 'I've got super sperm, you know that!' *Double cringe.*

I sniggered as I handed him my mobile. At moments like this, I could kid myself that I had nothing to hide. He could snoop through my phone all he liked, he wouldn't find anything dodgy. There were four clients' numbers listed, all under female names. I didn't need a degree in psychology to figure out that was the safest way of storing them.

'Oh yeah, you and your super sperm,' I said. Three of Alex's ex-girlfriends had children by him. I didn't feel too comfortable about it and tried not to think about it, which wasn't all that hard as he didn't have a lot of contact with them.

I went over to check on Freddie.

'Aw, poor Freddie needs water. You're a dry little thing, aren't you, eh, baby?'

'*What?*'

'Nothing. I'm talking to Freddie. He needs water. I thought he looked a little bit under the weather. Give me that spliff,' I ordered. I took a drag of the joint then gave it back to him and went to fill a pan with water. 'You know, it was really fucking irresponsible of you, getting those girls pregnant. What were you thinking?' I was determined to try to make him feel bad.

'How can you talk?' he asked. 'You told me that you've been pregnant.'

'Yeah, once. I was 16. I'd just come to London with my first boyfriend, Stephen.' I was starting to feel drunk. 'It was an accident. I'm entitled to one accident, for fuck's sake! But three?'

'Whatever. Come and do your line.'

'Let me just finish this. I left the heating on last night, that's why Freddie's so thirsty.'

'You're always leaving the heating on. Don't you care about bills?' I didn't have to – Joel paid them.

'Jesus, I've got to change this music. It's annoying the hell out of me,' Alex said, scrolling down the contacts list in my phone. He knew the name he needed, but he was clearly having a good old gander.

'Freddie's looking really unwell. I'm going to have to open the window and let some air in for him.'

'But it'll be cold.'

'No, it won't. My baby needs air. It'll only be for a bit. Anyway, Mr Super Sperm Extraordinaire, I'm sure you can handle a bit of breeze.'

'You and that friggin' plant,' Alex scoffed, ignoring my dig.

After a while, Alex got a text back from my contact. 'Give me a hundred quid, babe. The guy says he's outside in the car.'

'I don't know if I've got a hundred quid on me. Haven't you got any money?'

'No.'

'Is that it? "No"?' *Cheeky fucker.*

I didn't want to be seen going into the back of my wardrobe, where I usually kept about a grand in cash. Thinking quickly, I found a reason for having £100 lying around my bedroom. 'Actually, hang on. I went to the bank yesterday,' I said, wandering into the bedroom.

'Yeah, yeah . . . just get the money, Katie, come on.'

I was pissed off with Alex's tone, and my paranoia about where I'd really got the money from made me insist on explaining myself. 'As I was saying, I got this out the bank cos I thought I was going to get my hair done,' I shouted into the living room.

'Hurry up! He's waiting.'

'Why didn't you mention money before you bloody phoned him? I might not have had anything on me.' I handed over the cash reluctantly.

'You always have money on you. Why would tonight be any different from any other night, eh, baby?'

Whatever our squabbles, this white powder would evaporate any tension between us.

'What's that for?' Alex asked, holding the champagne that I'd just handed him.

This was the perfect time to give him the surprise I'd arranged earlier that day. He took the envelope and quickly opened it to reveal two travel tickets for a week's holiday in Turkey, leaving a few days later, when I knew he'd already booked time off work. He smiled, kissed me and that was that. I'd hoped for a bigger response, so I was disappointed, but I tried not to think about my feelings. *He is happy. I'm sure he is. He's just laid back, that's all.*

HOOKED

Later that night, I slipped my feet into sheer hold-ups and hoisted them up to my thighs. I put on very high heels with thin straps that tied around my ankles. I pulled on a tiny black skirt that clung to my bum, emphasising its shape, then clasped together a two-sizes-too-small corset, exposing a hefty cleavage. Alex loved this look. I was the picture of a stereotypical hooker. I found the irony amusing.

I slowly glided into the living room, an Amazonian queen of the night, ready for whatever was coming my way. Alex had dimmed the lights and lit more candles, and he watched me as I approached him silently.

He called me his high priestess. I got off on the eroticism of feeling revered. It was obvious that he wanted me badly and I knew I'd got him. When I was dressed like this, he was under my power.

'You look fucking hot,' he said tugging at his crotch. 'Looking like that you could make some money, honey.'

'What do you mean?' I lit a Marlboro, suspicious about what he was implying.

'Well, you know. You're a sexy woman, Katie. You should cash in on your looks.' He came over to me and traced the shape of my ass with his fingers.

'I don't know what you're talking about.' I was completely paranoid. The moment was lost.

'Yeah, babe, you could be a model.' He tried to kiss my neck.

'A model? Fuck off! Don't kiss me! I'm 24 years old. Are you taking the piss?' I snapped.

'No, course I'm not! Hey, steady! What's with the mood?'

'Mood? This isn't a "mood", Alex.' I swatted his hand off my rump. 'I'm just trying to understand what you're fucking on about, saying that I could make money from how I look.'

'Babe! Why the fuck are you swearing? What's wrong with you?'

'Why am *I* swearing? Hold on, you just fucking swore, too!

And don't fucking call me "babe". *Babe, babe, babe*,' I chanted as I poured another drink. 'I want you to be honest with me about what you were saying.'

I raised the glass to my mouth, banged my teeth and liquid trickled down my chin. I tried again, downed it in one long slurp, and for a moment Alex and I stared at each other.

He gripped my arm, pulling me towards him. 'Sit on here and shut up. I don't know what you're banging on about, but I'm sick of listening to you talking. I just want to eat out your pussy, but you won't stop fucking talking.' He sounded stern. 'If you don't shut up, girl, I'm going to slap you. Do you hear me?'

I didn't know if he meant it or not. I sat on the worktop and he tried to kiss me. I resisted. 'You're going to slap me, are you?' I managed to splutter as he tried again. 'Go on, then,' I dared him.

He pulled away, lit a joint, took a drag and said nothing. A pensive frown crawled along his brow as he blew the smoke into the room.

'Fucking slap me, then, if that's what you said you're gonna do.' I was seething.

I felt an impact on my cheek. His sudden action stunned me.

'You're a fucking *cunt*!' I shouted. 'What did you do that for?'

He raised his eyebrows slightly and grinned.

'What's wrong with you, you fucking idiot?' I shouted. I was confused yet turned on.

He took another drag of the spliff and gestured that I should take it from him.

'Fuck off.'

'Take it, Katie.' I'd forgotten why we were arguing, but we continued. He grabbed my wrist. 'Take the spliff, Katie.' I took it. He tried to kiss me. I turned away. 'Kiss me.' I did nothing. 'Kiss me.' His lips touched mine. He pulled away and sniggered. 'I knew you would.'

CHAPTER 10

'Wake up. Get up,' Alex said urgently.

'Why? What's wrong? Have I missed *Columbo*?' I was wrecked. Whatever sleep I managed to get, my body clung desperately to.

'*What*? Just get up. It's nearly one o'clock. I said we'd meet my sister for lunch. Her Bryan's taking her shopping.'

'Hmmm?' I groaned, still half asleep. 'Are you serious? I can't go. I'm sorry. I feel like shit. What day is it?'

'Saturday. Bloody *Columbo* isn't on today, Katie. Look, you're coming with me, babe, however you feel. I've told them we'll both be there.'

I was silently fuming. I wanted to outright refuse to go. My head was battered. I'd barely slept. 'Please can you just go by yourself and make an excuse for me? *Please*?'

'No, I can't,' Alex said pulling the duvet off me.

'Ahh! Don't do that!' I quickly curled into the foetal position.

'Get up now, otherwise we'll be late, and she'll tell me off if I'm not on time.'

'She'll tell you off?' I hadn't heard anyone say that since I'd been at school. 'She's your fucking sister, Alex, not your mother.'

Very reluctantly and very quietly, I manoeuvred myself out of bed and went into the bathroom. My breath smelled rancid. My tongue was laden with a thick white residue that looked like thrush. I stood sulking. I felt obliged to go for fear of appearing rude in the eyes of Alex's older sister, who clearly had a great deal of influence over him. And, of course, being bullied into submission helped my decision too.

*

'Lovely to see you again, Katie,' Alex's brother-in-law roared. He stood to greet me, offering a hearty welcome and a kiss that barely missed my mouth. He behaved as though we'd been friends for years. He took Alex's hand and slapped his back as Alex brushed past him to kiss his sister hello. I stood to one side to let them do the sibling bonding before I politely planted my dry lips onto his sister's cheek.

'You're late,' she smiled, not moving from her seat.

'By 20 minutes, Lauren,' said Alex. 'No one is officially late until half an hour after the designated meeting time.'

'You're such a smart-arse, Alex! I've been sitting here for nearly an hour waiting for you to get your lazy arse out of bed.' She looked straight at me. I wanted to tell her to get a life but said nothing.

'How's Katie?' she asked, addressing Alex.

'I'm very well, thank you,' I grinned, wishing that I wasn't there. 'How's Lauren?' Alex flashed me a look of disapproval. *I'm only being friendly.*

'Lauren's very well, thank you, darling. Sit down here.' She patted the chair next to her and I did as I was told.

Lauren was some ten years older than Alex, but she acted as though she was a generation removed. She and her husband seemed very different from each other, but for whatever reason their relationship worked; it was none of my business. Lauren was an attractive woman, but, despite drinking a lot, she seemed a little uptight and very bossy. However, as I watched the way Bryan glanced at me, I was certain that when given permission he would bang some of that out of her and give her a bloody good seeing to. I secretly imagined them dabbling in a spot of swinging. Not sure why. He was older than her, with silver hair. He'd 'made a few quid by having a flutter on the stock market', as he never failed to remind me.

As soon as we arrived, I started willing the time to fly by. My head wasn't clear and the thought of laughing made me feel ill, while the idea of listening to boring family chit-chat that had nothing to do with anyone I knew numbed me to the core. I was desperate for the drinks to come. Lauren had already barked the order for two bottles of wine, but where the hell were they?

'So, how are you doing, Katie? Everything all right in your world, eh? You two love birds getting married any time soon?' Bryan winked.

'They can't get married yet, Bry, you should know that. Not before she asks permission from me if she can run off with my favourite brother,' said Lauren, meaning every word. *Who is she, the cat's mother?*

'Everything's all right with us, isn't it, sweetie?' I looked at Alex for reassurance, trying to sound as though we were a united couple. He nodded and looked directly at his sister, who had an almost sympathetic look on her face, as if to say, 'It's all right. I know no woman will ever treat you as well you deserve. But bless the girl for trying.'

I immersed myself in a glass of Sauvignon Blanc as soon as the waiter had poured it.

'Is everything OK, miss?' the waiter asked me.

'Yeah, it's nice, thanks,' I answered, not looking at him. What's the big deal? It's only wine.

'How are you, Bryan? Enjoying work?' I asked, trying to sound like I gave a toss.

'Oh, it's grand.'

'I never see him. He's always out of the house,' Lauren butted in. 'Gives me chance to get my bit on the side round for a quick . . . *tipple*.' She glanced at her husband, who shuffled in his chair awkwardly.

'Well, you know that when I'm out, love, I don't do anything that you wouldn't do,' Bryan smirked.

'He's always like this. Tries to wind me up all the time, doesn't he, Licky? Tell the bugger to stop teasing me.'

Alex just said, 'Please, L, don't call me Licky, not here.'

'Why not? Katie, I've called him Licky since he was tiny

and he usually likes it. He's obviously got his knickers in a twist today.'

'I don't know about that, but I remember you calling him that last time we met and he didn't like it then, either.'

'When we're by ourselves he doesn't mind it. Or when it's just the three of us,' Lauren said, twirling her finger, indicating that she meant herself, Bryan and Alex.

I was astounded at her rudeness. I flashed Lauren a look, feeling embarrassed for her. She seemed oblivious to how she sounded. I picked up my glass and took a sip, trying to avoid eye contact. A silence swept the table. I couldn't believe Alex had said nothing to stick up for me.

'Anyway, how are your salsa classes?' Alex asked his sister.

'Bloody difficult, but I'm trying. Maybe you'd like to come along with me and be my dance partner sometime? How about that?'

'Get Bryan to go along with you. You'd go along to a dance class, eh, Bry?'

I was seething. I didn't care about salsa or anything else at that moment. I wanted to leave. I noticed a waiter smiling in my direction. Maybe he thought we were ready to order. I smiled back.

'Bryan can't dance, Lick. He's got no rhythm.'

'Hey, less of that! I *have* got rhythm. It was my ability to show you a few moves that got you interested in me in the first place, if I remember rightly.'

I was starting to think of the waiter as a welcome distraction. He was quite cute and looked familiar. Maybe he just had one of those generic friendly faces.

'That's what you think, love,' Lauren sneered, trying to sound sassy but instead coming across as bitchy. 'Come with me, Alex. Go on. You'd be all right with my little brother coming dancing with me, wouldn't you, Kate?'

'Eh?'

'Alex, coming dancing with me?'

'Oh, right, yeah . . .'

'You'd be all right with that, wouldn't you? Then maybe he could show you a thing or two.'

I suddenly realised not only that I couldn't stomach Alex's sister for a moment longer, but also that I'd fucked the friendly waiter. He'd been a punter.

'I'm off,' I said, standing up. I had to go. I couldn't stay.

'What do you mean?' Alex asked.

'I'm going home. I'm not feeling well. I have to go.' I dragged my coat on.

'What?'

'I'm off. I'm feeling really sick.' This wasn't entirely a lie. 'Sorry. Nice to see you again, Bryan,' I added just before I charged towards the door.

Alex followed me and grabbed my arm. 'You can't go, Kate. Not just like that.'

'I can and I am. I can't stand your sister. She's just rude,' I said in semi-hushed but very anxious tones.

'Keep it down, for fuck's sake!' he barked. 'People can hear you.'

'Well, they'll be able to hear you swearing at me too, then, won't they?'

I walked out, thinking solely about the waiter I'd had sex with. Alex called after me. I carried on walking. He ran to catch me up.

'Katie, look, I haven't got my wallet with me.'

'So?' I snapped. 'Oh, you mean you want me to pay for my unfinished glass of wine?'

'Er, no, it's not like that. Look, I promised Lauren that I'd treat her and Bryan to lunch today.'

Silence as Alex and I stared at each other. I got it. He didn't need to say any more. I retrieved my purse from my bag and gave him some cash, shaking my head. 'That should cover it,' I said, staring at his face. Yet again, I wanted a response from him. I wanted to see something. Nothing. I walked away as fast as I could in the direction of a taxi rank.

'Thanks, babe,' Alex called after me.

I'd been screwed – yet again.

*

Turning my phone on after the weekend always made me feel nervous. Alex had gone to work and I didn't know when I'd see him next. I was alone again.

Texts: Petra, Petra, Petra, the agency, Joel, Faye. Voicemail: five. Petra had been frantically ringing me and had left three messages. A woman from Dean's crew had called to arrange a rendezvous with some bloke who wanted nothing more than to give me cunnilingus while I wore over-the-knee boots. *Over-the-knee boots?* I didn't have any boots that went past my calf – not that they cared and neither, apparently, did they care about my request not to be disturbed over the weekend. The other message was Joel, whom I hadn't heard from for over a month. But as long as the rent was still being paid, which it was, I wasn't too worried.

The last time I'd seen him, I'd been in a panic. I'd only recently had my home phone installed. One afternoon, I listened to my voice messages and there it was, a woman's voice: 'Leave my husband alone,' she hissed.

Fuck! Joel's wife knew about our fling. *How?* Frantic, I called Faye and asked her to come over so we could discuss it. We sat down at the glass table, stony-faced, and replayed the message a number of times before analysing the content over some wine.

'Oh, bollocks,' Faye said. I stared at her anxiously, not knowing what to say.

'Pass me the lighter, please, babe,' was what I came out with first. 'She knows, doesn't she? That's Joel's wife, isn't it?'

Faye raised her eyebrows and shrugged her shoulders. 'Well, it sounds like it's her, Katie. It's definitely *somebody's* wife. Who else have you been seeing who's married?' She laughed and signalled to me that she wanted a cigarette.

'No one, you cheeky cow!' I chuckled, quickly coming back down to earth as Faye replayed the message. 'Fuck,

Faye! This wasn't meant to happen. What the hell am I going to do?'

'Well, I suppose . . .' Faye looked thoughtful. 'I suppose you could always call her and ask her over for a threesome!'

'You're obsessed with threesomes. Stop it! You need to go out and find yourself two girls to make your wish come true! Seriously, what should I do?'

'You need to speak to Joel.'

'Yeah, I know,' I said dubiously. 'Another thing I suppose I could do is call Joel's missus,' I said, playing Faye at her own game, 'and see if she approves of the design of the flat!'

'I can guarantee she won't like that rug you've got over there,' Faye cackled, snorting.

'Which rug? This is serious, Faye. I can't believe you're questioning my taste.'

'The one by the sofa. I reckon if Joel's wife did come over here, the hardest thing for her to believe wouldn't be that he's seeing someone behind her back, it'd be that you're prepared to live with that thing.' Faye was in hysterics.

'There's nothing wrong with that rug! That's a nice bloody rug, that is, Faye!' I half laughed. 'It was expensive.'

'Just cos it was expensive, doesn't mean that it's a nice rug, Kate!' She loved taking the piss out of me.

'Oi, look, we're getting off the subject. I'm fucking worried about this whole thing. What if she knows where I live?'

'She won't know where you live, Katie. I mean, how do you think she's feeling?' said Faye, shaking her head. I stared at her. I didn't want to think about that.

'This is the last time you're playing that message. It makes me feel sick every time I hear it . . . God, listen to her voice. She sounds really hacked off,' I said.

'Wouldn't you be?' said Faye. 'Personally, I don't think she sounds that angry, considering you're screwing her fella. She sounds as though she's just letting you know that she knows that you're having an affair with her husband.'

'I'm not having an *affair* with her husband, Faye. Don't

say that! I've been *seeing* her husband. It's only casual.'

'It's the same thing, Kate.'

The following day, as the clock struck noon, as arranged, the doorbell rang: Joel.

He lit a cigarette, 'I've missed you, my sexy girl! You look brown! Been sunbedding it, have you?'

'I always look brown! I'm mixed race, in case you've forgotten! I've missed you too.' That was a lie. 'Babe, just listen to this,' I said, before playing the message from his wife.

Joel's face fell and then a schoolboy smirk appeared on it.

'It's her. She knows. It's the missus.'

'It's not funny, Joel! How does she know? Jesus! I've only just recently got this bloody landline. I feel really bad – really bad. I don't want any shit, Joel, I really don't.'

I was worried sick and went to pamper Freddie to try to settle my nerves. His leaves were firm and healthy. Whenever I felt their coolness, it seemed somehow to ease my tension. Freddie certainly didn't seem to have any problems, unlike his keeper.

'She must have gone through my phone. Have you got an ashtray, sweetheart? And another glass. I can only find one.'

'You've got to sort your marriage out, Joel. The two of you need to decide what you're going to do.' My real concern was that I might end up homeless. 'Look, I suggest that after today you don't contact me for a bit while you work out what's happening at home, OK?' I handed him an ashtray, annoyed that he didn't seem fully focused on our predicament.

'If that's what you think.' He seemed more interested in finding a second wine glass. I was desperate to distance myself from the potential chaos that I saw looming ahead.

*

After I'd checked my messages, I dialled Joel's number. Had something happened with him and his wife? I hoped not. I certainly didn't want to start a full-on relationship with him.

'Can I see you?' he asked straight away.

HOOKED

Although I didn't see Joel often, when he did appear he was like a whirlwind. He was energetic and took life by the balls. He always seemed to be busy, but seeming busy while doing very little takes skill. I knew. I was doing it myself.

'Hey, baby.' I had to make him feel wanted. 'When do you want to see me? I can't make today, if that's what you're going to suggest,' I said in a cutesy, girly voice, adding a few 'aw's to make it sound as though I was genuinely disappointed that I couldn't see him.

'It doesn't have to be today, darlin'. Let's just see each other soon. Maybe later this week, or even next week.'

I breathed a sigh of relief. Short and sweet. It was basically a courtesy call. He was just making sure that I didn't forget him. I could deal with that. It wasn't that I didn't want to see him exactly, but it was awkward for me now that I was with Alex. I didn't approve of cheating. I had never been one for infidelity – by which I mean sex for free or even overt flirting. I'd never cheated on Alex, as far as I was concerned; I didn't see fucking a client as being unfaithful. I compartmentalised punters, placing them in a different category altogether from free sex. They were work. That was my job.

Nonetheless, I didn't want to do what I knew was required of me to keep Joel happy: being intimate, holding his hand, stroking his leg, kissing him – and what if he suddenly wanted sex? I couldn't have sex with him. Well, I could, but I really didn't want to. But what if he wasn't prepared to continue paying my rent? What then? Joel was no fool; he wouldn't have been too happy if he found out he was financing my relationship with Alex – which was taking place in his flat. I didn't see it as dishonest, though. After all, Joel and I had never had a conversation about our thing being exclusive. How could it have been? The guy was married.

My liaison with Joel had always been based on me massaging his ego. You can't have a relationship with a man who agrees to pay for your flat before you even have sex with him without understanding that the whole thing is about him and his ego; my part was to make sure that it was adequately stoked whenever we were in touch. It wasn't as though I'd been homeless when we'd met and he'd been the Good Samaritan, helping me off the streets. Sometimes I wondered what the hell he would have done if the sex had been crap. But Joel wasn't even massively into sex. I could tell that at one time he had been, but alcoholism had reduced his desire – and his physical ability – to near nothingness. He was proving his prowess and his status by 'keeping a mistress'. To whom he was proving himself, I don't know. As far as I understood, no one knew that he was renting the flat for me. In any case, he'd signed a year-long lease. He couldn't just walk away – could he?

CHAPTER 11

It was after 9 p.m. one night in April 2002. Petra opened the door to her tiny, one-bedroom, top-floor flat in Westbourne Park to me. No one would ever have called it a penthouse, but you could be quite sure she did. She was wearing a minute skirt and showing off her naturally pert DDs (lucky cow). I would never have had the guts to dress so provocatively, although it made me smile that Petra didn't ever hesitate to wear the skimpiest of clothing. She got off on it, and why not? The girl had it and she was flaunting it.

'Hey!' I said. 'You look nice. You all right? Babe, that music's loud . . .'

'Don't turn it down. I love Enrique Iglesias. He's just got such a soulful voice,' Petra laughed.

'Yeah, course he has . . . So how are you?'

'I'm OK. You look nice too,' she said, without even a glance, as usual. I was in my regular going-out clobber: low-sitting jeans à la Britney (that was one aspect of her style I was willing to take on; the bleached hair and belly-button piercings I left to other folk), a vest, a fitted tweed jacket (Vivienne Westwood-esque) and flat black pumps.

'We're waiting for Luca,' Petra said as she straightened her hair in the mirror.

'Oh, fuck's sake, is he coming round? I thought you'd have sorted it out already?'

'No, I haven't yet,' she snapped. 'Well, actually, hold on, I have . . . I mean, I was the one who called him to get him to come round, which is more than you did, Kate. So he's coming over to drop off the gear. You want some, don't you?'

Petra sounded like a schoolteacher.

'Yeah, course I do, clever arse. I just can't be bothered seeing that snivelling, twitching wreck. He gets on my tits. I like him, don't get me wrong; he just gets on my nerves. He's like a little weasel scratching around.'

'Well, you're going to have to see him if you want the stuff,' Petra said matter-of-factly.

Luca came in, as usual, to drop off the gear. And, as usual, he hung around. 'Nice to see you two lovely ladies. You both look gorgeous as ever.' *Cockney alert!* He kissed my cheeks, then slapped a gram of cocaine on the table in front of Petra.

'Hey, where's mine?' I asked, trying to sound jovial.

'I'm coming! I'm coming!' He thought he was so fabulous. I wanted to roll my eyes at him. Moments later, just enough time to make me wonder whether the stuff was coming, he placed a wrap into my hand as if he was giving me a really sincere handshake.

'Have you got another one?' I whispered. I didn't want Petra to know that I was getting two. Not that she'd judge – I just didn't want her dipping into my second gram when she ran out. She always bought one and then later she'd have to source some more, and that usually meant taking it from blokes who were out. I always had to have my own. It didn't matter to me if we were hanging out with men who had it. I never once, ever, went out and relied on anyone else for drinks, cocaine or money. Hell, that was what I sold my arse for.

'Sure,' Luca grinned, discreetly slipping me another wrap.

He was such an idiot, but he was totally unthreatening. He was always the same. There was no doubt whatsoever in my mind that he'd been caning as much cocaine as he was then every night for the majority of his 20s and the whole of his 30s. When I saw him, I was terrified of what I could become, but I just kept reminding myself that I was still young. Whatever. I couldn't be bothered to spend time thinking about it. Not then. Not before a night out. I just wanted a line. That was all I wanted. Cocaine – oh, and alcohol.

'Any more champagne, Petra?'

'It's Petronella!'

'Give me a fuckin' break. Don't start all that baloney.'

Luca bent over the table and sniffed a line. I heard the sound as my head was in the fridge.

'It's finished. Is that all you got?'

'There's some in there, Katie.'

'A thimbleful. Enough for a child's portion.'

'Kids don't drink champagne,' Petra said.

'No, they drink white cider instead,' Luca piped up, suddenly finding himself hilariously funny.

'Have you got anything else to drink? How about this vodka?'

'Yeah, take some of the Stolly, but I don't want any. I've got a drink already,' Petra said, rubbing her nose.

'Luca, do you want some?'

'Yeah, why not? Go on then, love, I'll have a bit of that. Vodka, innit?'

'Yeah.'

'Here then, sweetheart. Get this line down you.' Luca was staring at me. He raised his glass, said 'Cheers!' and knocked back his vodka. I held the liquid in my mouth for a moment before swallowing, knowing it would make me shudder.

'Right, you ready, P?' I was feeling in the mood to party.

'Give me one minute, OK? I need to get my shit together.' Petra looked dazed as she stood up from the table, walking around the room as if she was looking for something.

'Where you gals off to tonight, then?' Luca asked.

'Dunno,' I said nonchalantly, willing him not to ask if he could join us. I cut three lines on the table. There was always time for a quickie.

'Yeah, you do!' Petra squawked in a loud voice, smirking, knowing that I was trying to dodge Luca's question.

'No, I don't. How do I know? We haven't even talked

about it yet,' I responded crossly. She was trying to wind me up. It was working.

'Pass my drink, Kate!' she demanded.

'You're closer to it than I am, you lazy toerag. It's just behind you on the table. Get it yourself.'

Petra giggled and gave Luca, who was absent-mindedly pacing the room and sniffing profusely, a cheeky 'I'm such a naughty minx' type of smile; he wasn't even looking at her. It was obvious she was feeling full of herself; that would soon piss me off. 'Luca, pass me my drink,' Petra bossed, extending her arm as she bent down beside the sofa to pick up the second of a pair of black Jimmy Choos.

Luca picked up one of the tumblers and placed it in her hand. She took a slug and passed Luca the glass to put back onto the table. He did what was expected of him. Petra looked at me with a sly smile, and I told her to stop showing off. I sometimes found her games humorous, but most of the time they were just tedious. 'It's OK for me to show off, isn't it, Luca?' Petra said as she looked over her shoulder in the mirror, at her arse.

'Darling, you can do what the fuck you want. I don't care.' He finished his vodka and asked me for another.

'Give me your glass, then,' I said, puffing on a Marlboro Light.

'Hurry up, we're going in a minute!' Petra barked. I'd forgotten we were about to leave. She suddenly started coughing dramatically and fanning the air while clinging on to her cream, Louis Vuitton patent-leather purse. 'That cigarette stinks! You didn't ask if you could smoke.' She was trying to humiliate me, but only, of course, in the friendliest possible manner.

'Petra, you are fucking starting to annoy me now. Stop it right here, OK? You're acting like an arsehole and I'm not going to put up with you like this, all right? So don't try and embarrass me, belittle me or anything else apart from be all right with me, cos I'll fucking tell you where to go and I don't care where we are or who the fuck we're with, do you hear me? I'm just giving you fair warning before we go out and end up having a squabble.'

'Don't fight, gals,' Luca said dismissively. He started turning out his pockets, in a cocaine haze.

'You know I love you,' Petra said as she pinched my bum.

'And I love you.' I never felt genuine saying those words to her, despite our closeness.

'Come on then, girl. Let's go and paint this fucking town red!'

'Can I come?' Luca asked. We both looked at him silently. Our apologetic faces told him everything he needed to know. 'All right, then. Maybe see you later. Give us a bell whatever time you want. I aways have my dog and bone by my side, mate. This business ain't never closed, know what I mean? Twenty-four seven, mate, twenty-four seven, know what I'm sayin'?'

God, he was annoying. I understood perfectly well what he was saying. We had used his late-night/early-morning delivery service more times than I'd have wanted to admit. Luca headed towards the door to leave then suddenly he spun back round. *What does he want now?*

'Oops, nearly forgot my manners there.' Manners shmanners. It was just an excuse to kiss us both goodbye. He couldn't be invented. He was such a cliché of a dealer it was embarrassing. Of course, he had no idea of this and often referred to himself as 'the dog's bollocks', bless him.

'Thank God he's gone,' Petra sighed. 'I thought his job was to deliver and go.'

'He wants to get into your knickers.'

She grimaced. 'Stop it. It's you he fancies.'

'No, he doesn't!' I shook my head adamantly. 'I hardly talk to him. He does my head in. He should stop sniffing that stuff; it's turning him into a nervous wreck.'

'Pot. Kettle. Black,' laughed Petra.

'Very amusing. It takes one to know one, babe.' I prodded her. 'Imagine wot Luca's graaan must fink, eh?' I said, mimicking the stereotypical East End gangster's accent.

'For a minute, I thought you were gonna tell him he could come out with us. Anyway, come on, we're wasting time. Let's go!'

'Course I wasn't. But you didn't help the situation when he asked where we were off to.'

'Oh poo! It's already half ten. We've got some partying to do,' Petra said, linking my arm as the door closed behind us.

Sitting in the back of the taxi, I told Petra, 'I'm gonna take a few days off work next week. Alex and I are going to Bodrum in Turkey.'

'Ooh, nice.'

'Yeah, it should be. I need a break, you know. Work and everything is getting on top of me at the moment.' Petra nodded. She knew the score. All working girls need time out. The job would break you otherwise. 'I just want to pamper myself, you know. Hang out with Alex and forget London.'

'It's nice of him taking you away.'

'Well, I bought the tickets, so it's actually my treat.'

'What do you mean? Who paid for the trip?'

I should have known. 'I just told you – I did.'

'He must have been really chuffed with that!' She laughed. 'God, I'd never pay for a man to go on holiday. You're nuts, Katie.'

'No, I'm not! And yeah, he was really pleased, actually.' I was angry and embarrassed. 'It's a good job we're not the same person, isn't it, P? What the fuck is wrong with me treating him to a break? Just cos *you're* a tight sod!'

The truth was Alex had barely responded when I'd told him we were going on holiday. I'd bought the tickets, booked us into a cute boutique hotel – and he'd barely mustered a thank you. But I'd have rather gnawed off my right arm than admit that to Petra.

'Anyway, have you told that guy Dean you're not working?'

she asked. She was trying to wind me up by throwing a spanner in the works. For her, that kind of thing was light entertainment.

'Yeah, I've told them I won't be working. Why are you so bothered? Look, it's up to—'

'I was just asking,' she chortled.

'It's up to me if I take a few days off, Petra. God, it's not like I work in a bloody office. Stop shit-stirring! Do you ask that woman at your agency if you can wipe your arse? Or better still, hers?'

'Oh, shut up, Kate. I was just—'

'Don't fucking tell me to shut up, OK?'

'I was just wondering if you'd mentioned to the agency that you're taking time off, that's all,' she chuckled.

'You were trying to burst my bubble. I know what you're like!'

'You're just being paranoid.'

'I'm not. You're so fucking annoying sometimes, Petra.'

'I was teasing you, that's all. I know you hate having to answer to the agency. And stop calling me Pe—'

'Don't you dare start with that. Don't wind me up, please, just for one night. Sometimes I can't believe I put up with your crap. Jesus Christ.'

We sat in silence for a moment. 'Reece is in a mood tonight,' Petra said, changing the subject. 'He stormed out before you came round, saying he was going to his brother's place to watch football.'

Reece was Petra's long-suffering lawyer boyfriend, whom she lived with. He was tall, very good-looking, highly intelligent and black, which was a first for Petra. She'd never dated a black man before Reece, and in truth she'd never quite got used to the fact that her boyfriend was of African descent. Yeah, she'd fuck men of all ethnicities day in day out, but cohabit with a man who was anything other than white? I used to joke with her, saying that I was as dark a colour as she could comfortably handle. She just laughed and rubbished my comments.

Reece would do anything to please Petra, but it was never enough for her. She treated him like a toy. She wanted him when he wasn't there, and then when he was, she wished he'd disappear.

I had my reservations about him. I couldn't understand why a man so successful and stable in his working life would choose to be with a woman like Petra. It seemed to me to be proof that it wasn't just Petra and I who had issues. In my view, Reece must have had too, or he wouldn't have been with her. I had no real respect for him; I thought he was an idiot for tolerating so much crap from his girlfriend. Because, actually, you *do* choose who you fall in love with.

'I don't know why you two are together,' I told her when she said he'd stormed out. 'What's the point? It's always the same: either one or both of you upset. A relationship is meant to make you happy, isn't it?'

'I know, I know.'

'Anyway, I can't talk. Alex and I aren't exactly getting on brilliantly at the moment either. Maybe we should both leave our boyfriends, Petra.' I laughed. 'Reece hasn't got the balls to leave you, babe, so you should set the poor guy free.'

'Katie, tell me something. Why do you insist on calling me Petra all the time? Why can't you just call me Petronella like everyone else?'

'I didn't call you Petra. I called you babe.'

'Yes, but before that you called me Petra.'

'Oh, for God's sake,' I muttered. 'I call you Petra because Petronella's a mouthful, and I can't be bothered saying it the whole time. What sort of name is Petronella anyway? Listen, I thought you had a problem with Reece. Here I am talking to you about that, but you're more bothered about ticking me off for calling you Petra.'

She stifled a giggle. 'I can't leave Reece . . .' For a moment, she showed a glimpse of how vulnerable she was.

'You *can* leave him. You'd be fine. It's not all doom and gloom being by yourself, you know. I've spent lots of time without a boyfriend. Anything would be better than the misery you both go through being together.'

'I know.' She sighed sadly.

We walked straight to the front of the queue, ignoring the people waiting patiently in line to be admitted to Butterscotch. Stefano, the delectable creature who was standing at the entrance to the bar, smiled at us as we approached. However often I saw this guy, I never got tired of looking at him. I'd first been introduced to him at a party at the Met Bar in 1997. Somehow, a friend and I had managed to get our teenage asses in when we'd come to London for a few days. He'd been trying his luck with Meg Matthews, despite her being with Noel Gallagher, and had hooked up instead with a model who was a friend of the friend I was with.

''Allo, my darlings.' *Jesus, he's hot.*

'Hi,' we said, tossing our hair, as he opened the ropes and kissed our cheeks.

'How's things? I trust you're both well?'

He led us along a wooden footbridge that hovered above water with koi carp swimming underneath. On the walls were projected images of fairies flying around. Lanterns hung from the ceiling and a recording of crickets chirping was playing. The bridge was long and at first nothing else could be heard, and then – bang! There it was. From behind some immense glass doors the music was booming. We were itching to really get our night started. The place was trendy but not overly pretentious, and it was one of my favourite bars.

'What do you want to drink, ladies?' Stefano asked us with a grin.

'I'll have a glass of champagne,' replied Petra with a straight face. He looked at me and I nodded my approval, smiling gratefully. He pulled aside one of the waiters, who served up the drinks straight away. How we got this sort of treatment, I never understood, but I wasn't complaining. OK, we'd known him a little for a number of years, but, still, it wasn't like we were buddies.

HOOKED

I was checking out a couple of guys when I caught the eye of another of the managers, a French fella called Pierre whom I knew well; in fact, I'd sucked his balls and he'd licked my snatch – all for free. I'd made sure all my friends knew about this one. I'd fucked him for no reason except lust. He was a conquest any girl would be proud of: dark hair, pale-blue eyes, cute ass. He was tall, a bit skinny but strong, with an air of confidence that could make you believe anything. He talked a good talk, but when it came to the walk, I have to say I was disappointed.

Before I jumped his bones, I'd been convinced he was going to put me through my paces, and I was dismayed by his apparent lack of technique; he was barely able to find my clitoris. When I recounted my night of half-baked 'passion' to my friends, I played down his lack of skills, not out of embarrassment but to save his pride. He was a nice guy; it wasn't necessary to shame him like that. Women never forget. They'd never have looked at him in the same way again.

He always wore a close-fitting charcoal-grey suit, the trousers slightly tapered at the bottom, and an open-necked white shirt. 'Come with me, Katie. I'll get you a table,' he said, flashing us a glimpse of his overly bleached teeth. He looked so typically French that his only lightly accented English always came as a bit of a disappointment. His wink stirred my loins. Despite being rubbish in bed, he was still hot enough to be fantasy fodder. It wasn't as though I'd slept with him enough times to have that fantasy totally wiped out. He was still fair game for those lonely nights, just me and the toy. We'd had sex once; maybe he'd just been nervous. Whatever . . .

We thanked Stefano, who left us to go and flirt with other girls, and followed Pierre towards the VIP area. 'Excuse me, one moment,' he said, before wandering off. He was coming across as overly professional when he didn't need to be – I had seen his coming face, after all. I didn't mind sharing his attentiveness with Petra; the guy wasn't my boyfriend and our business together was done. In fact, even if he had been my boyfriend, I would have expected a man I was seeing to charm my friends and make them feel welcome and relaxed around us. On the other hand, if Pierre had actually been flirting with Petra, I would have felt offended. There's no need to target close friends of ex-lovers, or ex-lovers of close friends.

Two girls and a guy who, judging by their faces, had been turfed out of their seats so Petra and I could sit down passed us. I felt embarrassed, but I didn't dwell on it for more than the time it took to pass them. We were feeling important; our egos were being nicely massaged.

'More drinks, ladies?' Pierre asked, in full-blown manager mode. We'd only just received the drinks we were clinging on to, but who were we to refuse an offer of free booze?

'He could have got us a bottle, tight sod!' Petra grumbled as I lit a Marlboro Light, not knowing whether she was joking and not caring enough to ask.

We took turns to go to the bathroom for a line; it was strong stuff. Luca never let us down. He couldn't afford to. I'm guessing we were two of his most loyal customers. My nose was running profusely. During my first few lines, it was hard to distinguish between nervousness and elation. Despite having had a couple before I'd gone out, the change in dynamics now that I was in a bar with loud music and plenty of people made me feel as though I hadn't had any coke at all beforehand. Sniffing at home and sniffing when out are totally different experiences.

I called the process I went through to actually start enjoying the effects of the charlie 'levelling out'. Whenever I sniffed, the first two or three lines made me feel 'normal' after the activities of the day before. It was only after that that I'd start feeling the buzz I was looking for. It never used to be like that. At one time, two or three lines and I'd be soaring. But when sniffing and drinking became something I did religiously, the effect of the quantity that I once sniffed to get me high became negligible. That was when the amount required to take me beyond levelling out started to become ridiculous. And this change happened quicker than I acknowledged even to myself.

Petra and I were chatting about men we'd fucked for free, men we'd fucked for money, boyfriends, Petra's last shopping expedition and *Columbo*. Petra liked him too. Although I was underdressed compared with many of the women present, I felt comfortable. I couldn't be bothered to compete in the high-fashion stakes. As far as I was concerned, I was wearing what a bona fide model would wear on her day off.

We left Butterscotch and jumped into a black cab heading for Lolay, a bar/restaurant just off Park Lane. If there was anywhere in London that was the epitome of pretentiousness, this was it. It was Petra's favourite hang-out and had therefore become a regular haunt for me, despite the fact that I never felt I fitted in there. Bottles of booze sold from £130 for a spirit up to an unspeakable amount for champagne. We were allowed over the threshold of the place because two of Petra's friends were involved in a three-way relationship with the head doorman. He looked like a rogue of the highest order but sounded camp as anything. However, unlike at lots of other bars and clubs in town, here I had never managed to strike up a real rapport with any of the bouncers. They were aloof and cold towards me, or so I thought. I presumed this was because I never wore skirts up to my navel and half a MAC counter on my face.

We got a drink at the upstairs bar. The lights were dim. This was the restaurant section, where people paid a lot of money for very little food. If, like Petra and me, you weren't eating, you were only permitted to stand, unless you were willing to pay £350 for the privilege of resting your feet. If you did choose to sit at a table without food, the cost of an obligatory bottle of champagne would be added to your tab. It was the same downstairs around the dance floor, but without the option of food. Arses on seats equalled paying through the nose.

HOOKED

Petra and I were standing. The usual hip hop was playing and the vibe was posey. 'I've got to go speak to someone,' Petra said, heading over to a man who had just strolled in wearing a long camel coat. He looked like a middle-aged, southern European mobster. I was already willing her to hurry back; I hated standing alone on display. I might as well have made an announcement: 'I'm poor; I can't afford to sit down.' As my self-consciousness kicked in, it confirmed what I already knew: I *really* didn't belong there amongst all the footballers, Arabs in suits and overly made-up girls, many of whom I could tell were hookers. Time and time again, I'd try to persuade myself that I was cool enough to handle this, but the truth was, I wasn't cool enough, I wasn't pretentious enough and I certainly wasn't rich enough – not with a habit like I had – to pull it off in style. Looking round at the sexy chicks and the men they were accompanying, I could see that if these women weren't out-and-out hookers, a lot of them were gold-diggers. There was no other reason why these belles would be with the often rotund creatures that they were wrapping themselves around. Maybe these guys had 'nice personalities', but no doubt there are a lot of wealthy men out there with nice personalities who are also good-looking.

'That's one of my regulars,' Petra grinned on her return. 'He's fuckin' loaded, but you'd never know it. He kind of keeps a low profile, you know. Maybe we could both go and see him some time, together?'

'Low profile? Why's he in here then? There are paparazzi all over the place outside. It's not exactly the most discreet place to come. Anyway, what do you mean we could see him together? You know I don't fuck women, P. And I'm not even going to pretend to go down on you, so don't start getting excited!' I joked.

'Oh, no, babe, I don't usually fuck him,' Petra said casually, sounding posher than ever and more English than her friends in Dublin would have approved of. She'd clearly raised her game while talking to the mafioso lookalike. 'He usually just likes me to whip him and hang weights off his nipples or balls. You know, that kind of thing.'

'You're not serious?'

'Yeah, he's been talking for a while about wanting me to bring one of my friends along to watch.'

'You are serious, aren't you?' Petra started to smirk. I knew she wasn't kidding. 'Babe, I'd love to join you, but I've got better things to do than sit around watching some middle-aged, bored businessman who's searching for his next thrill getting flogged.'

'He'll pay you to watch. You won't need to do anything.' Petra started to laugh at the look of dismay on my face.

'He'll pay me to watch! What a weirdo!' I squawked. 'Fuck it, yeah, go on then. Where do I sign up?' We both got lost in our own thoughts for a moment. Petra was pouting, as she usually was when she wasn't talking. 'There are some oddities out there, you know, P,' I said eventually. 'We've got to be careful. You know, like that guy I saw the other day – he wanted me to piss on him.'

'God, I love doing that,' Petra said, straight-faced.

'Oh, please. Anyway, I couldn't believe it when he said that I was too nice and he couldn't let me do it. I wasn't going to, but before I'd had a chance to decline he'd already blown me out. I mean, what the fuck is that about? I think he wanted me to be some kind of ogre who was going to degrade him or some such bollocks.'

Petra laughed. 'You should have just got into acting mode.'

'As far as I'm concerned, I'm not a paid actress or piss-artist. I'm there for sex. Let's face it, bunny, you never know who or what you're going to find when the guy opens the door.'

'Don't start all this again, babe. Just stop thinking about it. We'll be all right.' Petra was getting irritated by my reality check. All she wanted was to look hot for any blokes watching her.

'Look, I was thinking about getting some Mace or pepper

spray. This whole thing is pretty fucking risky, don't you reckon?'

'Babe, you don't need to tell me about the oddballs that are out there,' Petra said, adjusting her cleavage for maximum impact. 'That guy, the one I just talked to, once wanted me to stick pins in his arse.'

'Please tell me you rebuffed his request.'

'Um, not exactly.'

'I can't hear you. What did you say?' The music had just got louder. It was past midnight. *Party time.*

'I said not exactly. I did what he wanted. A prick for a prick, I say.' I winced. 'Weirdos or not, Katie, I'm taking them for every penny their sorry asses have got to offer.'

'Fuck. That's dark . . . but I'll drink to taking them for every penny they've got.' We clinked glasses without really contemplating what we were toasting.

I lit a Marlboro Light. 'Let's go for a line when I've smoked this.' Petra smiled in agreement and started swinging her hips to the music. I'd easily get through numerous packets of cigarettes on a night out. Of course, it depended on how long the night went on. It wasn't unusual for us to go to an after-party when the clubs closed at around three or four and stay there until the following afternoon, evening or whatever, and then, of course, I'd smoke more. These parties were often surreal and always messy: people getting naked, playing grown-up versions of spin the bottle; exchange of bodily fluids and 'jokes' that only the teller got as night turned into day and elation to paranoia and suspicion.

I started to relax into my environment. Petra and I went off to the loo for a sniff. I had two lines and we returned, holding hands, to resume our position. More people were standing away from their tables dancing. A bartender came and stood beside us and I watched him as he opened a large bottle of champagne. He poured two glasses and handed us one each. I hesitantly took it and thanked him, bewildered. Petra shrugged and burst out laughing, then gained control of her excitement, pouting and running her fingers through her long hair. Things like this often seemed to happen when we were out. 'The gentleman over there sent you this bottle with his regards,' announced the waiter, flashing his eyes in the direction we needed to be looking.

An unattractive white man in his 40s with slicked-back, side-parted dirty-blond hair, dressed in Sloaney weekend attire – jeans, shirt and blazer – raised his glass and smiled.

'Take a look, P. He's quite sexy,' I said sarcastically.

'Oh God, is that him? Flippin' hell, he looks like a toad!' Petra said.

'We're gonna have to go over and thank him.' We both laughed and Petra let out a small snort, then quickly retreated to her usual uptight public persona. 'I don't want to sit with him,' I said, praying that I didn't have to go through another session of beaming like a clown for a stranger I had zero interest in.

'We're not going to! But you're right, we have to go over and thank him,' Petra agreed.

'Nice to meet you. I'm Petronella,' she said to the man, still holding onto her glass with both hands.

He nodded at her, clearly uncertain whether or not to shake hands, since she hadn't offered hers. He half stood – as any self-respecting public-school educated man would on greeting a lady – and turned to me. I dutifully thanked him, smiling, offered my hand and introduced myself. It was the least I could do, especially since Petra had been so reserved.

'Nice to meet you, Kate,' the champagne-buying posh bloke said as we air-kissed, literally – our faces didn't touch. He held intense eye contact for way longer than was necessary and I felt embarrassed. I broke his stare by looking stupidly at the floor. 'I saw you come in and thought you both looked in need of a drink,' he laughed in his rah-rah accent. (I mock, but I do like private-school accents. They remind me of my father and what I could have been had I not taken a major life detour.) I laughed along with him. He hadn't actually said anything funny; I was just being polite, playing the game.

'Well, have a good evening,' he said. 'I may bump into you later.' He resumed his seat. 'Oh, perhaps you might care to take my card?' We accepted then left, heading downstairs.

Was that it? Was that all that he wanted? He played it well. I liked his style, laid-back and moderately distant, but I was certain it was a ploy to make us feel obliged to let him tag along with us later.

CHAPTER 12

It wouldn't be so bad standing all night now we had free Dom Perignon to drink. On the stairs, we passed some of the usual Z-list celebrities who were always on the party circuit. A lot of them came to this place: children's television presenters off their faces on whatever, professional sportsmen desperately trying to seem controlled when in fact they were acting like it was Christmas, hordes of pretty girls sniffing around them like hyenas waiting for the opportunity to snare their prey, footballers clearly trying to figure out which of the women who were hanging around were looking to sell a story and who just wanted a stamina-driven, booze-fuelled fuck with no agenda.

Petra and I put our arms around each other as we headed to the loo for a piss and another line. Or two. In front of the mirrors in the Ladies, women were preening themselves – surgeried-up, tiny noses near crumbling point and plumped-up lips glazed with masses of gloss. Botox was clearly a favourite; their skin looked unusually taut and rigid. The most noticeable three girls were tall and skinny; two had porn-star boobs, covered but protruding, demanding attention in clingy designer tops. I saw these three out regularly and each time I'd try not to stare, but I couldn't help sneaking a glimpse as they stood side by side. The strong delineation of their cheekbones suggested that they too had had a little help from a skilled surgeon. As I quickly scrutinised their faces, I decided that only one of them had had cheekbone implants; the other two just needed to eat some food and put some meat on their bones.

They were caricatures of femininity, with their flawless features, long extensions in their hair and clothes that marked them out as lavishly expensive call girls. When you know, you know; nothing can hide it. They were members of the type species of the über-high-maintenance woman. I watched them silently reapplying their make-up, admiring the time, effort and money it took to look so immaculate. I wasn't willing to invest any of these myself, but this was the kind of girl that Petra tried to emulate.

The toilet cubicles had been stripped of all flat surfaces, including toilet lids, so nobody could rack up lines of coke. This trend was taking over all the bars and clubs I went to in London. It was a minor irritation, but nothing that couldn't be coped with. The lack of a flat surface wasn't going to prevent an avid user from sniffing. I dug into the side compartment of my bag, fished out a small wrap of coke and took out my credit card (or rather Joel's). Carefully opening the tiny, folded-up piece of paper that held the drug, with the credit card I shuffled the coke around, trying to avoid the larger crystals. Since I couldn't chop it up to make it more powdery, I had to take it as it came. I used the corner of my card like a small shovel, scooping up a little pile of the white powder on the tip. I sniffed.

My nose was running. I dabbed it with tissue and found fresh blood, which was trickling onto my top lip. I shuddered, not in alarm but in annoyance. I'd have to take my next hit into the nostril that wasn't bleeding. It didn't enter my head to just stop doing it.

It wasn't uncommon for my nose to bleed, but I didn't like to see it and for the most part I hated the idea of other people seeing it. There were occasions, say, at a house party, when I would get a sick thrill thinking about people seeing my nose bleeding and thinking of me as a hardcore user. At times, though, a nosebleed made me think seriously about the fact that I had a drug problem. I hated that. It was easier to live in denial. My nose had never bled in the early days, but it hadn't taken too long before it started. Bear in mind this stuff is cut with crap that isn't fit for human consumption.

HOOKED

The club was always crowded with tanned Eurotrash, black, Asian, white and Arab faces, everyone dressed in designer clothes and wearing expensive watches, with most of the women carrying overpriced bags. People went there to see and be seen.

As we approached the steps that led down to the dance floor, we saw Felix, a rich-kid male-model wannabe with whom Petra had once had a brief fling. I didn't like him, and the feeling was mutual. I thought he was an up-himself irritant who had an ego far bigger than those of the successful self-made men I'd met. And what exactly did he do? Nothing, except spend his parents' dosh.

He was a layabout. Some might have said that I was as well, but I worked. I worked hard, very hard. And at times the stress of my job was a strain, and the strain was hard to handle. Change career? I didn't know how.

Felix occasionally imitated my Northern accent, which narked me. Couldn't he at least have done it behind my back? He was a clever bugger, 19 years old and image obsessed; I knew he would judge me badly for my casual style. I had no doubt that he thought I didn't make an effort. Felix preferred girls wearing next to nothing that cost them more than two grand, but that was his problem – and that of the women who dressed like that. One thing I knew for certain was that I was good-looking and I knew he knew it, so there was little for him to say.

Felix seemed to come to Lolay at least as often as we did. He was laughing loudly, drawing attention to himself, gesticulating furiously as he talked. He was tall and blond with baby-faced good looks. Whatever our feelings, when we met, I would smile and we would greet one another with the usual kisses. Petra glided seductively towards him as though she was on a runway, forgetting that the two of us were meant to be heading for the dance floor. She wrapped her arms around his neck at the same time as he put his hands around her ass. They both squeezed in mutual brown-nosing.

HOOKED

Petra and I bopped to the music, chatted and giggled. She kept tossing her head so her hair would fly around the place; she was trying to hold Felix's attention. A random girl with cropped blonde hair came bounding over to our threesome and threw herself at Felix, ignoring Petra and me. She was whispering in Felix's ear to make herself heard over the music. The DJ clearly liked Ashanti's new track, 'Foolish'; as usual, he was playing it. I was buzzing. Petra looked at me, then at Felix, then at the blonde girl. I tried hard not to smirk. I knew what was coming. My friend was on a wave of cocaine-induced paranoia, which can be quite amusing when it's not happening to you.

I persuaded Petra to ignore Felix for five minutes so she could dance and enjoy herself without letting the guy spoil her fun. I peered down on the dance floor from the balcony, looking at one of the footballers I knew, whom I'd partied with and had a couple of rounds of free sex with on two occasions. He was surrounded by pretty girls. For him, whether he would fuck one of them wasn't the question; it was how many he would fuck at the same time.

I chatted briefly to a guy whose name I didn't know but whose face I recognised. Suddenly, I heard a shrill voice screaming behind me. I turned my head and caught the last seconds of some woman charging at Petra. 'You fucked my husband, you filthy whore!' she raged. *Oh. My. God. We don't need this.*

Her eyes looked ready to burst out of her head and her arms were splayed upwards and outwards; two men grabbed her, trying to hold her back while she fought for the freedom to scratch Petra's face to pieces. Before I knew what was happening, a drink had been thrown in Petra's face. The small but robust female continued throwing punches at the air and screeching accusations. 'I know what you do! You're nothing but a fucking tramp! A whore! You fucked my husband, you fucking bitch! That slut fucked my husband!'

My heart was racing. I heard Petra shout something. I

didn't know what to do. A crowd was gathering. Felix stood in the middle of the fracas. I manoeuvred my way over to Petra, grabbed her arm and dragged her away to the loo. My adrenalin levels had gone into overdrive. We didn't need this, especially when we'd been sniffing charlie. The incident had disturbed my buzz.

'Oh God, P! Are you OK? Who the fuck was that?' I was on high alert.

'I don't know! I can't believe she threw a fucking drink over my new Dolce & Gabbana top! Stupid cow.'

The bathroom attendant handed her some paper towels to dry her face.

'Shit, sorry I didn't do anything, babe. It all happened so quickly.' Petra was clearly in shock as I rubbed her shoulders. 'Are you OK? Did she actually hit you?'

'No, she missed, but she's soaked my new top,' said Petra, with a wounded smile. It was obvious that she was about to cry.

'Come on, you'll be OK. Dry yourself and let's get out of here,' I said urgently.

'Thank God I've got my make-up with me,' Petra sniffed. She squeezed past another woman to get to the mirrors and I stood behind her. Her face showed no damage other than a little smudged mascara.

'I wonder who she was,' I said again, paranoid and fully aware that if this stranger knew that Petra was a hooker, she probably knew that I was too. My heart was pounding. The thought of anyone finding out was completely unbearable – however high on coke and pissed on vodka I was. I simply couldn't contemplate the idea of people knowing how I made my money. It didn't matter to me that the place was swarming with hookers. That was not the point.

'Hurry up and let's go,' I ordered Petra, trying to sound calm.

Tears welled up in her eyes again. 'I'm not going. We've come for a night out. I'm not letting some fucking pissed poison dwarf ruin my evening. What did we do with that bottle of champagne?' she sniffed.

'Look, it's out there somewhere. That's the least of our worries. It's nearly finished anyway. I can't believe you're bothered where the hell it is. It's best we go, you know, really, Petronella. You don't know, that nutter might still be in the club,' I said, playing with her hair, thinking about my own hide, not just hers.

'I'm really upset,' she said, trying to be strong, although tears were trickling down her bronzed face. 'Look at me.' The other two girls who were in the bathroom were staring. 'Some fucking bitch threw a drink over me,' Petra told them disbelievingly; she wasn't sounding so well-to-do at that moment. They said nothing, but raised their eyebrows and made some sympathetic cooing noises, as is expected of polite women on hearing such news.

'Let's go somewhere else,' I said. I was staying calm in an attempt to minimise the situation, but I was desperate to get the hell out of there.

'No!' snapped Petra indignantly. Maybe I'd played it too cool. 'I want us to stay here. I want to talk to Felix. *Shit! How embarrassing! What's he going to think?*' Her pride was bruised.

'Look, don't worry about him. There's a lot more for us to be concerned about than that jumped-up prat.'

We went straight back to Felix, who was still chatting to the elfin blonde girl. He reassured us that the woman had been 'escorted' out of the club by a bouncer. I stood to one side, watching who was around, still eager to get out of there but resigned to staying. I started wondering who had noticed what had happened. Did people now think that *I* was a hooker? I mean, it was bad enough hanging out with someone who had just been accused of it.

Petra whispered something to me, clearly agitated. I snapped out of my trance. 'Do you think Felix likes that girl?' she shouted, trying to make herself heard over the music. 'Look at her! She can't leave him alone. She won't let go of his arm. I hope he's not into her, cos she looks like a chipmunk. That would be an insult: from being with me, to *that*.'

'What?' I asked, not hearing her properly, distracted. My attention had been caught by a married radio DJ whom I knew, vaguely, and had chatted shit with for hours at an endless house party in Wapping. Watching him made me smile. He was supposed to be such a positive role model for young people and here he was, by the looks of it ready to take the two girls who were hovering next to him back somewhere for a bit of extracurricular.

'Don't look, but do you think that girl and Felix are getting it on?' Petra persisted, gutted at the prospect that an ex-conquest was blatantly rejecting her for someone she considered less attractive than herself.

'No, I doubt it. Why? It's just chat, babe.'

Her eyes flicked in their direction once more. 'Do you think we should leave?'

'A few minutes ago, P, you said that you didn't want to go. Some woman attacks you and you're happy to stay, but some random girl is talking to that Felix arsehole and you want to go? No, we're not going. You're just being paranoid. There's nothing going on with those two. They're just talking! Come on, let's go get a drink and dance.'

'Do you think I'm being paranoid? Maybe I am. I don't know. What do you think?'

'I think you might be—'

'Might be right?' she interrupted. 'So you think there might be something in it? You think Felix likes her, don't you?'

'Petra, stop it! It's the coke. It's making you over-analyse things. Forget it!'

'We're going to the bar,' Petra shouted towards Felix. He smiled in our direction as we walked away, clearly not having heard and not giving a damn about where we were going.

I breathed in the scent of clean-smelling men as we squeezed past them, their expensive clothes clinging to bronzed torsos.

HOOKED

It was mainly men huddled around the bar; in this kind of place, there were never very many women buying their own drinks. The men were slick and overly gentlemanly, parting dramatically to make space to allow us to get to the barman. Even though a flashy appearance, over-styled hair and plucked eyebrows weren't what I found attractive in a man, the stench of testosterone radiating around the place still turned me on.

'What can I get you, girls?' the barman asked. He looked as though he belonged more in a hip indie band than working there. And judging by the bored look on his face, he thought so too.

'One large Sauvignon Blanc for me and two glasses of champagne, please.'

He handed me the drinks, I passed Petra two, then paid the £37.50 bill. I didn't flinch; I knew it would be expensive. It did piss me off, though. However much money I'd take out with me (usually £200 cash plus my credit card), it still stung paying so much for drinks.

'What's this?' Felix asked as I handed him a glass of champagne.

'It's for you.'

'Thanks so much, Katie. I've never had a drink bought for me by a girl,' he said in his public-school accent, smiling.

'You've never had a girl buy you a drink?' I replied in my comprehensive-school accent.

'Yah, seriously, never!'

'That's ridiculous! It shows that you hang out with the wrong girls!'

He leaned over and kissed my cheek. For a very brief moment we'd established a truce, thanks to my simple gesture. Then he sat down and our usual air of indifference towards each other was restored.

The music boomed, the bass rippling through the floor and through my body. People laughing, clicking their fingers, hips jostling for every inch of space. Petra and I stuck together, our skin glistening under the heat of the lights. The beat changed and Christina Millian's 'AM to PM' came on. 'Whoo!' I was squealing, along with half the club, everyone on their feet, boys up against girls, girls up against girls. Petra and I dropped down low to the beat.

I bumped into a big guy who spilt some of his drink over me; I apologised profusely and so did he. We started talking crap. I was focused on the moment and loving my life. I had no problems, no worries. I felt sexy. I was euphoric.

'Let's go to The Pelican,' Petra screeched in my ear.

Burly guy gave me his card – another one. 'Call me. I'll catch up with you later. We can hang out.' I like forthright men, don't get me wrong, but I'm not certain why some men (without any indication that the woman they're talking to finds them remotely attractive) so decisively let us know that we will see them later. Let's face it 'catch up with you later' in a club environment means 'I want more time to check out the other sexy girls, so you call me later in the evening and if I haven't got lucky by then, I'll come to wherever you are and try my luck with you.'

I had no intention of calling him later, or ever. But having said that, who knew what the night might bring? Anything was possible.

CHAPTER 13

'Time to make like a rock star, huh, baby?' Petra laughed as we stepped out of the taxi. We approached the crowd outside the club and Galvin and Nick, the two doormen I knew best, spotted us. Shouting at everyone to stand aside, they splayed their arms to ensure that no one was blocking our way. I felt like a celebrity. They opened the rope and greeted me with three kisses. I was never sure why three – they were both English – but I liked it; it added to the drama. The ritual was the same every time I went to the club. Nothing equalled the adrenalin rush I got from the attention; I felt so important in that brief moment – my grand entrance.

As we went in, a girl took our coats from us. We were led upstairs by Milo, a suave Italian maître d' type guy who was the manager Henrik's right-hand man. Around us were scores of smartly dressed men and striking women. Some of the girls were dancing to the DJ's choice of hip hop, others sipping cosmopolitans, surveying the territory, checking for the alpha males. We went through the VIP room and into the final, most exclusive room, his private domain.

Henrik was there, on his sofa, a two-seater opposite the entrance to his private lounge so that he could see who was coming in and out. The room, styled like a Bedouin tent-cum-opium den, had luxurious autumnal-coloured drapes hanging on the walls and across a number of the sofas and chaises longues. Beautiful velvet and silk cushions were scattered across the floor so people could sprawl across them and there were always several vases full of heavily scented flowers. Henrik stood when he saw us and welcomed me warmly. He was always a little distant with Petra, but I didn't really care. Henrik had a knack of appearing to be as pleased to see me each time as the last, even if I'd seen him the night before.

It was busy. When Milo took our drinks order, I asked for a Stolly and tonic, Petra for champagne. The boss signalled for me to sit next to him, in my usual spot. He looked good for his age, surprisingly muscular, and he always dressed slickly, in snugly fitting trousers that showed off his enviable packet and a glossy, usually black, fitted shirt. Petra, decided to 'have a walk to see who's here'.

Henrik liked me. I dare say that he would have called me a friend and he probably still would even today. In The Pelican I always sat with him, and always had an immense feeling of joie de vivre. I never really knew why he'd taken to me; it wasn't as though we'd ever had sex. He never propositioned me or even implied that he suspected what I did for money. It may have been that he recognised that I was relatively genuine and down-to-earth and Northern. He had an affinity with the North. I also guessed that Henrik was charmed by my naturalness when out clubbing. Everyone was excessively glamorous, but I went out to be carefree, not to be seen, and I think that was obvious in the way I dressed and behaved. Henrik treated me like his little pet and I lapped up the attention he gave me. We would sit together gossiping. He was very judgemental. He'd whisper derogatory things in my ear about some of the girls who were out to impress, their assets on display. The men were often the targets of his barbed comments too. He could be harsh, but then he could afford to be; he was king of his club.

I felt at home and, right there and then, life was good. I had nothing troubling me – nothing. Henrik and I exchanged compliments and made small talk about his work, travel and our love lives while we sat surveying the scene. I felt cool. I was in the hub of fashionable London, casual as hell, sitting with one of Europe's renowned playboys. Models wafted around, their skeletal physiques draped in understated Balenciaga and

HOOKED

Jil Sander or the latest Central St Martins graduate designs. The music was rocking. People sparkled under the lights, laughing, uniting, getting stoked. A small, pretty waitress came over offering nibbles, which I declined. There were a lot of things I would do for money, but I couldn't have eaten after using coke if you'd paid me. I'd seen this girl before and we always flirted a little with each other. She was hot. She sniffed too – I'd seen her in the loos rubbing her nose enough times to know.

Petra came back and we both started dancing in front of Henrik, shaking our hips and showing our wares. Once I was up, I took the opportunity to use his personal bathroom to have another blast of white powder. I was soaring as I strutted back, feeling sexy and fiercely alive.

The DJ suddenly stopped the music. The James Bond theme tune boomed through the speakers – very cheesy but also exciting. Heading towards us was a waiter holding a magnum of champagne crowned with sparklers. People started clapping. Henrik looked at me and said, 'This is for you.' I squealed ecstatically. The waitress handed me a glass and, as if it had been rehearsed, the clapping in the room stopped as I took a sip and raised it, beaming. I forgot about Petra. I forgot about my dad. I forgot about Alex. I forgot about all my worries. This was my moment. Everything looked pretty. Everyone was friendly. I had money in my purse, a beautiful home and I looked good. I was animated, exuberant and with Henrik. I was being indulged like a princess in her castle, with minions running around after me.

I was also wasted. Fucked. My ears were ringing and my mouth was dry. I kept wiping my lips to remove the creamy deposit that was building up. It was past 4 a.m. and people were leaving the club. Henrik usually sorted out a driver to take me home. I hated leaving. I would be alone. The party was over and I desperately didn't want it to be.

Petra and I kissed Henrik's arse before stepping outside, where Petra thundered, 'I can't fucking believe him! He's such a rude bastard. He gets you a driver, but what am I meant to do? Walk?'

'No, just get a taxi,' I piped up.

'Get lost, you!'

I felt slightly sick and unsteady. I wasn't exactly drunk in the conventional sense – charlie makes you feel wasted rather than tipsy. The cool outside air bashed me in the face. The sky had already cracked open, revealing a glimpse of the morning sun. The birds were chirping. I had the noxious feeling of restlessness that told me I was coming down. I got into the waiting car and the driver didn't say a word to me.

Welcome to the cocaine comedown. Paranoia, regret, loneliness and wishing you'd never done it . . . I was alone again, lost halfway between here and another planet. I didn't know what to do with myself. All I knew was that I didn't want to be alone. I was fucked. Petra had gone. She was different from me. She'd probably get into bed and manage to sleep peacefully.

I called the champagne-buying toff we'd met at Lolay. So what if it was past four? He picked up the phone quickly. I thought I was thinking clearly, but actually I wasn't thinking anything much. I just knew I felt alone. Waves of sickness kept washing over me.

'What a surprise, Kate. I'm glad you called, albeit late.'

He likes me – I can hear it in his voice. 'Sorry about the time. Are you in bed?'

'Yes, but I'm not sleeping. I'm feeling too horny to sleep. What are you doing, sweetie?'

Ahh, he called me sweetie. 'Not much.'

'Come and see me.'

'Text me your address. I'm in a car now and I'll come over. Whereabouts are you?'

'South Ken.'

I arrived outside the mansion block and rang the buzzer for his flat, wondering what I was doing. No one spoke but the door buzzed open. When I found the flat, I tapped lightly on the already open door. My head was banging. I hated this feeling.

'Hello . . . hello?' I called out.

'In here, down the hall, second on the right.'

The place was stark, very bacheloresque. It felt cold, but that was probably my comedown. I walked down a hallway floored with highly polished wooden boards to a room where I found the guy lying on a bed watching porn, wanking.

'Hiya,' I said cutely.

'Take your clothes off and get on the bed, darling,' the man ordered. 'Have you closed the door?'

I felt weird. I wondered why I'd come to this place. The guy wasn't attractive and this wasn't a job. So what was it exactly? A fuck for free? I had Alex. What was I doing? But I'd gone there for something – sex, presumably – so why pretend otherwise? *Fuck it, I'm here now. The least I can do is get an orgasm out of this idiot.* At least I wasn't alone.

The guy was domineering, and in small doses I liked that, so I followed orders and undressed down to a sheer pink thong. He looked at me almost angrily. Maybe that was his 'fuck me' face. He began to stare at the porn and I wondered again what I was doing there. I didn't want sex, I decided. I just wanted to be with someone.

'Come here, sweetie, and let me suck your tits. You've made me wait long enough.'

I remember thinking, 'Ahh, he called me sweetie again. He must genuinely like me.' I joined him on the bed. He stuffed a brown nipple in his mouth and sucked it so hard it hurt. Cocaine is an anaesthetic, so the fact that I felt the pain should have been a warning to me. I grimaced silently but didn't have the nerve to tell him to be more gentle. I didn't want to disappoint him; I wanted to please him. Instead, I tried to pull away slowly.

'What are you doing?' he snapped. Within seconds, he'd taken a condom from under the pillow and rolled it on. My mind was on autopilot. I remember his thin frame and the loose skin under his chin. I felt empty. Sex with a punter is one thing. Sex for free with someone I didn't fancy repulsed me.

'Come here, you little bitch.' I hesitated. 'What's wrong with you? You scared of my big cock?'

'It's not big, mate,' I thought to myself. I giggled nervously and said nothing. *What are you doing, Katie? Fuck's sake! Don't do this. Don't do this.*

'Come on then, what are you waiting for?'

My mind was blank. 'I can't just sit down on your cock. My pussy's not wet enough yet,' I said in a childish voice, wishing that I was somewhere else, with someone else, someone who would prevent me from feeling lonely.

'Make yourself wet then,' he sneered. I should have felt angry. I should have felt something, but I was numb. He's just trying to be dominant but he's getting it slightly wrong, I decided. 'Come on, you little bitch, I want to see you get yourself wet.'

My uncertainty must have shown on my face. 'What's wrong? You like men talking dirty to you, don't you? Isn't that what you're used to?'

'No, why should I be used to that?' My head was battered. I wanted to lie down and try to sleep. In our brief meeting earlier that evening we hadn't talked about sex, my likes and dislikes, or the fact that either Petra or I was a hooker. OK, so I'd called him at 4 a.m. But I was high. People do that. I hadn't been thinking straight, but it clearly hadn't been a problem; the guy was wide awake and had answered the phone within three rings.

'Touch your black cunt and make yourself wet so I can fuck you hard. You like it hard, don't you, eh?' He reached up and grabbed my face with his hand.

Black cunt? I still didn't say anything critical for fear of embarrassing him. *I can't believe he's just said that.*

'Aren't you supposed to get me wet?' I asked while I rubbed my clit slowly. I couldn't feel anything anyway; I never could with charlie.

'Come on then, get on my cock. I want you to ride this big cock.'

Before I knew it, the man had pushed my hips down, his pelvis up, forcing his penis inside me.

I screamed. 'That hurts! Stop. Please slow down, I'm not wet yet.' I grimaced. My head was spinning and the sickness hit my stomach once again. I wanted desperately to lie still, but I said nothing. He thrust harder. I felt pain. The entrance to my vagina had cracked open.

'You fucking love it. You love getting cock inside you, don't you, you dirty slut.'

He was frantic and I didn't have time to think. He pushed me off him and ordered me to bend over. I didn't know what I was doing.

'You're being . . . I don't want to do this,' I said, suddenly sounding very decisive.

'Shut up and give me your pussy, you fucking tramp.'

He grasped the flesh on my hips. I didn't know what hurt more, his grip or him entering me with such force.

'Stop it! Fucking stop!' I dropped right down. I was frightened and unclear about what was happening. I was disorientated. Was this a sex game or what?

'Get back up here, you black bitch.' He yanked my head back and I couldn't breathe properly. 'This is how you like it, isn't it?' he spat, and released my head. Then he slapped my ass repeatedly with heavy whacks. I howled and fell forward. Excruciating pain shot through me. I screamed and then began to cry.

'There you go, you dirty slut. I knew you'd like that.'

'Stop!' I shouted. 'Please stop. Please, I want to go home,' I begged him.

He forced his penis full throttle inside my anus and pulled my head backwards. I screamed and gasped for breath – then silence. Cocooned in my private hell, I realised there was nothing I could do.

Instinctively, I reached behind me and gripped the man's

thigh as viciously as I could with my fake nails, but I kept losing my hold because the intensity of the pain was close to paralysing me.

A cold flash swept over me as I slumped down and my body started trembling uncontrollably. There was nothing I could do to stop him. I couldn't hear anything, but I was fully aware of my body shaking. I put my head into the pillow and pulled it tightly round my face, trying to hide the fact that I was crying into the pillow. My mind was blank. Another rush of coldness. I wasn't sure if I was going to pass out. 'Stop. Please stop,' I pleaded quietly, talking to myself and God. Was this man going to murder me? Was I going to die?

Clearer thoughts came into my head, telling me to keep still and I could survive this. He thrust a few more times before releasing a loud, throaty growl. 'Is it over?' I wondered, still not daring to move. The bashing had stopped.

I lay still, taking in sharp breaths, wondering what was going to happen next. Where was he? I didn't dare move. My head was still buried in the pillow. A moment later, I heard the extractor fan and realised that he was in the bathroom.

I jumped off the bed and for a second I thought I was about to collapse. I had to get out of there immediately. I had to. Frantically, I grabbed my clothes. *Do I have time to get dressed?* I couldn't move fast enough as I tugged on my clothes. There were goosebumps on my cold skin. The toilet flushed and I couldn't find my bag. My heart was banging mercilessly. *Fuck.*

I suddenly remembered that I'd put it under the bedside table. I squealed. As I kneeled on the floor to retrieve it, I realised he was standing behind me. I felt something hit my lower back and half turned round. 'Please don't . . . please . . .' I whimpered, not knowing what I was asking him not to do. My face was covered in snot and I wanted to scream the whole place down.

As I yanked my bag from under the table, the guy was laughing like a demon that had been cast out of hell. I didn't think I was going to make it out of the flat alive. I stood up and tried desperately to open the heavy door, but I couldn't work out which way to turn the handle. I was frantic, frightened for my life. I was sure I wouldn't get out of there. I was sobbing but no tears came. He started saying something but I couldn't hear what it was. I remember him sniggering as I rattled the door manically.

'You've forgotten something,' I heard him say. 'Hey, I think these are yours.' I glanced fleetingly in his direction and he threw some coins at me, which fell to the floor.

Suddenly, the door clicked and I ran. I ran in bare feet, hoping that I was going in the right direction. I was. I frenziedly panted my way down the stairs, shoeless and jacketless, into the morning light to hail a black cab.

CHAPTER 14

I woke up at just past 3 p.m. to an abrupt text from Alex: 'Where R U? Wot R U up 2? Iv called U x6. Wots goin on??'

I felt battered. My mouth tasted like sewage. I was completely dehydrated and my head was banging like a troupe of African drummers playing the djembe. Every morning was the same. I never managed to get enough sleep; the cocaine wouldn't allow it. I stank of smoke, as usual. Peeling myself off the pillow I'd been dribbling onto, I wiped crusted coke residue from the corners of my mouth and looked around my bedroom at my going-out paraphernalia, strewn all over the place.

Guilt bombarded me. The previous night's events flashed through my thoughts. I shuddered, slumping back onto the white linen sheets. I pulled my duvet up to my nose and a sharp pain shot through my head. I cried silently. The light was hurting my eyes and the chirping of birds outside seemed to me derisive. I felt like a criminal as I tried to reconcile myself to what had happened the night before.

Turning on one side, away from the window, attempting to hide from the stark reality of daylight, I stared blankly at the wall, wondering how I should respond to Alex's message. 'Baby, I can't wait 2 C U. Hope yr ok? xx.' Sent. I burst into deep sobs.

He called me. I didn't pick up. He called again. I still didn't pick up. I had to call him back. 'Baby, I'm sorry I missed your calls. I was in the bathroom,' I croaked, wiping my eyes.

'Where the fuck have you been?' Alex was furious but trying to sound calm.

'I'm sorry, baby. I really am.' I wanted to scream. I felt so alone. Dirty, violated. 'Please don't be angry. I've got a really bad headache. My head's pounding.' I was sniffing as I tried to fight my pain.

'Yeah, that's cos you were out drinking again. I mean, what the fuck, Katie? I've told you that I hate you going out all the time and you still do it. What's going on?'

'What do you mean? Don't go on. I can't deal with this now. Look, we're about to go on holiday. I don't want any shit from you now.' Tears came to my eyes again and I tried desperately not to let them flow, believing that they'd never stop.

'We need to talk, Katie. I'm fucking sick of all this bollocks. You're always getting wasted without me. I'm pissed off with it. Why can't you just stay home, for fuck's sake? Am I going to see you tonight? Will you squeeze me into your busy social life?'

'No, I won't.' I was indignant. 'And no, I'm not always wasted. What are you talking about?' I wanted to not be living like this, but I couldn't ask for help. I didn't know where to start. 'You went out yourself last night, but I'm not giving you a hard time.'

'Stop talking shit, Kate.'

'Stop talking to me like a piece of shit, Alex. Listen, you get fucking wasted as well, you know. It's just that you think that I don't know, but don't kid yourself, boy, I know—'

'You know nothing.'

'Let me finish, for fuck's sake!' I yelled. 'You brought this up. Like I've said before, you can be so shady sometimes. I wonder what you really get up to. You were probably fucking someone last night.' This was a good diversion to help me stop thinking about what had happened to me that morning.

'I'm fucking someone? Don't be stupid!'

'Listen, I can't make tonight anyway. I'm seeing Faye,' I lied. I wanted to wangle a night at home to allow myself time to recuperate, get my head together, cry my tears and not have sex with anyone for money or for free.

'You're going out *again*?'

'Alex, fuck off. Stop it. I can't do this now. I'm in fucking pieces,' I yelled, breaking down and crying.

'Whatever, Katie! I'm off. Some of us have to actually get their asses out of the house to earn some cash, you know.'

What does he mean by that last comment?

'Oh, get a grip, Alex!' I screamed through my tears. 'I've already got one dad, I don't need another. That's what you sound like, the way you're always going on. Please can you stop bullying me when you know I feel rough. I don't do it to you when you're feeling shit. But I guess your comedowns are easier to deal with than mine since you smoke smack to bring you down,' I said, convinced that I'd smelled it on him on more than one occasion after he'd 'gone to find something in his car', which had taken him 15 minutes – and 15 minutes searching for something is a long time for someone with the patience of an SS guard.

Alex slammed the phone down. He was furious, but I didn't care. Right then, I just couldn't deal with him and I couldn't be bothered to try. I'd already had enough to cope with for one day. I was shattered, but still worried by his comment about going out of the house to earn some cash. Why had he used the word 'cash'? Who gets paid in cash, except . . . hookers. *Does he know? Nah, he can't know. Can he?*

So he was upset with me, and I suspected that his mood would probably last for quite a while, but that was his problem. I lay still, deadly still, as I thought about the early morning. My stomach felt as though acid was burning through my intestines. My head felt as though broken glass was being ground into the soft tissue of my brain.

I felt desperately alone and I was nurturing a brooding hatred towards the guy in South Ken as I lay motionless in bed. I vowed never to mention what had happened to anyone, ever. I would rather the man not be brought to justice than shame myself, be exposed as a hooker. I was afraid that if I went to the police, because of the nature of my work, I would be accused of being a bitter call girl who had decided to seek revenge on this poor, unsuspecting middle-class English gentleman, that I would have got nothing more than shame heaped on me, blame and revulsion.

My head was screaming at me never to drink again, my stomach was churning aggressively and my nose was running and sore. I promised myself I would simply never think about my ordeal again. If it came into my head, I'd have to force myself to think about something else. A line or a drink usually helped with those things. I wiped my top lip – the mucus had dribbled onto it – but I realised that wouldn't be enough. I needed to blow it. I couldn't bring myself to get out of bed, so I took the duvet cover and blew onto that. My skin was dry and taut, but I couldn't motivate myself to get up, wash my make-up off and moisturise. Visions of the night before battered me. 'Stop it, stop it, stop it, Katie,' I told myself over and over. I had to shut the memory out. The flat was hot – as usual I'd left the heating on full throughout the night – but I just couldn't get up and turn it off. I didn't dare move. I couldn't move. I thought I'd fall apart.

'I can't do this,' I muttered to myself. 'I can't cope with this shit.'

Go to an NA meeting. Just phone them and go, Nice Kate was thinking.

You can't just go to a meeting by yourself, Katie. You'll feel really fucking self-conscious. Don't bother; you're just having a 'moment'. You'll get over it. You'll be all right with everything again in a couple of days. Goblin Kate was forcing her way into Nice Kate's thoughts.

I touched my face and felt pus-laden spots on my chin. I squeezed one and felt it pop. I took a look at the clear liquid that was on my forefinger and thumb and wiped it onto my pillow. I started thinking about work. I couldn't work that night, but soon I'd have to. Alex and I were about to go on holiday. I had to get more money. I had to. But at the thought of sex with a stranger, an acute wave of sickness jolted my tummy. Couldn't I give myself a break even for a moment? My head never seemed to shut up. *I've got to change all this. I can't carry on. Fuck, I'm cracking up.*

My heart was racing. I raised myself from my bed. Off balance, I stumbled into the bathroom. I put the toilet seat up and a barrage of vomit forced itself out of my mouth, the slimy waste crashing into the toilet bowl. A foul deposit tainted my cracked lips. I knelt on the bathroom tiles, panting, waiting for the hot flush to pass. My teeth chattered as a chill made my body tremble. This wasn't so unusual. But getting raped was.

Back in bed, I grabbed my phone and called directory enquiries to get the number for the Narcotics Anonymous headquarters. My goblin was chattering at me not to waste my time – but I had to do this. I had to make the call. I spoke to a woman who gave me another number. I was shaking. I wanted to cry, scream, hit myself, be whipped in public, anything as punishment for living as I did. I just wanted relief from myself.

I battled with myself about whether to call the second number. Goblin Kate vetoed anything that could be deemed good for me. I called regardless, and spoke to another woman who told me that there were NA meetings four times a week near my flat. She could arrange for someone to pick me up and take me to one the following evening if I wanted. I did want, very much. But did I dare? I just didn't know.

'Do you mind me asking,' I said, 'how long have you been off drugs?'

'Nearly five years,' she said.

'Really? So there is hope, then?'

'Most definitely.' The woman laughed. 'All that is required is a heartbeat and a desire for things to change.'

That was what I needed to hear. I certainly had a heartbeat. I was determined to take my life by the balls the moment I got back from holiday. Tomorrow was too soon. I had to sort out my finances before going to Turkey.

You won't change, Katie, the goblin snapped.

C'mon, stop that chat. You can change. You can, you can, you can. Start the day you get back from holiday, said Nice Kate.

*

Alex and I arrived in Turkey excited and ready to take in all the area had to offer. I was happy. I had a week away from London with my scrummy boyfriend. I just wanted this time away to be perfect for Alex. It wasn't going to be difficult. What could go wrong? It would be idyllic – just the two of us together.

So what if I hadn't yet been to an NA meeting? There'd be plenty more times. I was feeling fine now. I could go when I arrived back home. What was the big deal? The sun was beaming and Alex was with me.

We wheeled our luggage outside the airport and the heat smacked me in the face. The air was sticky and heavy. A stench of sweaty bodies lingered as people crowded together waiting for transport to take them to their hotels. Alex approached a taxi and tried to explain to the driver where we wanted to go. He didn't understand English and we didn't understand Turkish. They both spoke slowly, trying to be understood but without success.

'Hang on, babe. Let me find the details from the travel agent,' I said, wanting to sound like an organised citizen. I was hot and sweaty and desperate to get to the hotel to have a drink. We hadn't had any booze on the plane, which I was sure was Alex's way of exerting some control over me. He knew that I'd want to, but he also knew that I wouldn't want to set up a confrontation by drinking alone, especially on a morning flight. His urge to dominate was stronger than his own desire for alcohol.

I searched and searched through the detritus in my bag and got angrier and angrier when I couldn't find what I was looking for. 'I can't find anything in here!' I barked.

'Just chill, babe. It'll be in there.' I hate anyone telling me to 'chill', even more so when that is exactly what I need to do. It's a ridiculous expression that takes the recipient's feelings and places them down the nearest drain.

'You look!' I snapped, standing up. I was annoyed. Alex was doing nothing except staring at me with pursed lips. I didn't like that look; I'd seen it before and it made me feel judged. 'Babe, *please* will you look?' I said calmly. I didn't want a row.

He snatched my bag. This time the taxi driver stood watching us, smoking a cigarette with one hand on his hip, calm as you like. 'It's here, *stoopid*,' Alex scowled. I hated him for calling me stupid, even though he was at least pretending to be playful.

Why couldn't I find things for myself? I asked myself this question time and time again. I was constantly misplacing and losing things. Faye took pleasure in teasing me about being a 'scatty airhead' who could never concentrate on one thing at a time. Charming.

Of course, the drugs didn't help, but even when I was growing up, my dad used to call me a 'butterfly' because I'd 'flit from one thing to another', never concentrating on or finishing anything. 'I'm worried that the die has been cast,' I remember Daddy saying to me. 'You're going to have to change your ways, Kate, otherwise you'll fail.' *Fail? At what?* As a prepubescent child, I didn't understand what he was trying to tell me.

The taxi travelled into hilly terrain and we stopped to admire the distant ocean. The sky was a cloudless azure and the sun blazed through the rear window onto the back of my head. I clung to Alex's thigh. He slipped his Oakley sunglasses from his head onto his nose. I looked at him. In his three-quarter length skater-boy shorts, the hair on his chunky calves gleamed in the sun's rays. God, he was hot. I was so content in that moment.

HOOKED

Alex was very masculine, and physically I found him hard to resist. I looked at his profile, the shape of his perfectly formed ears with their soft downy hair, barely visible without bright light, his prominent nose jutting from his face. A wave of lust pulsated through me.

Sensing me staring, he turned to me and smiled, lips closed, almost a pout. He raised his sunnies off his face and his eyes flickered. Flecks of green could clearly be seen in the blue irises. He put his hand on the back of my head to pull me closer to him and firmly kissed my lips, which were plump and ready. Our lips were in sync. The taxi stopped and the driver said something. We'd arrived at our destination.

'It's quite far from the beach, innit, darlin'?' Alex commented. 'Never mind.'

I couldn't believe he'd just said that. '*Sorry,* but I did tell you it wasn't by the beach.'

He put his arms around me, but the damage was already done. He kissed my forehead and we followed the porter up to our room.

'Wow, babe, this is great!' He'd changed his tune. But he was right: it was lovely. I said nothing, though. I was too busy sulking.

He went into the bathroom. 'Katie, come here!' he called. 'Look at this!' I was standing on the balcony, angry about his comment about the beach, and I pondered for a second whether to ignore him. 'Come here, princess,' Alex called again. I went inside and found the porter still standing in the room. Alex came through from the bathroom and asked, 'Have you got some change for this guy?'

'No,' I said dismayed. 'You must have something.'

He gave the porter a note. Then he took my hand as the man shuffled out of the room, leading me to a large jacuzzi bath with ocean views and a two-person shower.

'Why don't you run a bath, stare out of the window and imagine you're on the distant beach?' I sneered.

'Thank you,' Alex said, wrapping his arms around my

135

shoulders, ignoring my sarcasm. 'Thank you so much for doing all this. It means a lot.' Despite my annoyance, I was pleased he was happy. Whatever it took, he was worth it.

It was late afternoon, but the sun was still high in the sky and relentlessly powerful. Alex suggested we go for a walk and although I felt exhausted, never one to be kind to my body, I agreed. 'Let's walk up this way,' Alex said, as he headed towards a steep incline. 'We'll see more from higher up. We might even get a glimpse of the ocean.'

'God, we've got a comedian on our trip,' I sniggered and we both laughed.

The great outdoors wasn't my natural habitat, but if that was what my boy wanted to do, that was what I was going to do.

Just past our hotel there was a small farmhouse sitting on the edge of a large field. It was stone and had a rickety roof that made it look barely habitable. We were walking along a makeshift pathway of rubble and I was concentrating on not breaking my neck or getting munched on by creepy-crawlies. The field was dry, seemingly barren except for a handful of trees rooted in its rocky earth. Oranges were hanging off the branches, adding vibrancy to the arid surroundings. No doubt at some point this land was well tended with hard work and care, but no longer. It had been left to fend for itself. I imagined an elderly farmer and his wife, both with brown, leathery skin, who had once lived in the deserted-looking house but had become unable to take care of their land and abandoned it to nature.

After walking for a while through prickly grass along the bank of the hill, we stopped to take in the scenery. There was virtual silence. The cars were too distant to intrude, but the crickets reminded us that we weren't totally alone. I yelped occasionally, thinking I was coming under attack from insects. I didn't mind, though; it only reinforced the fact that for that week I wasn't sniffing cocaine in toilets and sucking off strange men.

HOOKED

As far as the eye could see, there were defined strips of colour, starting with the radiance of the blue sky melting into the darker blue of the distant ocean. The closer the ocean was to the land, the lighter and more inviting the water appeared. The ivory sand of the beach was dotted with hundreds of specks, people compressed together. Past the beach, nearer to us, there was a thin but prominent wedge of white, flat-roofed houses and hotels, clearly catering for the hordes of tourists that would visit the area in the summer. Beyond that, we could see a busy road. The area immediately below us was a rich, dark green, full of short olive trees that were crammed so close to one another it seemed that they were one thick hedge. The separation of colours reminded me of the patchwork of farmers' fields in Yorkshire. The air was dry and heavy. I took in some deep breaths in an attempt to taste it. Together with the stillness, it reminded me of Africa. Although I hadn't returned to Zambia since I'd left at the age of five, there were certain tastes and smells that transported me back in time to when I was climbing mulberry trees in my father's back garden.

I could feel London and my usual life receding as the relief of being in a place where no one knew me, and where the phone wasn't about to ring to take me to a job, took hold.

'We're gonna get a convertible tomorrow to use for the rest of the week. My treat,' Alex said. I squealed excitedly. I'd never been in an open-top car before and I'd never experienced Alex paying for anything either.

As the sun started to sink lower and turn the sky pink, we meandered back past the haunting little hilltop farmhouse to our hotel, hand in hand, in silence.

*

'You look pretty,' Alex said, when he walked back into the bedroom after taking a shower. I was casually dressed, as usual: chocolate brown linen trousers and a tight white vest that pushed my boobs together. I rarely felt comfortable showing off my body in public, but I was more relaxed than usual.

HOOKED

'Come on, let's grab a beer by the pool,' Alex said. So many people use 'grab' in this way, and it irritates the life out of me. I always think that the user thinks they sound really cool, which I find ridiculous. But in this instance, my focus was not on 'grab' but on 'beer'.

I had mixed feelings. Naughty Kate wanted to grab more than a beer; she wanted a large vodka to kick-start the evening. But the Kate who didn't want to expose herself as a slave to booze was scared of drinking, knowing what would happen. I wouldn't be able to stop once I'd started. Alcohol would take its hold and other people's feelings would be disregarded. This was the part of me that insisted that drinking and sniffing coke were not a waste of time, they were fun. This was the side of me that was out to trip me up at any opportunity. As usual, however, I took the risk and tottered to the bar holding Alex's hand.

A beer. What harm could that do? After all, it had been his suggestion, not mine. Alex looked fit, dressed in baggy jeans and a casual sage-green Comme des Garçons T-shirt that I'd bought him. Designer clothes were for other people; I never bought them for myself.

We drank beer sitting on high stools near the pool, stroking one another's hands as they rested on the high table. We discussed what we wanted to eat. Moments like this were a little out of the ordinary for me. My mind was usually preoccupied with what excitement could be had next, not mundane options for day-to-day activities such as eating. Small talk wasn't something I did a lot of. As the chat continued, my mind flitted onto the argument that Alex and I had had by the river in Putney about me going food shopping without him. I wanted to remind him and tease him about it, but I decided not to in case he became irate. Food was not one of my big priorities in life, so I was happy to do whatever Alex wanted. Most of the time, I didn't care about having a voice or a choice so long as my boy was happy.

We trudged down the hill, arms around each other in the

darkness, the crickets chattering invisibly around us. That night, Alex and I talked in a way that we hadn't ever before, at least not without the help of cocaine. Strangely, I didn't feel like I needed it. OK, I might have wanted a little, but not enough to source some. In any case, I certainly wouldn't ever have suggested to Alex that we go and score. I managed to sip my wine without guzzling it, and it was only for a moment that I hankered for a second bottle as the first one was emptied.

When it came to my booze consumption, I always planned ahead. I hated to run out and liked to have the next one in front of me before finishing what I was drinking. It made me feel secure. I remember that a very dear friend, whom I rarely see these days, used to remind me of a time when I was 17 and I went round to her place. She had one bottle of wine, with no possibility of getting more. Even at that tender age, I realised that a glass or two of wine would trigger me into wanting to get blasted, so instead I refused to drink any, not wanting to put myself through the mental torture of starting something that I couldn't finish in the manner that I wanted. It would have put me in a horrible mood. I thought of it like awakening the dragon, teasing it with the smell of food, then walking away without feeding it properly. You only aggravate it. Pointless.

*

The next day, Alex and I did exactly what he'd said we would and hired a car. Each day we drove away from the touristy areas, heading high up into the hills, hoping to find more secluded beaches along the coast. We wanted to be alone, free to bask in the sun without people milling around.

I hadn't done any coke for a few days and I enjoyed the tranquillity of our environment. I was feeling very grown-up and we were doing what I considered to be 'grown-up stuff' like sitting quietly together reading. After three or four days, though, I was finding it really hard to keep my attention focused on being still. I could feel myself getting twitchy. The beast needed to be fed.

HOOKED

The holiday was about me and Alex bonding and taking our relationship to a new level. I knew that. But the desire to get wasted was bubbling inside me. I started to feel that I was torturing myself by having three or four drinks a night then stopping. I was lusting after something to take me completely out of myself for a while. It wasn't that I wasn't enjoying myself there with Alex. It was a compulsion, a drive to obliterate myself that was virtually impossible to resist.

I tried to sleep away my urges and instigated frequent sex so that at least for a short while I would get some kind of buzz. I just wanted something. It was becoming difficult for me to keep a lid on it. My worries felt like irritating mosquitoes buzzing around my head, needing to be swiped away. The only way I knew how to stop the buzzing was by getting messy. I lay in the sun trying to pretend that I was one half of a 'normal' couple but I was all too aware that there was very little that was conventional about me or my relationship.

My weird state of semi-sobriety was starting to piss me off and a couple of glasses of wine in the evening wasn't enough to numb me sufficiently. My need wasn't yet screaming, but the call was getting louder. I was very aware of how my demons manifested themselves – I couldn't have done months of a 12 Step treatment programme and not be aware of it – but fighting my compulsive behaviour was something I had not spent enough time trying to do after I'd left rehab – otherwise I'd have remained sober. There was a long, difficult road of exploration to go down before I could become the Kate I wanted to be, and even embarking on that would be asking a great deal of myself.

*

Alex and I found secluded areas away from people. We'd kiss and he'd pick bits of shrubbery out of my hair, which I didn't bother straightening for the whole week. He liked to see me like that, he told me, without make-up and with hair untamed. He told me I looked like an Earth Mother – nice compliment, but unoriginal. We talked about our future and how we wanted to be together, always, and I believed him and encouraged those hopes.

On the one hand these conversations sent desire flooding through me, but on the other I felt anxious, because I was still married. In spite of my secret marriage, I did want to share my life with Alex, and there, away from everything, all things seemed possible. In the heat of the sun and the warmth of our lovemaking, little else appeared to matter apart from what Alex was telling me – not even cocaine, not even booze.

Why shouldn't we stay together? We both wanted to, so it was up to us to make sure we did.

CHAPTER 15

MAY 2002

I tried to ignore Mick the driver, who was chatting to me, passing the time of day as he took me to a job. I was feeling a lot more anxious than usual. I needed to stop all this; I hated myself for it. But how could I make money without qualifications or even basic computer skills? Who the hell would employ me? And doing what? Sweeping toilet floors? I wasn't ready for that. Did I even dare take the risk of seeing what else was out there for me? I was so used to making money through opening my legs that the prospect of legitimate work terrified me. I was aware that at some point in my life I'd have to try to live a socially acceptable existence – but just the thought of it scared me witless. I asked myself the same questions regularly, but it was easier to pretend that I didn't have to put myself through that life change for a number of years. Sometimes I'd question why I had to stop hooking at all. *Maybe I don't have to. Maybe I can be an escort all my life.* Although some women claim to have managed to live that life for many years, I knew that it wasn't genuinely an option for me, for one simple reason: I wasn't happy. Not at all, not one tiny bit. Nothing and no one was easing my pain.

'Can I smoke, Mick?'

'You always ask me that, love. Course you can, feel free. Go ahead, darling, you're all right.' He was so friendly I wanted to cry. Any genuine kindness, however small, touched me.

HOOKED

I knew from conversations that Mick and I had had that he felt sorry for the girls but did this job because the money was fantastic. He easily earned two to three hundred pounds tax-free per night, and as a man with a wife and four kids to feed, he'd managed to cast feelings about the morality of it to one side.

I wanted to change. I'd made my decision. My mind wandered onto my options, and the thought of rehab reared its head.

To hell with that, snapped my goblin.

It'd be good for you, whispered Nice Kate.

Shut up! Shut up! I felt constantly bombarded.

The aftermath of rehab had been the most gruelling and challenging test that I had ever gone through. After months in a residential rehabilitation centre, it had seemed easier in the end to go back to what I knew – drugs and alcohol – than to face up to the real emotions that I'd buried throughout my life, and which, without the option of self-medicating, I had to face every minute of the day. I would rather have been publicly flogged naked in the middle of a traffic island than endure again the debilitating feelings of hopelessness, fear and sadness that I had experienced in rehab.

When I'd entered the treatment centre and stopped using chemicals, I'd felt exposed; I'd reverted to being the vulnerable girl who'd opted to start taking drugs in the first place. All the feelings I'd tried to escape had been body-slamming me every waking moment, without the usual anaesthetic. So although I knew I had to change, going back into treatment was an option I wanted to avoid.

Thinking about all this, I suddenly blurted out, 'Please turn round and take me home. I don't want to do the job.'

'What do you mean, Jasmine, love?'

'Please take me home. I want to go back home. Now.'

'All right, darlin',' said Mick, not asking me any more questions, 'but I'll have to call them in the office and let them know.'

HOOKED

I nodded and he phoned the agency. They weren't actually shouting, but they were clearly annoyed. I didn't care what they thought or how they were feeling – I was going home and stopping all this, and that was that.

I gave Mick 20 quid and got out of the car, closing the door on the agency and prostitution for good. I sighed with relief. I was never selling my arse again, not for anything. It was over. I untied my high ponytail and stepped out of my black wraparound dress and open-toed tan sandals. It was now time for me to focus on my relationship and try to live a normal life.

The thought of doing a real job surrounded by normal people scared me to death, but I knew what the alternative was and I was determined to make a go of it. I picked up the Yellow Pages and searched under 'Recruitment', feeling excitement and sprinklings of terror at the prospect of venturing out to start a 'clean' life. This was an opportunity for me to do something different, away from the sex trade. I'd had a few new starts in my life and, as Jim always reminded me, they proved that I was still trying. To me, though, these attempts just proved that I was still failing. But getting kicked in the teeth wasn't something of which I was unduly afraid, and at first I felt sure that things would work out very nicely.

I'd make appointments to register with job agencies, they'd find me a job, I'd start work, and a new life would be in place. It wasn't going to be difficult. Or so I thought.

But sitting in the test room of a recruitment agency, in mid-May, I could feel myself burning up. I stared at the computer screen and didn't know what to do next. I was on question one in the first of a series of three thirty-minute tests. I'd answered the first question but didn't know how to get on to the next. Two minutes, seven minutes, fifteen minutes passed, and finally, more than twenty minutes after I'd sat down to start the competency test, I realised that I had to call for help. My heart was racing and as usual when that happened I'd started sweating. I didn't know if it was just anxiety that made my body react this way; it was more likely to be a combination of extreme nervousness and toxins oozing out of my pores.

'Are you stuck?' the smiling recruitment consultant asked me.

'Er, yes. Um, how do I get *this* . . .' I said, pointing at the cursor, 'how do I get it to go onto the next line so I can answer the second question, please?' I was shaking with embarrassment. In an attempt to calm down, I persuaded myself that (a) it was a fair question and (b) maybe there was a fault with the computer.

'Sorry, what do you mean?' came the puzzled response from the still perky consultant.

I started thinking I hadn't explained myself properly. Not only did I not know what I was doing, but now this woman, who spoke perfect English, as I did, couldn't understand what I was talking about.

'Um . . . I'm here,' I said again, pointing at the cursor, willing it to move.

'Yes, question one,' said the woman, smiling a little less.

'And I want to get here,' I said, pointing at the screen. I could feel my face burning up.

'Ah, OK.' She sounded confused. 'You just press the return key.' There was silence and neither of us moved. That was it – simple! *Just press the return key.* If only I'd known what that was, it would have been easy – but I hadn't a clue.

My heart was thumping, a voice was screaming in my head, telling me to grab my bag and run. The woman leaned over my shoulder, tapped a key and the cursor moved.

'OK now?'

I felt a complete fool. My eyes were fixed halfway between my lap and the screen. I was mortified. She'd made it look so simple. The woman left the room and I followed shortly afterwards. With tunnel-vision focus, I headed through the open-plan office, praying to the Almighty that no one would spot me.

'Kate, are you OK?' I heard a loud voice call. *Shit. Ignore it.*

Ignore it. Ignore it. 'Kate?' I couldn't ignore it a second time. I half turned my head and answered into the air, 'Yes, I'm fine, thank you. Er, I have to go. Sorry!'

I walked straight out of the door and into the nearest pub, crying, feeling pathetic.

Who could I call who wouldn't laugh or think I was an inadequate idiot. *Jim?* I couldn't handle a lecture. *Petra.*

'You won't believe what just happened to me,' I told her, ordering a large wine. The first one of the day went down so well, especially in a state of emergency such as this. 'I just went into a recruitment agency and——'

'You did *what?*' Petra asked in disbelief.

'I know!' I could barely believe it myself.

'What do you mean? What did you do that for? Anyway, listen, do you want to go out tonight?'

'Petra!'

'It's Petronella, Katie! For God's sake! Look, I've got tickets for some premiere tonight in Leicester Square.'

My head was all over the place. 'Petra, listen, I've just had a fuckin' horrible, cringeworthy thing happen to me.'

'Babe, what is it?' she said impatiently. 'Why don't you tell me tonight? What time do you want to meet? It starts at 7.30. I'll get us some fairy dust. We're going for drinks at the Covent Garden Hotel afterwards, OK? We'll do the sniff then. Can you imagine sitting through a film after having a couple of lines?'

She always spoke so fast. She had an irritating habit of sounding inappropriately businesslike, the way some of the upper middle classes do when having a conversation, making it sharp and abrupt, thinking it sounds like they're just *sooo* busy they don't have time for chit-chat. But Petra wasn't upper middle class. Her manner could come across as cold or, more bluntly, rude.

'I'll let you know later,' I said.

'No, tell me now!' she snapped, pretending to be teasing. 'Where do you want to meet?'

HOOKED

'Petra, I'm getting off the phone. I'll speak to you later, OK?'

'Don't let me down, will you?' This was more of a statement than a question. I wanted to tell her to fuck off, but instead I swallowed my anger and ordered another large Pinot.

The Eagles' 'Hotel California' started playing over the speakers. I felt like topping myself. I sat smoking my cigarette with my glass of wine in front of me, feeling totally alone. The hell I was in was as real to me as the table I was sitting at. I was gripped by darkness.

I thought about the ordeal in the job agency and shuddered with embarrassment. I wanted to block it out, so I took a gulp of wine. Thoughts of the man who had attacked me made my stomach lurch, and the question of why I'd gone to his flat in the first place started whirling round my head. Then I thought of a client, a man in his late 60s with thinning white hair, who had wanted his tongue all over my body. It sickened me and I started shaking my head. I needed to block it out, so I gulped down more wine.

Then the internal name-calling started. I had a habit of doing this. I'd call myself names: *dirty slut, piece of shit, fucking useless*. I'd tell myself that I shouldn't be alive, that I was alone, that my dad didn't love me and my mother hated me. I'd say these things over and over and over. Sometimes I wasn't even aware of doing it until I actually mumbled a profanity out loud and someone asked me what I'd said.

I felt as though I was sinking into the chair. I wanted to disappear off the planet. I peered round the pub at the lunchtime drinkers. *Have I fucked anyone here? Does anyone know what I do? Can they tell? Can they tell I'm a whore?* I lit another cigarette and lowered my eyes, hoping that no one was looking at me. My phone rang; it was Alex. I ignored it. I couldn't talk to him and pretend I was happy and bubbly, the way I normally sounded. It would be too much hard work right now. I didn't have the energy or the inclination.

I started chewing the sides of my nail extensions and picking at skin that wasn't even hanging off. I felt irritable and angry. I was fed up with myself and worried about the possibility that I'd never be able to do anything except be an escort. Surely I wasn't trapped in it for life? *But what if that's what's been pre-ordained for me from a higher source? What if I've been put on this planet to get used and fucked by men who always discard me?* I felt that the darkness that was rooted deep in my psyche forced me to do the things I did.

But from somewhere there still came a tiny, quiet voice in my head telling me that the idea that I had been placed on this planet to be abused was ridiculous. I had Jim, who loved me unreservedly, and my dad and Elaine, who wanted the best for me.

After a moment's clarity, however, I was reclaimed by my usual thoughts of self-loathing, until a man came to my table and asked me for a light. I gave him one, which was certainly not intended to instigate a conversation. That was the last thing I wanted. I felt awful and was sure it was etched on my face.

'So, are you meeting a friend here, darlin'?' he asked in an East End accent.

I couldn't be bothered to talk. The truth was the guy wanted to know if he could fuck me – simple. The answer would have been no if the survival of the species had depended on it, and since I thought he had a damn nerve to even try chatting me up, I answered with a sharp 'No.' I should have said I was meeting someone.

'Oh, so can I join you?' he asked me.

'I'm about to leave, sorry.'

'Well, can I buy you a drink instead? Maybe you could sit and have a drink with me before you go? What do you say, sweetheart?' He spat before coughing his guts up.

'All right, then. I'll have a large brandy,' I said, managing a smile but making sure I didn't add 'please'.

'That's the spirit,' he said with a throaty chuckle, thinking he'd just made the joke of the century, searching in his pocket for some change. I kept a straight face. Most people would be taken aback by someone having a double brandy at 1.20 p.m., but not him, not here. This man, I could see from his weathered red face, was in this pub constantly – except, I imagined, when he went to beg for money from his hard-working son on his market stall. Judgemental? I didn't care. Maybe my disdain towards him stemmed from shame over the similarities between how he lived his life and how I lived my own.

'There you go, love. Enjoy it,' he said, placing the brandy on the table with pride, having bought a pretty girl a drink.

'Thanks,' I said, securing my bag on my shoulder. I stood up, downed it in one and walked out.

CHAPTER 16

I'd usually wank thinking about the men I fucked for money. The men I hated most were the ones who got me off more than any others. The more anxious I felt, the more I fingered myself. The more I imagined men who disgusted me fucking me, the more ashamed and guilty I felt after allowing myself to climax. Other than that, there was shopping. I was spending without thinking about my lack of income. I hadn't heard from or contacted the agency for nearly a month, and I felt that I could breathe. But relax? That wasn't coming so easily.

Plodding around the flat in my knickers, smoking fags, masturbating, drinking tea, sleeping, wanking some more and waiting for Alex to arrive back from work was my daily life. At one time, the antidote for my worries had been seeing him, but somehow that wasn't easing my anxieties any more. In fact, his presence was pissing me off. He was just a distraction, some entertainment to take me through the evenings. He wasn't a wizard who could cast a spell over my life and make things better. He had practically moved in and the pressure of trying to appear carefree while he was around, when all I felt was panic, was a massive struggle. I couldn't possibly contemplate my life without him around – that was too much to bear – but still I questioned if I really wanted him. I was confused. I didn't know what I wanted. My sudden change in lifestyle was proving hard to adjust to. I tried to immerse myself in sex with Alex in an effort to escape my feelings.

Money was running out fast. I had to find a job, a *proper* job. I was skilled at talking myself into things and I was sure that if I got an interview, I could nail a job offer. But when it came to the practical side, my fear of failure prevented me from even trying. I wasn't able to admit my financial situation to Alex. How dodgy would it have looked? I'd always had money, then suddenly I had nothing. He'd surely have questioned why. My credit cards were maxed out and I avoided conversations with Joel about finances since his name was embossed on the cards and he got the bills. I just couldn't face chatting with him about it. There was no one to whom I could voice my concerns except Faye. Jim got too upset if I talked openly about my work and money, so I avoided putting him through that.

Faye was the only person other than Jim who knew the things I got up to. Petra knew, of course, but I classed her as a player in the same game. And in times of need, I wanted advice from someone who wasn't directly involved in my chaos.

When Faye was around, I felt calmer. She didn't have the issues that I had. Her family was large and they were close. She worked hard and lived what I considered to be a 'normal' life. No drugs, no sugar daddy, no husband floating around, no scrapping with her partner. She had masses of integrity, which I admired. She lived how I wished I could: with regard for her emotional stability, content being herself and living the life that she led. She wasn't grandiose and she wasn't constantly searching for something outside herself.

I needed to see Faye, so I asked her to meet me for a drink. 'I don't know what to do,' I said, clutching a large glass of wine.

'You don't know what to do about what?' she asked.

'Everything. I'm stressed out. I'm not thinking straight. I don't know what's going on in my life.'

'Has something happened?'

'No, not exactly. Not yet. But I can feel it's going to.' I was aware of how I sounded. I had lived with a sense of impending doom all my life; it had started with the conviction that my dad would leave me like my mum had done. 'I can tell I'm going to fuck things up,' I said, lowering my voice.

'Fuck what up exactly?' asked Faye.

'Everything. Alex. Everything . . .'

'Apart from Alex, what else are you worried about?'

'Where do you want me to start?'

'You've stopped working now, haven't you?'

'Yeah, but I still don't know what to do, you know – for money, about my dad, with Alex. I mean, everything's a lie.'

'I think you need to go back into rehab, Katie,' said Faye, staring at me, waiting for a reaction. For at least a minute, neither of us spoke a word – just eye contact and understanding grimaces.

'I can't,' I said finally. 'I can't go back into treatment, Faye. God, can you imagine what Alex would think? He knows that I'm a bit chaotic but . . . I haven't told him I was ever in there.'

'Well, I reckon Alex needs to go in there himself, so he can't talk!' said Faye impatiently. 'A *bit* chaotic!' she chuckled. 'Sweetheart, this isn't about Alex,' she said. I loved it when she called me 'sweetheart'; it sounded how chocolate felt. 'Who cares what he thinks?'

'I do.'

She tutted. 'Remember how you were for the months straight after your treatment? You know, before you relapsed?'

'Yeah, I was a bag of nerves.'

'Well, at least you were clean. You weren't drinking and you started that computer course.'

'I lasted two two-hour sessions! I couldn't do it. I didn't understand a word of what was being said. The tutor might as well have been speaking Japanese. Faye, I can't fucking do anything.'

'Maybe at that time you just weren't ready. It was too soon. But at least the motivation was there.'

'Yeah, but listen to this, babe . . .' I cringed, realising I was about to confess my latest computer disaster. 'I went to a recruitment agency the other day, without realising that I'd have to do a test before they'd find me a poxy receptionist's job—'

'Oi, you! "A poxy receptionist's job" is a respectable job, missy! Don't knock it.'

'OK, OK, you're right. Anyway, so I went there and I didn't even know what the fuckin' return button was!' We both started laughing. 'It's fuckin' ridiculous, innit? The woman made it look so simple. I mean, do you know what it is?' Faye nodded. My laughter was quickly subsiding. 'Well, I'm still not sure. But seriously, Faye, one good thing is that since I stopped working I've eased off on the coke.'

'Yeah, but what about the drinking? And has Alex eased off on that cocaine shit too? He's not exactly a great example of clean living.'

'Yeah, I'm drinking less as well. I've had to ease off on it. I'm broke.' I avoided answering the question about what Alex was getting up to. I wasn't sure myself. 'Anyway, he's always watching like a copper, so I can't drink loads, can I? He's at the flat every fucking night.'

'Well, he should watch himself. He's a bit controlling, babe. I never know what to think about Alex. You don't sound too happy about him being with you all the time. I thought that was what you wanted?'

'You always say he's controlling. He's OK. He's not that bad,' I said defensively. 'I do want him around, don't get me wrong, but it pisses me off that I can't have a friggin' drink whenever I want.'

Faye started to laugh. 'Babe, you know this isn't all about drinking. This is about *you*. Your attitude, the chaos . . .'

'Well, what should I do about it? I know,' I joked, 'I'm gonna go out tonight and find myself a rich old man, fuck him senseless and take all his money!'

'Hey, just make sure before you ride him to within an inch of his life that he's changed his will so that everything comes your way. You'll give the poor sod a heart attack. I've heard about the way you shag.'

Shag? Ooh, that word makes me cringe. 'No, you haven't! You've just *guessed* that I got skills from when you heard me in the bathroom, when we were in Greece that time and you had your ear up to the wall.'

'Yeah, while rubbing my snatch.'

'Stop it, for crying out loud, woman! Enough!' I giggled. 'I don't want to think of my best friend listening to me having sex.'

'But it's OK for me to play with myself while *thinking* about you having sex, right?' Faye laughed.

'No! Course it's not!' I said, shaking my head. 'Look, Faye, I'm in a right pickle over here . . . What shall I do with myself? I'm fucking totally lost.' My heart sank. 'I wish I could hand my life over to someone else, cos I don't know what the hell I'm doing. I just don't get what's happening in my life. Everything's changing and I'm not coping.'

'You're asking me what you should do with yourself? You should know, honey. You've been where you're at now before. You know what you need to do, Katie. Do the things you did when you were sober for that time before. Go back to AA and NA meetings. Don't keep everything bottled up inside.'

'I'm *not* – that's why I'm here talking to you.'

'Yeah, but I can't help you really, can I? You need to talk to someone about some of that stuff you carry around with you. Those secrets, all that stuff about your mum, the things you never talk about,' Faye said. I didn't flinch. I couldn't go into that now. That would break me for sure. 'I know it's not easy for you, Katie, but I also know that only *you* can help *you*, babe.'

'You sound like you've been on a friggin' counselling course, Mrs!' I laughed.

Faye smiled. 'Well, you know what we've all gone through with my stepdad. It wasn't easy for any of us. Once we all realised that there was nothing we could do to sort him out and that it was down to him, that's when our lives became easier. But Mum had to go through some therapy for her to understand that, and then educate us about it all.'

'God, yeah, I'm sorry . . . I'm sorry.'

'And, you know, for my mum, being a proud Northern lass, counselling wasn't something she eagerly wanted to do, but she didn't know what else to do about it all,' Faye said sadly.

'Babe, I'm sorry. I can't see past my own nose sometimes. I'm going to shut up now. Just talking to you now has helped me. Thank you. It's been good to speak to someone who knows what the hell I'm on about.' I got up out of my seat, walked round the table that was separating us and wrapped my arms around my friend. Faye took my arms and put her hands on them as I kissed the side of her head. 'As for those meetings,' I said, 'they're depressing. I can't go to them.'

'You say that now, but they helped you to keep sober and start looking to the future.'

'Yeah, you're right. OK, I get your point. I'll think about it.'

'You'll think about it while you weigh up your unlimited options, then?' Faye grinned sarcastically.

I arrived back home to deathly silence.

Alex would be back shortly to breathalyse me. He was boring me. Everything was boring me and the urge to release my tension would, at some point, become intolerable.

I called Petra and heard an international ring tone.

'Where are you?'

'I'm in Monaco. I told you I was going. I asked if you wanted to come, but you said you couldn't because of Alex. Fuck, Katie, I've already made seven grand and I've still got another three days to go! You should have come. It's fucking great!'

'Bloody hell, really?' I was jealous. 'What's Monte Carlo like?'

'I haven't seen much of it, to tell you the truth. I've mainly seen the inside of hotels,' she giggled. 'I've done two overnights. They pay really well here, sweetie. One guy gave me a thousand-euro tip.' She'd 'sweetied' me; that meant she was excited.

'Amazing! Well, back here I'm bored, and I thought I'd

let you know that that pays you shit!' I was laughing at myself.

'Aw, babe! Let's go out when I get back and get trolleyed, yeah? Listen, I'm going now. I'm paying for this phone call.'

'No, you're not,' I tutted. 'I called you.'

'Yeah, but I think that's how it works. It's something like that anyway. I end up paying for received calls, so I'm off.'

'All right, then . . . Bit skint, are you? You can't handle a poxy phone bill?'

'Don't be like that, Katie. Listen, I'm off, OK? Bye.'

Minutes later, Alex walked through the door, smiling. 'Hey, babe, what's going on? You OK?'

'Yeah, I'm OK,' I answered, fed up seeing him every goddamn day. I couldn't even be arsed to muster a smile.

Alex walked towards me and I offered him my cheek. The cheek kiss – always a bad sign in a relationship.

'What's wrong?'

'You've been asking me that a lot recently. I wish you wouldn't,' I snapped. 'Nothing's wrong.'

'I know what's wrong with you.' He sounded patronising. 'You're upset because you're not getting wasted every day like you were before, right?'

How does he know? 'If you think you know what's wrong with me, then why are you asking me all the fucking time? No, it's not that! I don't know what's wrong. I'm fed up. I'm fucking bored.'

'Come on, Katie. Why are you swearing like that?'

'What do you mean? And why the fuck are you talking to me like I'm a three year old?' I scowled. 'Look, Alex, I like fucking swearing, that's why I swear, OK? I swear a fucking *lot* because it makes me happy. In fact, it makes me very fucking happy. And if you don't like it, you can piss off.'

'Steady . . .'

'There's a lot about me that you don't know, Alex.'

'Like what?'

'Like lots! I don't know. I'm stressed out at the moment,'

I said, wondering what I was on the brink of saying. 'Yeah, you're right, I'm fed up with my life and I'm sick of feeling like you're watching me the whole time.' I reached into the fridge to find a bottle of wine. Anger was making me defiant. Alex was standing in the living area with his hands in his pockets, staring at me. 'You know what? I'm trying. I've been fucking trying the whole time we've been together. I don't know what else I can do to make you happy, but I know one thing: I'm fucking miserable right now. I've got so many worries.' I stopped ranting for a moment to pour myself a drink. 'If you knew . . . I'm telling you, the stuff I go through . . .'

'What are you on about? I don't know what you're talking about,' said Alex angrily.

'Do you *really* want to know what's stressing me out?' Adrenalin was pumping through my veins as I lit a cigarette. 'You'd never understand. This whole fucking thing is a mess and I just can't cope any more. I'm fucking miserable.'

'Katie, tell me what you're talking about. You're getting on my fucking nerves, talking in riddles like this,' Alex snapped. 'No doubt you'll be blaming me for something when the actual reality is that, simply put, you're a friggin' alco—'

'*I'm a what?* Alcoholic, is that what you were going to say? How dare you accuse me of that, you fucking wanker!'

'Don't call me a wanker, you stupid bitch. You're in a strop cos you're not pissed every day, cos I won't let you.'

My rose-tinted glasses were barely balancing on the tip of my nose. I was livid. 'Do you know what, Alex? I'm sick of hearing you constantly accusing me of having a drink problem. Where do you get off with all this finger-pointing? You're the one bringing coke into my flat and rolling a spliff with it and trying to keep it hidden from me. No, actually, mate, for once my problem isn't about you and your constant fucking whingeing, it's about me being broke. Go on, give yourself a pat on the back for not being the cause of my misery for once in this fucking sham relationship.'

He steamed over and gripped my throat with both hands.

His eyes looked as though they were ready to pop. I started grinning, showing my contempt. 'Let go of me,' I tried to say, my voice strained because of the pressure on my windpipe.

'You're fucking doing my head in,' Alex seethed before releasing my neck.

'What are you trying to do, you fucking idiot? Are you trying to kill me now?'

His grabbing my neck momentarily calmed my anger, replacing it with fear. I'd rather have cut my right hand off than show it, though.

My internal pressure cooker had been bubbling for a while and it had just about started to whistle. Soon the steam would have to be released. 'Up until now,' I continued, aware that I was provoking him, 'you've done nothing in this farce that we call a relationship.' I was trying to gauge his anger. 'Have you ever thought if that might be a problem for me, Alex?'

He sat quietly on the sofa, rolling a spliff. He didn't need to speak; I knew he was listening.

'This is all wrong,' I said pouring myself more wine.

'What is?' Alex asked after a moment's pause.

'This. You and me. I haven't got a job. I haven't got any fucking money.'

'Katie, you've never had a job the whole time I've known you, but you've always had money!' he sniggered. 'What's so different today from, say, last week?'

My rose-tinted glasses toppled completely off my face. He wasn't even looking attractive right now. If he wasn't doing it for me physically, what the hell was left in the relationship? 'This is what I'm on about, Alex: your shitty attitude towards me and your lack of thought. The whole time we've been together, you've never seen me work, even for one day, and you've let me pay for this, pay for that, pay for virtually everything—'

'Just wait a minute there, you ungrateful cow!' he started, as if he were talking to a stranger. 'I bought you that nice bottle of wine when I went on that work trip to that vineyard.'

'Oh yeah, you're right, darling, you did . . . Anything else you've ever bought me that you can think of? In fact, can you think of anything that you've ever done for me? I mean, anything? I don't think you've ever even run me a bath.'

'Don't be funny with me, Katie,' he said threateningly.

'No, Alex, I'm sorry if you thought I'd suddenly turned into a comedian. Actually, I'm *really not* trying to be funny. I'm just asking whether you can think of anything else *you've* ever paid for or done for me in the time we've been together? Do you realise how many times I've bitten my tongue and not said anything to you about this before?' I said, smoking manically. 'Do you realise how worthless it makes me feel when my boyfriend, the man I love and who I share a bed with, can't put me before himself sometimes?' I started sniffing, but anger was keeping me strong. 'I know you've given me a line of coke before your hit or you've let me light a joint when you've just made it,' I said, half laughing at the shock realisation of the truth, 'but I don't think there's anything you do that could possibly make me believe that I mean anything to you, except good sex and a free ride.'

There was a moment's silence, then I released a loud yelp of frustration. *What the fuck are you saying, Katie? Shut up! Why are you saying these things? He'll probably whack you. Be careful*, half of my brain was thinking. But the other half knew that it was absolutely necessary for me to finish what I'd begun. *You're starting an argument, Katie, What if he walks out? If he walks out, fuck him. I'm sick of him using me like this. If he hits me, fuck it, I'm going to stab him. There are knives in the kitchen drawer.*

'I'm just amazed that you didn't mind taking continually without ever a thought about where I was getting the money from. Did it never cross your mind to ask me? Did you even think about it?'

You're going to regret saying all this if you don't shut up now. Stop it! You're going about this in the wrong way.

No, say it! Continue, Katie! The fucker needs to hear it and you need to get it off your chest. This geezer's been taking the piss for too long.

Alex started pacing the room, head down, hands still in his pockets looking for a lighter. 'You want a lighter?' I asked him. 'Here's a light,' I walked over to where he'd been sitting and handed him the lighter that had been right beside him. 'Alex, are you listening to me?' I said, in his face. *If he hits you, grab a knife.* 'Did you or do you ever fucking wonder how I cope with the pressure of you taking, taking, taking from me all the friggin' time, eh?' *Good on you. Tell him what you think. Just say it. You've been a financial doormat for this guy for too long now.*

There was a knock at the door. I never had random visitors. 'Will you get the door, please?' I said, shaking. My mind was buzzing.

The second he walked off, I froze. In an instant, I knew who was knocking. I don't know how I knew, but I did.

CHAPTER 17

I successfully dodged the questions from Joel about who the 'good-looking young chap' who'd answered the door was as we walked down the road to the local pub.

'I hope he's not living with you?' he asked, trying to sound matter of fact. 'I'd feel a bit stupid paying the rent on the place if you've got your boyfriend there too.'

'God, no! I'd never do that to you,' I answered, hoping that he wouldn't ask me anything more. He didn't.

'OK, girl, I trust you.'

He trusts me? I was sure he knew 100 per cent that Alex and I were together but he was too dignified to make a fuss. Whatever. There was little I could do about it.

'Are you working?'

By 'working' Joel meant a legitimate job. Part of the deal about getting me the flat was that it was so that I could save some money. He thought I was a temping receptionist.

'Nah. I guess that's what I'm worrying about,' I said, thinking about Alex, the fact that I was skint and what my boyfriend's response to it was going to be.

'Sweetheart, the idea of paying for the flat was that you could work and save some money,' Joel said in a responsible, fatherly way. The last thing I wanted right now was a lecture. Jim did that for me. My relationship was in pieces, my adrenalin was flowing and I didn't need Joel dumping his two penn'orth on me.

'Hey, I thought the idea of paying for the flat was so that you didn't have to pay hotel fees whenever you wanted us to fuck,' I retorted angrily. 'Of course, you were helping me out

161

cos I was living in a "shithole", as you put it. But the rest of it, the part about you and me not working out, that wasn't my fault, was it?' Joel had never heard me being anything other than sugary sweet. He stared at me in disbelief but said nothing, apparently choosing to ignore my outburst. We drank a bottle of Rioja as he talked about his wife and work. I wasn't interested in what he had to say. I asked for a large Courvoisier and drank it quickly.

'I've gotta go, babe,' I told him.

'So have I,' Joel said, 'but just sit with me for a minute longer. At least let me finish my glass of wine, darlin'.'

'Hurry up, then,' I said, trying to sound like I was joking.

Joel stood up and we held each other in an uncomfortable embrace for a few seconds before I pecked his lips and drunkenly walked out of the pub towards home.

*

'So?'

I was feeling defensive. 'So *what*? Who was that guy? Is that what you mean?'

'Yeah, Katie, who was that fella? And why did you go for a drink with him?' Alex seemed to be trying to remain as calm as he could, but his anger was etched on his face.

'I went for a drink with him because it was the least I could do.'

'Who is he?'

'Look, I didn't tell you about him before . . . you never asked me about my situation with the flat and how I afforded it—'

'Katie, just tell me who the fuck he is!'

'Fucking calm down, will you?' I snapped. My heart was beating quickly and I was trying to gather my lies. 'It's weird how this has come up today after our earlier—'

'Katie! Who is he?'

'I'm trying to tell you . . . I'm glad this has come up today after our conversation earlier,' I repeated, desperately stalling for time. 'The guy is called Joel, and he and his wife Gerry have helped me out for years.'

'Helped you out?' Alex yelled, clearly not believing a word of what I was saying – and I wasn't even in full flow yet.

'Yeah! What's wrong with that? They're friends of my parents and they felt sorry for me here in London, fending for myself.' Alex was pacing around the room. It looked like he wasn't even really listening to me. 'They pay half my rent.' I gulped, waiting for his response.

'You're a grown woman and they feel sorry for you "fending for yourself"? Bollocks! So that guy pays your rent?' He glared at me.

'No, him and his wife Jenny *help* pay it.'

'You just said his wife is called Gerry,' he said with an incredulous smirk.

'Alex, stop it!' I shouted, feeling trapped. 'His wife is called Gerry, OK, and they help me out here and there.'

'Does he pay your rent, Katie?' Alex asked, seething.

'They're really nice people.'

'Katie, answer the fucking question. Does that geezer pay your rent?'

'I get on really well with his—'

'Katie, for fuck's sake! Answer the fucking question!' Alex bellowed as he charged towards me. 'Does that bloke pay your rent? Does he pay your fucking rent?' he screamed as he shook my shoulders.

'No!' I shouted back. 'He doesn't pay my fucking rent, OK?'

'You've been drinking, haven't you?' Alex asked calmly, turning away.

'Yes, I have! I've had a glass of wine. What's the fuckin' problem? I'm sick of you telling me what I can do and who I can see.' I had to come back at him with something. 'You drink, sniff coke, smoke spliff and fuck knows what else, but I can't do anything without you breathing down my neck.'

Alex was grinning contemptuously, still pacing, occasionally squeezing his hands together. I was watching him, trying to assess what was going to happen next. 'You're a friggin' control freak, Alex.' I looked at his face to see how he was responding. 'I'm sick to death of you and your attitude. If you don't want me, then leave me.' I swallowed hard.

'All right then, I'm going.' His voice was trembling with anger.

'What do you mean? Going where?' He ignored me. 'No, you're not. Why are you going? Cos I've had two glasses of wine? I'm not even drunk.' I reached out to touch him.

'Don't do that.'

'Do what?' I asked, on the brink of tears. 'Alex, don't leave me, please, babe. No man has ever made me feel like you make me feel, you know that.' Tears trickled down my face. I didn't even believe what I was saying to him.

'I've had enough of this. I've had enough of you,' he snapped. I felt worthless. I just wanted him to cuddle me. 'I can't be doing with this. You're messing up my life.'

Those words did it. Sod the cuddle. 'Oh, right, so you're going, are you?' I said venomously. He hadn't wanted me to touch him. He'd rejected me. 'I'm messing up your life, am I?' I taunted. 'You always tell me that you love me when we're having sex, but since I told you I'm fucking broke, now you're off?' Again I felt tearful.

He headed into the bedroom.

'Where are you going?' I shouted. The tears were on pause.

'I'm going home.'

'Back to Mummy?'

Alex spun round, launched himself towards me and stopped just before grabbing me.

'If you go, Alex, never come back, do you hear me?' I screamed. 'Never come back!'

I turned around, my mind awash with fear of being alone. Feeling confused, I started pacing the room. 'I knew this would happen, I knew you'd fucking leave me. What did I do to make you leave me?' I started ranting. 'I've tried to be good to you, Alex, for the whole time we've been together. I've been making a fucking effort, but you're still gonna walk out on me?'

He said nothing as he went towards the door to let himself out. I ran in front of him and stood guarding the door, eyes wide open and tears dripping from them. 'Alex, please don't go. Please don't go. I haven't done anything wrong. You can meet Joel and his wife, they're nice people . . .' I knew I was losing control of the situation.

'Let me out, Katie.'

'No. Why? Why are you leaving? Please, baby . . .'

'This isn't about Joel and his wife,' Alex began. 'This is about *us*. I'm not happy and I haven't been for ages.'

'How can you say that? After everything? How the fuck can you say you're not happy?' I was angry.

'Let me out of the door, Katie.'

'NO!' I screamed. 'No! You're not leaving me! You promised you would never leave me.' Alex walked away and I followed, crying. 'Baby, please. Please don't go, please don't . . . don't leave me.' I was finding it hard to catch my breath.

'Fuck off.'

'But you said you loved me,' I sobbed. My cheeks were bright red. I'd been shouting so much that a build-up of white saliva sat in the corners of my mouth.

Alex looked at me. 'I made a mistake.'

I stared at him, my chest heaving. 'You made a mistake about telling me you loved me?' I was crushed.

Alex looked at me standing there, childlike in my need for forgiveness. 'Yes.'

My mind went blank and I silently walked away from the door. 'OK. OK, if that's the case you'd better take your stuff with you.'

I went over to the TV where the large metal rack full of his CDs sat and picked it up.

'Where're you going with those?'

'I'm taking them outside to your car. I'm helping you move your stuff. You said you're going, right?'

Alex said nothing as I walked towards the front door. I was void of all feelings. My nose was still running but the tears had stopped. I put the rack down to open the front door. Feeling a gust of cool wind smack me in the face unleashed a lifetime's feelings of abandonment that hit me with the ferocity of a tornado. I felt rage at his rejection and hate towards myself for accepting a relationship with a man who cared only for himself. I picked up his CDs and, with a guttural scream, threw them onto the drive, using every molecule of power in my body. I manically started stomping on them, trying my hardest to break every one into tiny pieces.

Alex rushed towards me. I flinched, waiting for his counter-attack. I stopped stomping. He grabbed his near-empty CD rack and charged back into the flat, muttering under his breath. The sound of breaking glass pierced the air. I cautiously edged my way into the sitting room. There, in the name of retribution, Alex was using the piece of metal to batter my television again and again and again and again, unleashing the fury that he could have taken out on me. My heart was thudding, although I felt calmer than I had been a few minutes earlier. Within moments, he'd silently steamed past me without a glance and violently slammed the door shut. I didn't move. I stared at the TV and started smirking, the same smile a defeated gladiator might exhibit, showing bravery in the face of his assassin. I was wounded. In pieces. Broken.

I spied on Alex as he sat in his car, head in hands, for about 15 minutes before he drove away. He was gone and I wasn't getting him back.

*

Brandy had become my drink of choice. It numbed the pain far quicker than anything else; even vodka couldn't compete. I spent my days trawling around a variety of different pubs in the area, alone, invariably chatting to/up strangers, mainly men, telling anyone, whether they wanted to listen or not, about the break-up of my relationship.

My money had just about run out, and I felt that I had no choice but to go back to what I knew. This realisation stung me, but thinking of other options seemed futile. Would a trained lawyer leave his job, then decide to work on a building site with hardly any knowledge of the industry and even less confidence that he could do the job?

I didn't know what else to do. I couldn't think of another practical solution to my immediate problems. But still, in an attempt to find a different way, I called the Narcotics Anonymous helpline. They gave me the number of a local woman, Janet, who would be willing to take me to an NA meeting.

It was nearly six years since I'd been to an NA meeting, and I felt nervous as we headed to the church hall where the meeting was based. Janet was a friendly woman in her early 40s, with two children and a husband from whom she'd recently split. She had been a heavy cannabis smoker and alcoholic.

On our way to the meeting, she opened up about her own situation. 'He stayed with me throughout everything,' she explained. 'But when I started to get well and was no longer dependent on him, we started to have problems, then eventually we split up. It's such a shame, but these things happen,' she said sadly.

'In hindsight, our relationship was based on my instability and inability to cope with simple day-to-day living. His role was to be my saviour, but, of course, he was never going to save me. Only I was going to save me,' she said with a wry smile.

We got a cup of tea and perched ourselves towards the back of the meeting room. I felt edgy, but I knew that I was OK there. Everyone was either in the same emotional mess as I was or they most definitely had been at some point and understood thoroughly what I was going through and what I would have to overcome to get better.

'Katie?' a woman's voice called. 'Is that you?' said a smiling face as I turned round.

'Hey! How are you?' I asked Samia, a woman I'd met at two meetings I'd been to years earlier.

'God, it's good to see you. I won't ask how you are,' she grinned knowingly, offering herself up for a hug. I reluctantly indulged her. 'Welcome! I only just came back in myself six months ago, after relapsing,' she said, shaking her head. 'It was like a war zone out there for those eighteen months.' *Tell me about it.* 'I thought I'd been through it all just before I went into treatment nine years ago, but, hell, man, it was fifty times worse during my last dabble.'

'Sorry to hear that,' I said, not really wanting to hear it. I was tired. I just wanted to be well without having to go through listening to other people's battle stories.

'But for today, I'm clean. Just for today.' I'd heard that a million times. Clichés, clichés. 'That's all we've got, isn't it?' she smiled. 'I'll see you after, OK, babe?'

I cringed hearing the expression 'just for today'. All that saccharine niceness would get on my nerves. I watched as Samia walked off to hug another one of the attendees. Without a doubt, it felt good to be amongst people who understood me, even if I didn't know them personally. I also knew, though, that I wouldn't be able to allow people to hug me willy-nilly as everyone seemed to do. I needed space. It never occurred to me that it might be odd that I could fuck a naked stranger but not hug a fully clothed one. I knew people in NA understood part of me that others who had known me all my life never could, but that wasn't a pass for them to invade my personal space. Sometimes hugs were all right. But only when it suited me.

At the end of the 90-minute meeting, having heard people talking honestly about their lives, feelings, struggles and joys, I realised that I had no other choice left but to go for it. I winced slightly listening to people rabbiting on about their drug and drink use and their failures, but at least it confirmed to me that I wasn't the only fuck-up walking the streets. That was reassuring and very necessary. As we were leaving, Janet stopped for a moment to talk to a young woman, Amelia, to whom she introduced me. I was about to be offered a hug, so I stuck my hand out.

'How are you feeling after that?' Janet asked as she drove me home.

'I guess hopeful,' I smiled. 'I want this to be a good year. It's my birthday today. I really want to do this, Janet, but I'm not sure about doing ninety meetings in ninety days.'

'My God! Happy birthday! You shoulda said.'

'I wasn't feeling up to celebrating.'

'I understand. There'll be plenty more. Look, don't worry about ninety meetings, blah, blah.' That made me smile. 'It's just a suggestion.' Another of the clichés – my face fell. Don't forget, there are no rules in NA or AA; everything we get told is 'just a suggestion'. *Zzzzz* . . . 'You take out of it what you want.' In spite of my cynicism, however, I truly wanted to be free from myself.

I slept soundly that night, a deep restful sleep, although, of course, all my problems were still there when I opened my eyes. I talked a lot and thought a lot about getting free of booze and drugs for good, but if I stopped for a day or two, I thought of myself as clean. I was nowhere near ready to give up in the sense that someone else would have understood it.

And in the meantime, I still needed money. There was no time to learn computer skills or anything else. I had my trade and for now I had to utilise the tools that I'd developed; later I could attempt to find a job in a world that I didn't understand. I would have to make a call. It didn't mean I had to give up on meetings. *Hell, no.* Earning some money by selling sex would only be a temporary thing.

*

'Dean, it's Jasmine. How you doing? What's going on? I told you guys I wanted my job back ages ago and your son said it was OK, but nothing's been happening.'

'Nothing's come in for you, honey, what can I say?' he said coldly.

'What? Don't give me that! There can't have been nothing. Even if a client asks for a blonde, you'll send a brunette. What's going on?'

'Have you been drinking?' he asked me. 'You're slurring your words.'

'What's it got to do with you? It's got fuck all to do with you if I've been drinking or not, you fucking—'

The phone went dead.

Meanwhile, the regulars at my local pubs were clearly getting fed up of having some perpetually drunk woman constantly talking at them and scrounging drinks – and so was Faye. I wasn't stupid. It was time for me to stay away.

I would do things my own way. To hell with everyone. *Fuck 'em.* The problem was, I was desperate to talk to someone – anyone except Jim. I was too ashamed to be spewing verbal vomit on him the whole time.

Phone calls.

Alex: No reply.

Dad: 'We're not speaking to you while you're drunk. This is not on, Kate. You're an adult and you need to get yourself together.'

Alex: No reply.

Alex: No reply.

Faye: 'Sweetheart, I can't speak now, I'm just going out for a bit.'

Me: 'But I'm calling your mobile.'

Faye: 'Sorry, sweet, I really have to go.'

Joel: No reply.

Faye: No reply.

Faye: 'You sound drunk. You need to sort yourself out, Katie. This is getting silly. What are you doing to yourself, babe?'

Alex: No reply.

CHAPTER 18

There was an eerie stillness in the flat. I was lost in my own thoughts. There wasn't one definable problem; there were hundreds moulded into one. Prostitution; Alex; my parents; my friends were all fed up with me. With a swig of brandy, I would try to cast those thoughts to one side. I'd think about how Dad and Elaine didn't want to speak to me and I'd choke up. Another swig of brandy and I would become indignant. Anger was my protective armour. The thought of Alex, and him never wanting to see me again, made me sob uncontrollably, but with yet another swig of brandy I hoped to find some consolation for his rejection.

My friends were distancing themselves. Yes, I had Petra, but I couldn't even face seeing her while I was in this state. Besides, she was too consumed with herself to be unduly concerned with how I was feeling. I called Joel, who didn't pick up. *Who else is there?* Jim. But the guilt I felt about his constant love and my constant fucked-up-ness prevented me from talking to him.

Feeling morale slipping away, I realised that I had to take decisive action. Immediately. I was a survivor and survive was exactly what I was going to do. I needed to sleep and try to physically give my body a break from the torturous chemical excesses. I knew that. I ran a hot bath. I had almost no toiletries left and no money to buy more, so I put the dregs of a bottle of shampoo into the water to produce bubbles. I wanted to create a sense of 'taking care of myself'. The steam made me drowsy as I stared at the water churning around in the tub. After a while, I snapped out of my daze and went into the living room to check on Freddie.

HOOKED

I touched his leaves, which were firm and healthy. 'How you doing, Freddie?' I asked, my voice cracking. I was sick, sick, sick of crying. Freddie felt fresh and cool and looked the picture of health. He seemed to have flourished under my care and I was proud of that. Tears began to well in my eyes.

I refocused on my bath and being good to myself. I needed to eat, but I couldn't face walking to the supermarket. I couldn't face people. The realisation that I couldn't get motivated to go to the shop caused more conflict in my mind. I knew I was being lazy and paranoid, and I started to scold myself, calling myself names, wishing I was dead. As a compromise, I spent some of the very last of my money ordering pizza and chips to be delivered to the flat. As I placed the order, a small voice in my head, my goblin, questioned whether I *really* wanted the food. *That money could be spent on booze.* I went ahead and did what I knew would be best for me. Would my head ever shut up? Would my life be an eternal series of arguments in my own mind whenever I thought of doing something nice for myself? I couldn't possibly live the whole of my life like that. I couldn't and wouldn't do it. I'd rather kill myself. For now, I had food, a home and a DVD – six back-to-back episodes of *Columbo*. It could just possibly all be all right.

*

I called Janet to arrange to go to a meeting and when she told me that she wasn't able to make it that day my heart sank. 'But I'll give you Amelia's number. She takes care of the literature at that meeting tonight. Why don't you give her a call and see if you can meet her beforehand?' I wasn't confident enough to call a virtual stranger. I couldn't possibly. *No, I can. I've got to do this.* Then my goblin sprang to life. *Don't call her, Katie. Just leave it.*

Trying to ignore the cunning demons that made destructive choices look like reasonable options wasn't easy. Throughout my life, I'd steamed into chaos, offering myself up for pain with a smile on my face.

HOOKED

The stillness in the flat was giving me the creeps. I turned round, sensing something was there, and as usual there was nothing. I sat back, heart racing. My eyes darted around the room, searching. I thought about what would happen if I sat there for the whole day without moving and realised that nothing would change. Faye would still be at work, my parents (*shit, my parents*), well, they'd still be upset with me. The bloke upstairs would still be going to work every day. The postman would continue to deliver letters that I never opened. I could sit all day wishing that Alex was there and still I'd be alone. I could sit there for a week and still nothing would happen. 'If nothing changes, nothing changes' was a slogan that I'd seen at one NA meeting. I needed help, fast, and I didn't know who else to turn to except Janet, so I did as she suggested and called Amelia, who agreed to meet me later that evening.

My head was chattering with ideas about drinking and sniffing. I badly wanted to do both. My urge to use was making me very restless, but I understood the basic principle of recovering from an addiction: abstinence. Sounds obvious? Not to an addict with an active goblin residing in her head. At that moment, I could just about cope with my desire. However, I knew it could quickly turn into an all-encompassing craving, and if that happened it would feel to me as though any resistance had been taken from me. I had to try and fight it by any means necessary. Sobriety wasn't simply going to wash over me, that was very, very obvious.

Just go and buy some wine. It's OK. Everyone drinks wine. It's normal. Goblin Kate.

No, you'll blow it if you do. Nice Kate.

What else is there to do? Nothing. Just get pissed. You'll feel so much better.

No. Don't do it.

Do you really think you can resist me? What's the point of trying? You know you can't do it.

My head, my thoughts! Would I ever have any peace? Probably not.

I arranged a last-minute doctor's appointment. I didn't know what else to do and I had to do something – anything but indulge my obsessions.

'What's the problem?' the doctor asked.

'Everything.'

'Can you be more specific?'

'I'm not coping.'

'It's OK, take a deep breath. Take your time.' The doctor smiled sympathetically.

'Everything's wrong. I don't feel at all right. I feel I'm cracking up. I drink too much. I don't know what to do. I've got problems and I've got no one to turn to.' I started whimpering. The doctor was silent, letting me carry on. 'My life's a mess. I'm really lonely. I need help. Please . . . please can you help me?' I looked into her face and her warmth made me sob out loud.

'Apart from drinking too much, is there anything else?'

'What do you mean?'

'Drugs?'

'Yes, cocaine.'

'How much?'

'As much as I can.'

'How much is that?'

'Quite a lot.'

'Right . . . OK . . . have you ever thought of joining a group or some sort of club or a night class or something to ease your loneliness? Maybe get a hobby?'

'Er, no, I haven't.' I stared at her. 'I think the problem is a little bit deeper than that.' I was confused.

'Do you speak to your parents about how you feel?'

'Um, no. We rarely talk.'

'You don't even talk to your mother?'

'No. I don't know her. My dad brought me up alone.' The number of times I'd said this throughout my life was innumerable and people's reactions were always the same: sympathy and curiosity. Knowing this and wanting to avoid it, I changed the subject. 'Um, I sell my body in order to pay for the coke,' I blurted out. 'I feel like I'm sinking.' I accepted a tissue.

'It's OK, we'll help you.' She sounded gentle. I wanted to hug her. I wanted her to stroke my hair. I wished she was my mummy. 'Try and remain as calm as possible, OK? You'll be all right. Now, do you have any suicidal thoughts?'

'Yeah, but I'm not going to kill myself. I've had suicidal thoughts on and off all my life. I want to change and live differently, but I'm not gonna kill myself.' I tried hard to smile. More than anything, I wanted to be held, to be soothed and for someone to tell me that everything would be all right.

'I'm going to give you a prescription for antidepressants, OK? And arrange for you to see one of our therapists here. You'll get a letter offering you an appointment within the next two weeks. Now, I can see in your notes that you've got a history of addiction. OK . . . and you seem to have psychiatric reports from when you were around 15 years old?'

'Yeah.'

'Well, let's try and get this resolved for you this time, all right, Kate? There's just one thing: you're not to drink when you take these tablets, otherwise they probably won't work.'

Not drink? I nodded. I wanted to do it. I really did. I walked out of the doctor's surgery clutching a prescription for Prozac, which I took to the chemist on my way back home. I popped one of the pills as I walked down the street, then another, despite being told that I was to take only one tablet per day. The stuff was non-addictive – so what? Things couldn't feel much worse than they already did.

*

Amelia was cool. She was funny, sassy and full of self-confidence. She'd been clean for nearly two years. This was how I hoped recovery would be. The woman was 32 years old, she had a job, which wasn't her dream job but it paid the rent on her flat, she was skint a lot of the time but cared little about it. We hung out and laughed and drank lots of coffee, at least she did – it made me feel too manic. Watching her and listening to her gave me hope that I was going to be OK. Sobriety wasn't gloomy. On the contrary, it was clear that Amelia was having the time of her life. She told me that the first year of her new life had been tough, but things were getting better for her each day she went without drugs and drink. It wasn't going to be easy – no one had told me that it would be – but first and foremost I desperately wanted the compulsion to drink and use cocaine to leave me. I doubted it ever would, but Amelia assured me that it would. She couldn't guarantee when, but it would as long as I didn't continue feeding my demons.

For me, though, it wasn't that simple. Not yet. While I was attending meetings, I was able to give up drinking for a day or so at a time, and drugs for longer, sometimes. But I was unable to stop for a long enough period to really change things. In my head, although I was still drinking and taking drugs, the fact that I was even trying to ease off meant that I was heading in the right direction.

Towards the end of June 2002, I made up my mind that I would work in a flat. Not in a brothel (that was illegal) but in a flat where only one woman worked at any given time. It would tide me over until I could think more clearly. The doctor had said it would take a few weeks for the antidepressants to start working. I didn't have time to waste. I needed to be out earning money within days. I'd made a decision to make a go of improving my life and I had already started implementing changes; now I needed money. I'd never worked a flat before and didn't know the ropes, but fucking was fucking. *How difficult can it be?*

'You don't take black girls?' I asked the woman on the other end of the phone. *What the hell is this all about?* 'There must be men in Wimbledon who want to fuck a black girl,' I insisted as I flicked through the back of the paper, where there were scores of adverts looking for working girls.

'Maybe there are, love, but not here. Try somewhere else.'

Finally, a girl answered who sounded keen to get me on board. She was opening her first agency, out in Ruislip. She wanted to meet me. 'We'll pick you up from the Tube station tomorrow morning around ten for an interview.'

'We? Who do you mean by "we"?'

'Me and my boyfriend.'

'I'm not comfortable with your boyfriend being there, to tell you the truth.'

'Well, it should be OK, cos if you get the job . . .'

'If I get the job, what?' I sniggered. 'If I get the job, I get screwed all day by strange men, right?'

'Er, well, yeah, hopefully you will. It's more money for you, babe, know what I mean?'

'And what cut do you take?'

'We'll cover all that at the interview, OK? See you tomorrow,' said the aspiring madam before putting the phone down.

I laughed to myself at being told I was having an 'interview' to assess my suitability for getting rutted by random men for less than a hundred quid a pop. I knew it was appalling money but couldn't bring myself to beg Dean for my agency job back, and it hadn't even entered my head to join another agency. This would have to do for now.

I couldn't face the 'date-like' aspects that often come with agency work; you're required to be conversational and charming as well as good in the sack. Agency work required so much more of a girl than I imagined sex in a flat would. Guys paying £300 an hour expected the girl to be well maintained, with perfect hair and nails, and plenty of ego massaging was required. I was in no frame of mind to be making an effort with punters. My usual exuberance had been put on hold as I had more pressing issues to deal with, such as getting money. I was sure this new job would be 'fuck and go' – perfect.

HOOKED

Immediately after I'd spoken to my prospective employer, I received a text from Joel: 'Darlin, U knw the lease is up @ the start of September? Im not goin 2 renew it. Sorry. x.'

Icing on the cake.

CHAPTER 19

Interview over and down to work. The 'maid' – the woman who answered the phones – came in, all 4 ft 11 in. of her, with the biggest pair of boobs I've ever seen. Lorraine was a skeleton with a layer of skin draped over it, clearly an active drug user who was past her best years. She'd obviously had her boobs enlarged at a time when she was prettier, more glamorous and had all her own teeth. She was lovely, a friendly woman who must have been in her 40s if she was a day but dressed, sounded and behaved as though she were 17, and had the body of a 13-year-old girl who'd had her birthday-party balloons stuck onto her chest. She had overly long, stringy, mousy-brown hair and a haggard face, with just four, posssibly five, brown teeth in the front of her mouth.

We got on brilliantly, although when I first met her I was scared by her appearance. She was funny. She was a working girl herself, but, as she told me in her Birmingham accent, she was 'trying to go straight, know what I mean, darlin'?' Yes, indeed. I knew exactly what she meant. It was always a matter of *when*.

The flat was in a block just off the main road to Ruislip from central London. It was OK, nothing special but certainly not a hovel. It was just a bland, ordinary flat. It was basic but clean. The wallpaper obviously hadn't been changed since sometime in the very early '80s and the kitchen units had no doubt been in fashion at some point in the past 20 years. The bathroom had a green suite, no shower and a broken window. I had to sit in the bath rather than stand under a shower to wash myself after every couple of clients. If I'd thought about it, I'd have had to scrub myself with disinfectant after each guy. But for the time I was there, I was on lockdown. I couldn't spend time pondering what I was doing.

Lorraine and I arrived any time between 10 and 11 a.m. We'd sit drinking tea, eating, popping Valium, of which Lorraine always had a supply, and we'd smoke, watch TV and laugh a lot. I loved pills such as Valium. They made me feel hyper, not sleepy. Whenever the phone rang, the punter would ask for a description of the woman and if he wanted to fuck me, Lorraine would give him the address and he'd come, ring the intercom, come up the stairs, go into the bedroom and discuss what services he wanted, then hand over the cash. There was a baby monitor in the bedroom so that the transaction could be heard in the sitting room by the maid, which was supposed to prevent whoever was working the flat short-changing the madam.

Hookers we were; stupid we were not. I realised after my first client that I could simply switch off the baby monitor. What were they going to do? Sack me? It was only me they had working for them so far, and in the first three days I'd raked in more than 1,400 quid. I was good at my job, and besides, a new agency and a new woman always attracted attention.

Usually a flat has a different girl working every day, but not this one. It was new and the girl who was running it was lazy and just happy to be getting some income without having to do jack. She wasn't going to get rid of me. The price was £80 to £100 a pop (take that as you will). It wasn't based on time; it was about a quick bit of whatever they fancied, an orgasm and they were gone. I charged the punter what I wanted and gave the naive madam whatever I felt like, enough not to arouse suspicion, in case Lorraine was in cahoots with her. I trusted no one.

I usually pretended that the punter had just wanted a blow job, which cost £30. I'd take half of that, give the flat half and pocket the rest. So, from a quick fuck that cost around 100 quid, I gave the flat £15 and kept the rest. *To hell with them.*

HOOKED

Who's doing the work here? I had to make and save as much money as possible, not only because making money was the only thing giving me focus, but because it bought me freedom to drink and sniff as much as I needed to keep numb.

I also had to find somewhere to live, which would be a struggle considering I had more chance of living on the moon than getting a flat through an estate agent without a huge initial payment. Those damn credit checks were a pain in my butt. There was no way that I'd have been able to live in the flat that I was in if it hadn't been for Joel. Moving back into a dingy bedsit like the one I'd lived in before Joel had agreed to sort me out was not something I wanted to imagine. Regardless of the fact that I was earning lots of money, saving enough to pay six months' rent up front to get my foot in the door of a swanky flat was going to prove very difficult.

One day during my third or fourth week in Ruislip, I arrived as usual late morning and waited for hordes of men to come and give me some cash so they could use my snatch. Lorraine was already there. In the bathroom, there was a smell that I recognised instantly. I breathed in the sickly, chemical smell that was making me shudder and I could practically taste it: heroin.

Once you've smelled it and tasted heroin smoked on tinfoil, you never forget its distinct, putrid stench. It's like nothing else. I had done my time with heroin when I'd been in my late teens. It made me feel calm, completely took away my perpetual nervousness and rounded the edges of my awkwardness. The thing that terrified me about heroin (and which I'd never forgotten) was a period of time when I had used it for three days consecutively and on the fourth I'd woken up suffering with cramp in the backs of my legs. That morning I was vomiting from my mouth and anus – the first signs of physical addiction. I wasn't wholly certain that the symptoms I was experiencing were a direct result of the H, but I guessed that they were.

HOOKED

Not only did it wipe me out, but it took me in a vice-like grip within days, ready to squeeze any bit of resistance out of me. Even though I enjoyed the effects of heroin and I thoroughly embraced the calmness that it induced in me (after I got over the initial burst of vomiting the first couple of times that I'd ingested it), I was very wary of its power.

It would have been easy for me to view my foray into taking heroin as simply another part of my drug-using career. My saving grace, preventing me entering a life of physical dependency on the drug, was my stint in rehab. It was normal for me to experiment. I wasn't aware enough about what was happening to me to realise that when I wasn't using, I was actually just going through the motions of my non-using life, not really participating, more accurately observing. Everything bored me. I enjoyed nothing. All that really mattered was my next hit of whatever. When I was sent to treatment, I was nonetheless relieved to be placed somewhere where my compulsions could not immediately be acted on. And after those months in treatment, when I relapsed, I avoided downers.

So I escaped heroin addiction. But I convinced myself that if I used only stimulants and alcohol, I'd be all right. After all, alcohol wasn't a drug, was it? Er, of course not. So what if alcoholics suffered the worst withdrawals of anyone in rehab? So what if alcohol killed more people than illegal drug abuse?

Most people don't bother to find out which drug suits them best, but I believe I was a classic example of how an inability to cope with one's emotions can lead a person to seek out a reprieve from the pain. I was actively searching for something to ease my feelings of inadequacy. I had an obsessive nature, so whatever it was that I chose to use to escape, I'd have got addicted to it. My three most enduring obsessions – cocaine, alcohol and sex – ran concurrently with one another. Cocaine and alcohol were in joint pole position, with sex tailing them. Before I started selling my body, I'd used sex as comfort, seeking validation from men, confirmation that I was desirable and lovable. By many people's standards, I was a late starter. I didn't have my first snog until I was 14 years old and lost my virginity two weeks before my 16th birthday. That was with Stephen, the boy I moved to London with, with whom I did heroin, by whom I got pregnant and who died of an overdose in his 20s.

The smell of heroin in the Ruislip flat shook me up. I wasn't craving it; the stuff intimidated me. I understood its potential. It made my skin crawl thinking that Lorraine had just confirmed to me what I actually already knew but had wanted to ignore: she really was an active junkie. Still, I decided to say nothing.

Cocaine use and heroin use were as similar, in my mind, as the taste of cheese and the taste of strawberries. They had no connection. I didn't think in terms of 'drugs are drugs', despite being told this when I had been in rehab years before. It was easier for me not to think like that. There's so much elitism amongst druggies. People who smoke weed and drink think that everyone else is scum. People who sniff cocaine think that people who smoke weed are hippies or gangsters and that everyone else is scum. People who use heroin think that cocaine users are up-themselves arseholes and that weed smokers are lightweights. And people who use crack don't think anything. They just want their next hit.

The phone rang. 'You're gonna get screwed in 20 minutes, love, you'd better get ready,' Lorraine chuckled. My heart leapt. I was about to fuck a punter; adrenalin was preparing me for combat. I scurried into the lounge and grabbed my bag to take into the bathroom so I could change into some underwear. Yes, I was coy. I'd never change in front of Lorraine, although she often did in front of me before leaving work for the day. I was pretty shy for a whore. The thought of leaving my clothes on the back of the bathroom door when the client would more than likely use the bathroom after he'd finished and might touch my personal belongings repulsed me. Fingering my pussy was tolerable – a means to an end –

but fingering my personal effects, that was forbidden. I waited in the bedroom for the intercom to buzz.

'Ah, excuse,' said the short Asian man, with a sleazy grin, as he was shown into the bedroom. *Oh, fucking hell.* He was gross.

'You beautiful.'

I gave him an insincere smile. 'So, what is it you want?' I asked, checking again that I'd turned the monitor off.

'You got nice bottom. Is nice,' he grinned.

I ignored that, feeling self-conscious about his comment because my arse was the part of my body that I was most insecure about. Why should I care what a complete stranger, particularly a punter, thought about it? I did, though. 'So, is it full sex or what?' I asked, forcing myself to speak softly. It was either that or I'd have spat in his face; he disgusted me.

'Yes, yes. Full. Everything,' he said eagerly, nodding his head again while furiously unbuttoning his shirt.

'A hundred quid, then.'

He stopped grabbing at his shirt, put his hand into his trouser pocket and pulled out a wad of notes. I took the money, thanked him and opened the bedside drawer, put the money inside and took out a condom and some KY.

He came over to me, his semi-erect cock desperate for attention. 'Suck. I want to suck,' he said pointing a finger in my direction. I was about to put the condom onto his cock when he lunged forward, trying to kiss me.

'No,' I said sternly. 'I don't kiss.' Well, not this guy.

Whore protocol dictates that prostitutes, even when talking to other working girls, must try to keep the moral high ground and remain non-committal when discussing affairs between themselves and their clients. But the transaction often goes far beyond the exchange of cash and the physical act. There is so much more emotion to this game than hookers are willing to admit. That's why they always deny kissing.

'OK. No kiss.' He sounded disappointed. 'Let me suck . . . lick,' he said.

HOOKED

'Me? You want to lick me?' I finally realised what he was talking about. He nodded. 'That'll be another £30.' *Fuck it.* He was a horrible, unkempt, unshaven little thing, but at least I'd get an extra 30 quid out of him. I'd pretend to come within moments; he wouldn't know any better.

I lay down, his hot sticky body between my legs. I could smell him. The backdraft as he got onto the bed was hideous. I grimaced as he started furiously licking my pussy. I put pressure on his forehead to move him back, but he was relentless. Suddenly, without warning, I felt a powerful throbbing between my legs. This foul-smelling, rat-like man was turning me on.

'Stop now,' I said half-heartedly, ashamed for letting him arouse me. He raised his head up and I looked down at him and he carried on. Deep down – and I didn't want to admit it to myself – I wanted him to continue. Moments later, I could feel the beginning of the pulsations that were my last opportunity to push him off me if I didn't want to climax. I said nothing and came intensely. I desperately wanted to hide it, but I couldn't. I pushed his head away and placed my hand over my cunt so he couldn't continue. He sat upright and I reached over to the side of the bed to grab a condom. I hated this man and I hated myself for allowing myself to orgasm onto some grotty punter's tongue.

As with kissing, prostitutes don't generally admit to climaxing with clients. I'm sure a lot do, though. Many men see call girls for something that is probably more important to them than the actual sex: an ego boost. Now, a girl can pretend to orgasm, of course she can; but let's face it, sometimes, when faced with a guy who is pressing all the right buttons and you've got him there between your legs, you might as well get something out of what starts as a nerve-racking experience. The man can be so not your type that you need to shut your eyes and climax in order to get through it. It's virtually impossible to fuck for money without going with the flow, otherwise you wouldn't be able to get through the ordeal of someone touching your skin for a second, never mind your genitals for minutes, or potentially hours, without getting something from it – and sometimes money ain't enough.

One of the hardest experiences I have ever had was with a man who was in his late 60s. He had flown from Ireland for our four-hour rendezvous at a Heathrow airport hotel, after which he would be flying straight back again. It was very unusual to get booked for that length of time by a client I'd never met before. Four hours is a fuck of a long time. I presumed that we would be sniffing and drinking throughout the course of our appointment, which would break up the time spent actually rutting. We didn't. Alarm bells started ringing when I got a call from the agency telling me that I shouldn't admit to smoking cigarettes because he was vehemently against it. Thankfully for me, his flight was delayed by an hour. Of course, he still paid me for that hour, since I'd been waiting.

From the moment we got into the room, he wouldn't leave me alone. His creepily soft tongue relentlessly covered every part of my body. He had white hair. He was an old man. I thought I was going to have a panic attack. I was freaking out. I felt like pushing him off me, punching him, strangling him, killing him. I excused myself and went into the bathroom. I sat on the toilet, head in hands, heart banging, muttering about being unable to finish what had been started. I wanted to scream. Then I thought of the money. I needed it. I wanted it. I wanted cocaine. I wanted the booze that would go down so easily with a sniff. I gave myself a talking to and made a decision to 'enjoy myself'. A tongue is a tongue, whatever age it is. I focused on climaxing. I had to. If I hadn't, I would never have been able to get through it, and that wasn't an option.

Now, in the flat in Ruislip, I couldn't look at the client after I'd come. I unwrapped the rubber, handed it to him and watched as he rolled it onto his small dick. He lunged forward and pummelled my pussy like a baboon. Less than a minute later, he came silently inside me.

As he pulled away and got up, I looked at his cock. 'Shit! The fucking johnnie's split.' I was horrified. It had never happened before. 'That condom has burst and you've just come inside me.' *You fucking cocksucking wanker, tosspot, dickhead.*

'No, no,' he said softly, as if denying all knowledge of what had just happened would make it less true. He ripped the torn rubber off his deflating penis and dropped it onto the bedside cabinet. Why do men think it's their right to drop used condoms wherever they feel like?

I jumped off the bed and grabbed a towel to wipe myself with. *How many other women has he fucked and had that happen? Most girls that work in flats aren't like me, clean, non-intravenous drug users . . . They're fucking filthy old birds trying to raise a few quid to feed their six kids and get their next hit of crack . . . My game is different.* I was thinking in my usual delusional bubble.

The man dressed quickly and left the room. I was having palpitations as I sat on the edge of the bed trying to squeeze the come onto the towel. I cursed the man, cursed myself, cursed my life, cursed everything.

That was the last day I worked at the flat: 20 August 2002. I never returned and never explained why. All I knew was that I had to go and get an HIV test. Fast.

CHAPTER 20

Despite changing the sheets and gathering all of Alex's belongings together, I felt the pain each time I walked past his stuff. I'd made sure I'd packed literally everything, from his boxer shorts to a lip salve to a lighter that I knew was his. It was too painful to have any traces of him lying around.

Alex was still there; at least, in my mind he was. Thoughts of the tender moments that we'd shared, snuggled up on the sofa as he twirled my hair around his fingers, made me more sad than I could bear. The way he'd made me feel desired. The way he'd touched me. When a relationship ends, you forget the hurt and crave to go through the same experience again, like childbirth.

Five days had passed and I still hadn't had the bottle to go to the clinic and ask for an HIV test. The thought nearly killed me. I still thought a lot about trying to get clean, but I was miserable and there was nothing to do except sniff and drink; if only I'd had the energy, I'd have tried to free-fuck myself out of depression. I was taking the Prozac, but the tablets didn't seem to be taking effect yet, probably because I was still drinking and my mind and body were wrecked.

I sat beside the table, Alex's table, and stared blankly at nothing. I was still, frozen, consumed with more pain than I knew what to do with. When I allowed my mind to focus on a specific thought, let it dwell on a bad memory for long enough to make me recoil with shame, I'd aggressively and repeatedly punch my hands into the sides of my head. *No, no, no, no. Stop it, Katie, stop it.* It was as if I was trying to hammer the thoughts out of my mind. I found comfort in it. It was certainly no worse than bashing myself with the monotonous cycle of drugs, drink and indulging in abusive sex by sleeping with men I didn't want to be with.

Jim called. 'What's going on, Katie? I can never get hold of you. There's something wrong. What's happening?' he asked.

'What do you mean you can never get hold of me? You're talking to me now, aren't you? I've told you before, Jim, if you continue asking me, "What's going on?" I'm not going to answer the phone to you, OK? I'm all right. Nothing's going on. Absolutely nothing. That's maybe part of the problem,' I barked.

I was practically friendless, I felt useless, I was most definitely boyfriend-less, almost homeless and now I was jobless. The resilient spirit that had enabled me to live through overwhelming emotional turmoil was barely keeping me going. My survival mechanism was on overdrive as I forged on, somehow believing that things weren't always going to be like they were then. All I could do was ride through the next month and see what happened. I was alone.

Then Alex called me to say he'd be coming round. I'd already had warning that he was going to. He'd sent a text days before suggesting a time he could come and pick up his belongings. I started making the flat the cleanest that it had been for a number of weeks. I washed my hair for the first time in a long time then poured myself a brandy before I began work on straightening it. As the tongs were smoothing out my frizzy mop, I started wondering if I would be able to mend my relationship with Alex.

He arrived eight minutes late. My skin was smooth, my top lip was waxed and make-up had been carefully applied to give the appearance of none. I wore a short linen skirt (easy access), a white vest without a bra (nipple alert) and had put my hair up, knowing Alex loved to see the length of my neck.

'Why didn't you use your keys?'

'They're your keys, babe,' he said, handing them to me.

I was anxious. I closed the door and joked that I wasn't going to barricade him in this time.

'I know you're not.'

I felt awkward. He seemed like a stranger, yet I still loved him in a way. 'I'm sorry, I'm so sorry,' I said. 'Can you forgive me?'

'I've forgiven you. It's all right. I've moved on.'

I didn't dare ask what he meant by that. 'Baby, can we get back together? I've missed you so much,' I said in his ear. He didn't respond, which convinced me that he simply needed a little persuasion. 'I'm so sorry about everything, Alex. I was stupid. I don't know what came over me.'

'OK. But we can't get back together, Katie.'

'Why? Please . . .' My eyes filled with tears.

He started shaking his head. In a desperate attempt to get ahead in what seemed to be a losing battle, I started rubbing his crotch.

'Don't.'

'Why not?' I asked through my tears. *Has he already met someone else?*

'It won't help.'

'Yes, it will.' I tried to muster a laugh, attempting to lighten things up. 'Come on, just once.' I was certain that if we had sex, he wouldn't be able to walk away from me so easily. I continued tampering with him.

'Stop it, babe.'

'Why? You want to.' I placed my lips on his, he returned my kiss and we went to the bedroom.

During sex, I was on top and we didn't use a condom. Alex's sunglasses, which had been perched on the top of his head, fell onto his face and for the remainder of the sex he kept them on. It wasn't until I thought about it afterwards that I realised he hadn't wanted to engage fully in what we were doing. More to the point, he didn't want to fully engage with *who* he was doing it with. By leaving his glasses on, he kept a degree of distance between us.

Immediately afterwards, he got up and said he had to go. 'Why? Baby, why are you leaving?' I felt nauseous. There was a long silence. 'Why?' I asked again, reaching my hand out to touch his arm.

He looked at me, blinking quickly. 'Self-preservation.'

Self-preservation? I was dismayed. *Self-fucking-preservation? Who the fuck does he think he is?* My sadness was replaced with anger as I realised that Alex was blaming me for everything that had been bad in our relationship.

'Right. Well, you'd better fuck off then, hadn't you, Mr Holier Than Fucking Thou?'

'What?' Alex said as if he hadn't understood.

'You heard me. Piss off out of this flat then, you fucking idiot. Go on! Fuck off!' I screamed, thumping his arm furiously.

'Stop this, Katie. I'm warning you!' Alex bellowed.

I screamed and flung my arm back, ready to put all my weight into attacking him. Suddenly, I fell onto the sofa then rolled onto the floor. The force of Alex striking me in the face had caught me off guard. The next day, I could see bruising at the side of my head and discoloration under my eye.

The door slammed behind him. He left and I never heard from him again.

CHAPTER 21

A few days later, I got up the courage to call the STD clinic, my hands trembling. They told me that I could go for the tests in two days without making an appointment, but I had to turn up at around 8.30 a.m. *Half eight in the morning? Bit early*. But I knew that I had to do it.

I was pacing my living room with my hands cupped over my mouth to prevent myself from screaming as panic gripped me. I stopped still for a moment and heard the silence. I stared blankly at nothing, then sharply turned my head to look over my shoulder, sensing something there – something or someone. It felt like a shadow. But my rational mind knew that I was in the flat alone. My eyes scanned the room; my heart was racing. I was scared. *What the hell is happening to me?* I placed both hands in a prayer gesture covering my nose and mouth. I could feel the swelling under my blackened eye. I sensed movement behind me again. I thrust my body round to confront my fear and to prove to myself what my logical mind already knew: I was alone. I took a deep, slow breath in, then with as much control as possible I breathed out loudly as I crept towards the sofa.

Maybe Faye was right. Maybe rehab was the answer if I wanted to regain a sense of reality. Somehow I needed to start dealing with the mountain of problems that I felt I couldn't cope with. As I sat still and quiet on the sofa, the realisation that I'd ridden Alex's cock without using a johnnie flooded my thoughts. I squealed and squirmed my way to the kitchen to pour another brandy. The sleeping pills that helped bring me down after a night on the sniff seemed like a welcome solution to my worries.

HOOKED

The South Kensington guy clattered into my head and a vision of the attack brought me out in a hot sweat. I jumped off the sofa and went over to the stereo to put on a CD, hoping that music would drown out the noise in my head. I lay back down. Primal Scream started playing. A track that usually made me feel relaxed helped me now to release some of my pain and sob quietly.

*

I told no one about my HIV test. I had to trudge through the next two days alone. I was used to keeping things secret.

I called my local dealer. 'Also, have you got anything to help with the comedown?' I asked after he'd agreed to drop off an eighth of charlie.

'Yeah, a bit of B.'

I knew what B was, but he threw me off guard offering it. 'B?'

'Yeah, B,' he said again.

B equals brown, brown equals smack, smack equals heroin. 'Yeah, cool. Bring me a bit of that, and some sweets if you've got them.' Sweets equals downers, downers equals sleeping pills/tranquillisers.

'All right, love. I'll be with you within an hour.'

What the fuck are you doing getting smack? a tiny voice shouted in my mind, but the voice might as well have been shouting from Timbuktu for all that I listened to it. *Fuck it. Why should I care? I might have a death sentence handed to me in two days. Why care now?*

He dropped the gear off and I handed him his 140 quid. 'Do you want to stay for a drink?'

'I've got another drop, so I better not. But I'll give you a buzz in a little while. Maybe we could hang out later if you're free. I ain't got plans for this evening.'

As I closed the door, I curled my nose up. I didn't even like the guy. Why was I asking him if he wanted to hang out? I knew Luca, in fact he'd probably say that we were 'mates', and I didn't even like hanging out with *him*, so why ask some dodgy middle-aged geezer who should be babysitting his grandkids rather than running around Surrey in his souped-up beemer thinking he's a teenage hood rat? *Fuck's sake, Katie. Come on, girl, sort yourself out.*

*

My breath was knocked out of me and I thanked the nurse profusely, then I thanked God. *That's it. I've gotta change my lifestyle. I can't and won't live like this for a moment longer. I've gotta take control of my life.*

I had an appointment to start seeing a therapist just a few days later. I'd been lucky, there'd been a cancellation. I felt things were on the up. I'd kept myself to myself for the past few days and, truth be told, I was looking forward to talking to someone, even if it was a stranger who was being paid to listen.

I've gotta do this. I don't want to live like this any longer, I was thinking, as I ignored the voice in my head that was questioning what the hell I was doing as I tipped the last bit of coke down the toilet and flushed it out of my life.

Think about the money you just wasted, said Goblin Kate.

SHUT IT! Fuck the money. It was dirty money anyway.

I'd fought with my internal demons and victory was mine. To celebrate, I texted Janet and arranged to go with her to an NA meeting. Not that day, but maybe tomorrow if I felt human(ish).

I'd hidden the heroin high on a kitchen shelf and hadn't used any of it. *Cocaine is my problem, not smack*, I decided, so I kept it there for the time being. I'd enjoyed the restful sleep that I'd had the night before, and maybe a small toot would help me replicate the same peace again. It would help me sleep and stop me from feeling so anxious. I knew how to use it without letting myself get physically dependent, so I grabbed the wrapper from the shelf.

The counsellor was kind, patient and vague, as it was her job to be. She left me with 'thoughts' rather than advice; but the simple experience of a little human interaction raised my morale and gave me a confidence boost, if only for the duration of the session. There were tears, tissues, questions and confessions.

Another week and there would have been more if it hadn't been for the fact that after spending another few days staring at the wall I began wondering why I'd flushed the wrap of coke down the toilet and what exactly I had to live for. My lease on the flat was up and I had no fight left to sort something else out. I had nothing left. I made a decision: I was leaving London and, unfortunately, Freddie.

CHAPTER 22

SEPTEMBER 2002

There were two used condoms on the bedroom floor and my head was banging. I was dehydrated as hell. I attempted to move and experienced what felt like lightning erupting inside my skull. The downside to not sniffing coke was the blazing hangovers.

'Are you OK?' a deep voice asked.

Where am I? In Gambia. *Who the fuck is that?* I'd done it again.

I'd arrived in Africa less than 48 hours ago and here I was with a strange bloke who was asking after my health. I wanted to pretend that I was still asleep, but my thirst wouldn't allow it. I lay still for a moment trying to remember who I had brought back with me the night before. I hadn't come to Gambia for this – men, sex, getting pissed. I was meant to be on an expedition of self-discovery. I'd left London to get away from my usual shenanigans, supposedly.

I turned round and there he was, eyes wide open, looking at me. 'Are you OK?' he asked again. His face looked vaguely familiar, but I didn't know his name.

'Not really. I'm desperate for some water.'

He got up – jeans, no top, exposing his black skin and ripped muscles. He had a huge tattoo that covered half of his torso and swept down his arm. He was tall, which wasn't a surprise, because I am, so I usually go for taller men, and had a shaved head. 'Did you have a good night?' he asked.

HOOKED

I didn't answer. Instead I propped my head up on the two flat pillows, folding them in half. The guy handed me a bottle of water and I glugged it down. 'I feel like shit,' I said.

He had a husky laugh and an unusually deep voice. I kept looking at him and I couldn't decide if he was good-looking or not. There was something sexyish about him, but my mind was not made up. He got back on the bed and started rubbing my tummy. *Very confident.*

'You were pretty drunk last night, Katie.'

'Yeah. I was fuckin' plastered.' I started laughing but soon stopped. I thought my head would burst with pain. 'You've got an American accent?'

'Canadian, man. Had you forgotten?'

'No, not really. I was just saying . . .' Of course I'd forgotten. 'What time is it?' I asked.

'Around eleven.'

'I should get up in a minute and take a shower. I hope there's water.'

'Yeah, there's water. I've already taken a shower.'

'How are you feeling?' I was hoping he felt at least half as bad as I did.

'OK. I feel all right.'

'Fuck. How do you manage that? I feel really fucking ill. My head's banging.'

He was quite cute on closer inspection; I just wished I could remember his name.

'Take a shower and let's go and get some food, man.'

Hmm . . . decisive. I like that. But 'man'? I'm not a man.

'OK, give me ten minutes.' I got up and tripped. I was still drunk. Water came freely out of the shower head. That made a change. I'd been to Gambia before and understood that for half of each day you got either electricity or water. If you had one, you didn't have the other. Then the other half of the day, you'd get what you hadn't had earlier. Complex, but that was how it was.

'You good to go now, girl?' I can't bear that Americanism.

'Come on. My car's over here. Let's go get some food, man. I'm hungry.'

'Oh, OK, you've got a car?' Thank God I didn't have to walk anywhere. I felt awful.

'Yeah. Haven't you?'

'Here?'

'Wherever.'

'Here, I haven't, no.'

'But you got one at home, though, right?'

'No. I don't drive.' I wasn't even thinking straight.

'You should. How do you get around London if you don't drive?'

'I get taxis,' I said, not wanting to admit that I usually got public transport. That didn't sound too sexy.

'You get cabs? Fuck, man. That's expensive, huh?'

I raised my eyebrows, thinking about the impression I'd just given, aware that I'd started my usual trick of making myself sound like I was someone I wasn't, someone with money. I often did this, but it had to stop. Alex had said to me the last time we'd spoken, 'Maybe you should try and be yourself, Katie. Stop pretending to be someone else.' I hadn't understood what he'd meant at the time. But time had passed and I was getting it.

'So, where in Canada are you from?' I asked as we drove slowly along the dirt road in his new Alfa Romeo.

'Toronto.' He was actually pretty good-looking from the side, and he made me feel quite shy in a strange kind of way.

'What are you doing here then? Are you on holiday?'

'Yeah, I'm visiting my mama.'

'How long for?' I desperately needed painkillers. My head was still banging.

'I haven't decided yet. Maybe a month.' He had a beautiful voice. I could imagine him whispering dirty things in my ear, but I couldn't remember the sex we'd had.

I didn't ask him about his work; I didn't want him to ask me about mine. But if he did, I'd be vague, of course, and tell him I worked in an office – my usual receptionist baloney.

We went to a restaurant, where we sat away from the main concourse. The guy picked up the bill – a rarity in Gambia. I knew from my previous trip that I could expect to pay most of the time, since most people didn't have a decent income and certainly didn't have the money to eat out.

'Take it easy, babe,' he laughed as he dropped me back at my flat. 'Rest your head. And, hey, no more drinking!'

'Not until later, er . . .' *What the hell is his name?* 'Yeah, see you, mate.'

Mate? Get a grip, Katie! That wasn't even a natural way for me to talk; I only called people 'mate' when I was angry with them.

*

The mosquitoes were rife. I was ambushed as I sat alone in the sweltering bar. I slapped them viciously, taking no prisoners. I was focused on defending myself against malaria and being eaten alive when I heard a loud laugh that I recognised. The guy walked in. A bright-yellow T-shirt, dark Levi jeans and Nike Classics – not too shabby at all. He touched the back of my neck and kissed the side of my face. *Very sweet. Well played, boy.*

'Hello, sir,' said the meek bartender, who looked about a third of the guy's size.

'What are you drinking, babe?' he asked me.

I was thinking about how gutted I'd be if someone had said hello to me and I hadn't received a hello back, but I replied, 'I'll have another beer, please.'

'Get me a beer and I'll have a fruit juice,' he told the bartender. No please. No thank you. English etiquette didn't apply. This was Gambia and these were Gambian rules.

I was fiddling with a beer mat, working out how I could find out the guy's name without having to ask him. I'd slept with him. I was too embarrassed to admit I couldn't remember it. Somehow I had to orchestrate a conversation that would get me the information I required.

'Thank you,' I smiled at the barman when he brought over my drink. 'Er, I'm sure I'll see lots of you, I'm just staying next door. My name's Katie.' I hoped he'd continue the conversation.

'I'm Modou,' he said.

I looked at the stranger who'd just kissed me hello, and he stuck his hand out and introduced himself to the barman as Hassan.

Beautiful. I smiled broadly. I could relax a little now. He'd eaten straight out of my hand and given me exactly what I needed. Now I was determined to use his name lavishly to make up for not remembering it before.

After a long conversation with *Hassan*, I tried to get my head round the fact that *Hassan* didn't drink. Nope, never. He was teetotal. He was Muslim and this was the only part of Islam he faithfully followed. The thing I found hardest to take in was that the poor guy had never tasted alcohol. Never even tasted it. But he sure as hell wasn't anything like my idea of a teetotaller. He was funny, he loved to dance and he was confident. But I didn't want to get too involved with anyone. Well, I did, but I knew what I was like: obsessive. If I allowed myself to indulge, I'd end up getting clingy, however hard I tried not to.

I thought I should lay my cards down and tell him that I wasn't looking for a boyfriend. 'I don't want you thinking something's going on here, OK?' I said after a while. 'We're only having a drink.'

'That's cool. We'll just hang out,' he smiled.

'Yeah, maybe. But, you know, I don't want this to turn into something.'

'Hey. It's OK. Listen, I'm gonna leave you my number, and you call me whenever you want, OK? I can come pick you up and we can hang out. I mean, you're here by yourself and so am I, but the difference is I know a few people. Listen, don't be scared. I'm not going to do anything to hurt you.' He laughed.

'I'm not *scared*!'

'Whatever you say, boo-boo. Listen, I'll speak to you soon, yeah?'

'Maybe.'

'You'll call me! I know you will. You don't want to admit it, but you will . . .' He walked away laughing. *Cocky git.* That was it; I screwed up his number. I knew he'd be back – *Cocky? Who?* – and I knew I wanted to see him again soon. But he was right – I didn't want to admit it.

*

'I'm just not sure it's a good idea, me moving in with you. I mean, we've known each other two weeks,' I told Hassan. The way he had presented the idea to me made perfect sense. He had a lovely home, a friendly family and I liked him. The family didn't appear to want anything from me. That seemed unusual to me, though. I was suspicious of people who didn't barter in life, and especially in Africa, where poverty ruled and the opportunity to escape Gambia for Europe was one most people would not miss out on if they could see a possible opening. But why should I worry? Hassan was just visiting from Canada. He wasn't untravelled. The guy was streetwise and knew his shit. But regardless of the signs pointing to everything being above board, I tried to keep an open mind but also a healthy degree of scepticism about his intentions.

'My mum would welcome you with open arms.'

'How do you know?' I asked him.

'I've already talked to her about it.'

That was a good sign. He was genuinely keen. I liked him too, but what was the rush? I had met his mum, who had seemed like an austere woman who kept a close eye on her son's acquaintances. I'd noticed she'd been keenly observing my mannerisms and general demeanour, as I had hers. Luckily, I understood that levels of respect had to be high when talking to anyone older than myself, regardless of their status within the household. It wasn't the done thing to be casual with elders.

HOOKED

I learned to ask twice how the person I was talking to was. Also, I had to ask how their family members and their respective partners were between the two queries about themselves. In turn, I would be asked twice during the same exchange about my own health, and twice I'd lie about it. I was always 'very good, thank you'. And, of course, it would have seemed rude, despite it being tedious, if I hadn't been asked about the health of my father and my family (which was my father again). I enjoyed the rituals of Gambian life, although at times my patience was tested. Everything moved at a very slow pace. There, I was able to catch a glimpse of my heritage. I was fascinated, knowing that part of my ancestry lay there. I was part of that earth, part of those people. I listened intently. I watched everything. I stared at some of the exaggerated silhouettes of femininity – women with wonderful, firm curves who looked strong and regal.

My mother was Zambian, not Gambian, but still it was a gift that I could spend time with people who would have understood her values. I moved into Hassan's family home and decided that I would give Gertrude, his mum, some money as a gesture of good will, so I wouldn't feel in any way beholden to them and so they wouldn't think that I was freeloading. It was gratefully received, although she insisted it was unnecessary. By Gambian standards, and even by European ones, they were wealthy.

The fact that the family were Muslim (as are the majority of people in Gambia) fascinated me. It added another interesting dimension to an already intriguing experience. I listened to people talking, unshakeable in their own beliefs but still respectful towards other people's philosophies and religions. I would sit and talk to Gertrude and her friends, who were mainly women in their 50s, and ask them about their attitudes and feelings about the fact that their Muslim husbands were allowed more than one wife. I found comfort in spending time with them. In their faces, I saw my mother. I saw who I hoped to grow into: a wise, honest nurturer, at ease with herself and grateful for everything that God has given her, even if that isn't much.

I was shocked by their honesty and honoured by their openness. They let me into their thoughts and feelings about their personal and cultural issues. Being at the house reignited the desire for knowledge that my father had instilled in me when I was growing up. I was fired up, ready to better myself and ready to move my life forward. I didn't have any major worries as long as I kept focused on the present. I had some money, which would last a little while; how long was unclear, but whenever anxiety stirred in my belly about this, I would remind myself that most people around me had less. As long as I didn't think too much about London, I wasn't panicking about anything. I missed nothing about England except watching *Columbo*; I wondered what had become of my Freddie but guessed he'd be safe and well looked after by the next inhabitant of my ex-flat.

I felt better and more hopeful than I had done for a long time. Despite this, I was aware that the demons hadn't left me. After a period of relative calm after the night I met Hassan, the inevitable urges reared up again. The itch needed to be scratched. The compulsion to get out of my head was beginning to take hold. I wanted to fight it, but I knew I couldn't. I had cooled down from tearing around London, I wasn't sniffing charlie, I wasn't selling my arse, so why bother putting myself through the strain of trying to avoid having a few drinks? After all, I was on holiday, I told myself.

I let rip with bottles of moonshine, making easy work of at least a litre a day, plus beers if it was particularly hot or cloudy, or if I was especially happy or down, or if I was going to a bar or staying in, or if I was laughing or crying. *What the hell is wrong with that?* 'I'm enjoying myself,' I'd say if I thought someone disapproved of my drinking habits. I'd say it to the barman who would raise an eyebrow when I ordered my sixth lunchtime beer. 'Just cos you don't drink. Leave me alone,' I'd chunter moodily. 'The beer here is like water . . . Oh, it's 5 per cent, is it? I didn't realise. It doesn't taste that strong.' *What the fuck are people's problems?* 'Stop going on about it, Hassan. I'm on holiday. It's OK, I don't drink like this at home.'

Hassan was a real 'lad'. In a way, I could imagine being with him in London, although he'd have to stop watching all those endless kung-fu flicks. I thought about us together with my friends, sitting by the river like Alex and I used to, having a romantic drink and a stroll home hand in hand, ready for a quiet night in front of the TV before I got up the next day to go to an office job. That was the fantasy. That was what I wanted. Not necessarily with him, and I wasn't sure if I would actually be able to live the dream, but I wanted it. 'Wellness' would not just come searching me out, offering its services. I had to find it for myself. I wasn't sure where or how, but I knew nothing would change unless something changed.

Hassan told me he'd help me. He could see some of my flaws – my drinking, disorganisation and erratic moods. He tried to suggest that we stay home some evenings, but every night we'd go out and laugh non-stop while I got drunk in the scent of the Gambian night. Sean Paul's *Dutty Rock* had just come out and 'Gimme the Light' was booming all around us, the bass rippling through the trees. Thankfully, most of the bars and all the clubs had generators, so when the light cut out, we could continue to party.

'You should marry me, I'll sort you out and stop you ruining yourself with all this drinking bullshit,' Hassan would go on.

'Oh, stop it, babe. Not again. I don't need this hassle.'

I was already married and I wanted to forget about that. I didn't want to be reminded every time Hassan mentioned wedded bliss between the two of us. Of course, Hassan didn't have a clue about my situation with my first husband, Sam, and I wasn't intending to tell him.

'Look, I'll move out and stay in a hotel if you keep badgering me about marrying you, OK?'

HOOKED

'Baby, you know I love you.'

'Yeah?'

'So why don't you want us to get married and have children? You know I only want the best for you, boo-boo, so don't get angry with me when I try to help you.' I felt patronised and irritated. 'Besides we shouldn't be having sex outside of marriage,' he said, stroking my hair.

'Don't give me that bollocks.'

To be precise, I wasn't in fact having sex outside of marriage. I was married – just not to him.

CHAPTER 23

Sam's mum and I spotted each other instantly. She was with her daughter, who had grown into a very pretty teenage girl. I panicked. I wanted to order Hassan to drive away, but I couldn't. My mother-in-law was ten yards away from the car, if that. The windows were already wound down and she came over and leaned in, asking me how I was, smiling with hatred in her eyes. I wished the road would crack open so that I could escape into the ground. I didn't bother asking her how she was. I could tell by her face she wasn't at all happy. Her daughter peered into the car. She started speaking Wolof in a raised voice, gesticulating furiously. *Steady*, I thought. *You're 14 years old, you cheeky cow.* I didn't need to speak the local language to understand that the torrent of abuse was for me. The mother piped up in a spookily calm voice, clearly asking Hassan what his name was. She said something, pointed at me, then the two of them walked away.

'I knew I'd see them at some point,' I said as calmly as I could manage. My heart was racing. I'd already told Hassan that I'd dated a Gambian before, in an attempt to cover my arse if this situation arose – but of course I'd never mentioned that I'd married the guy.

'So, what did she say?' I was shitting myself. I knew full well what she'd said and I didn't know how to respond when he repeated it. I liked Hassan, I didn't want him to walk away from me now. I didn't want to feel alone again. 'She said that you're married to her son. Are you married, Katie?'

Shit. 'Of course I'm not married, baby. C'mon, if I was married, I wouldn't be here with you, would I?' I said, leaning in to kiss him. Guilt must have been oozing out of me. 'You know how it is here. If you've ever been out with someone, they refer to you as that person's wife. Just ignore her.' I was trying to sound as nonchalant as possible.

He kept silent.

'Did she say anything else?'

'She said that you're a bad person.'

'What?' I was horrified. '*A bad person*? Is that what she said? Shit, really? God, that's horrible.' I was genuinely hurt. 'Baby, do you think I'm a bad person?' I felt acutely anxious.

'No, I don't,' he said quietly. 'She didn't actually use the expression "bad person", though.'

'So what did she say, then?' I asked, bracing myself for the answer.

'She said you're a witch and I should stay away from you.'

*

If someone had offered me a million pounds cash if I could explain why I did what I went on to do, I still wouldn't have been able to answer the question.

Five days after my marriage to Hassan, I woke from my drunkenness. The magnitude of my decision crushed me like a ten-ton boulder bearing down on my weak, toxin-saturated body.

I had married Hassan and I was still married to Sam.

I lay motionless, staring at the floor, where my ivory wedding dress lay scrunched in a heap. I pulled my left hand from under the pillow and there, sitting smugly on my finger, was a silver and gold wedding band.

I needed to get out of there. I feared for my mental health. I had to leave Gambia immediately. I'd been there practically a year. I'd done my time. I'd absorbed a little African culture. I'd witnessed how my life could have been had I stayed in Africa. But now it was time for me to leave. This was the final straw. I had committed a crime. I was now married to two men at the same time. I could barely believe the horror of what I had done. Breaking the law was not what frightened me most – it was the irrationality of it.

I added my torturous feelings of regret to the casket that held the rest of my problems. Marriage is sacred. I did believe that. At heart, I'm an old-fashioned girl with traditional values. So why had I done this? I couldn't understand and I didn't want to wait around while I figured it out. My feelings weren't like the manic desperation that I'd experienced when Alex had left me. No, this time I felt somehow still and very, very lonely.

Looking at the bedside cabinet beside me I saw packets of sleeping pills, which in England one would need a prescription to obtain. All the packets had been opened and, by the looks of it, consumed. I must have taken them during the binge I'd been on for most of the past week. Any glimmer of sanity I had held on to was all too quickly avalanching downhill.

'Have you murdered anyone?' Jim asked me when I cried to him over the phone.

'No.' *But I'm a bigamist.*

'Well, then, you're gonna be all right. But, Katie, at least for today, try not to drink.'

Hmmm . . .

*

Smuggling drugs was the only way I could think of to get money and avoid selling my body when I got back to England. I had nothing, literally. Since I'd been in Gambia, I'd had Jim send me money over on three or more occasions. I had also rung Faye, who'd sent me £800.

I couldn't bring myself to have sex for money. I just couldn't do it. The thought made me panic. I'd rather do anything other than that. But I needed the security of having money; I felt even more vulnerable and lost without it. So this was my practical solution to an obvious problem.

I'd had to buy a ticket via Amsterdam. It had been that or wait three weeks for a direct flight to Gatwick. I couldn't wait. I needed to get out of there urgently. I was a bigamist. That word persecuted me. So my plan was to fly from Banjul to Amsterdam, travel from Amsterdam to Rotterdam on a train, then take the overnight ferry to Hull, where Jim would meet me. He lived less than 50 miles away.

I wasn't thinking about the consequences of being caught. I was thinking of the consequences if I didn't try. I knew I'd be having sex with strangers for money again within days. I was penniless and in debt. I had to do something. I knew no other means to make some cash, and quick cash at that. My body was the tool of my trade and I wanted to give it a rest. I was going to take the risk smuggling the weed. I was crapping myself, but all I kept thinking of was how desperately I didn't want to open my legs to a stranger. I drank to top up my alcohol levels and to prevent myself feeling shaky. I didn't allow myself to dwell on the risks involved. My mind was made up.

The day I left, I thanked Gertrude, we hugged and the family matriarch shed some tears. Not being comfortable with goodbyes, I made it brief and jumped into Hassan's Alfa Romeo. The kids who played outside the house came to wave me off, frantically squealing my name. I just wanted to get the hell out of the country. I didn't talk. I felt a bleak awareness of what lay ahead and I was on emotional lockdown.

We set off and I realised I'd left 200 cigarettes in the flat. 'Can we turn back? I haven't got money to buy more.'

'No. It's not good to turn back when you're on a journey. It brings bad luck,' Hassan said.

'I don't believe in all that superstitious stuff,' I insisted.

'Yeah, but I do,' Hassan said, puffing on a cigarette.

'Give me one of those.' He passed me the packet. I lit one and stared out of the window. The cling film was tightly wrapped around my waist and my skin was itching. I stubbed out my fourth cigarette before walking into the airport. We had 20 minutes until check-in time began for the Amsterdam flight. We went to the bar and I drank two large vodkas. I had started to shake. Hassan and I were silent as we walked over to the entrance to passport clearance.

'OK, I'm going to say goodbye here,' I grimaced. We hugged.

'You take care,' Hassan told me. 'I'll see you soon. And don't worry about me. I'm your husband. I love you, you know.'

The word 'husband' made me cringe. I didn't want to hear it. It was wrong. I'd got myself into one helluva pickle and if I thought I'd have trouble getting out of the original mess I'd got myself involved in with marrying Sam, now I had this to sort out too.

Hassan and I looked at each other. Tears filled my eyes and he held me close. I held onto my hand luggage and hugged him with one arm. I was crying silently.

'Do you think you'll get the visa quickly?' I sniffed, fearing my loneliness when I arrived back in England, if indeed I made it that far.

'As quickly as God allows,' Hassan said, kissing my nose. 'Everything will be OK, Inshallah.'

'I'm going. I need to go. Wait for me here. Watch me go through,' I said.

I turned and headed to the queue, ready to show my passport. I stood quaking. My eyes felt as though they were on stalks.

'Please take your luggage over there to be checked and they will weigh it for you,' said the check-in assistant.

I followed the instructions without question. I was in a haze similar to that which had controlled me for the majority of the time I'd been there. Alcohol and sleeping tablets were anaesthetising me to an extent, but nonetheless I felt agitated. I wanted to get through to the next section. This was nothing. They wouldn't check me here, just my bag. My hold-all was opened and two security guards started rummaging through my stuff. I knew at a time like this I needed to be more perky and flirt with the guys a little. That would distract them from the fact that I looked nervous as hell.

The guards were laughing and joking. I tried to join in

but couldn't focus on what was being said. I kept fighting an urge to turn around and look at Hassan. My heart was thumping erratically in my chest. *What the fuck am I doing?* I asked myself over and over. The guys seemed to be having a whale of a time noseying through my belongings. Usually, it was here where I'd be most paranoid, worried that the customs people would stumble across my dirty knickers, but I didn't care a jot about knickers, dirty or otherwise, on this occasion. If they found any, they could have them for all I cared.

All I wanted was to pass through the body scanner without detection. *Please, God, don't let me get arrested.* The air conditioning was emitting ice-cool air, which was much needed. Sweat started streaming like tears from my underarms. I'd passed one check, now for the main one.

I can't describe the degree to which my heart was racing as I approached the security guard, even before the alarm started screaming at me. The situation felt surreal. I knew I'd been caught. I was sure of it.

The guard came towards me with a hand-held scanning device and waved it at my waist, looking me straight in my eyes. *Here we go. Show time.* At this point, my mind was empty. I felt as though I was about to collapse. I felt sick. I was convinced I was about to keel over. He said, 'That's it. It's your belt. That's why the alarm keeps bleeping.'

'Oh, right,' I said, holding my breath as I gripped the belt over the top of the kaftan that was hiding the weed. I didn't dare move. Sweat trickled down my brow. I was uncertain if he was joking or testing me to see what my reaction would be. *Does he want me to take the belt off?* I was motionless, trying to evaluate the situation.

'Get your bag, miss. You're free to go.'

I still didn't move, convinced it was a trap. I stared at him. I wiped my forehead and for a moment I believed I was about to faint. 'God, it's so hot,' I said. My mind was racing. Maybe undercover drugs police used this as a tactic before they grabbed the smuggler in the departure lounge or maybe they'd arrest me in Amsterdam after informing the police there.

'Hey, you're in Africa,' he grinned. 'It's always hot here! Go, madam – please walk through.'

Madam? He'd been calling me 'miss' a minute ago. 'Is that it?' I asked.

'Yes, that's it. I will see you in London some time, OK?'

I took that as a sign that he meant he'd see me when he turned up in court to testify against me. I tentatively collected my bag. I burped and I thought I was about to throw up. I walked very slowly into departures, waiting for someone to tap me on the shoulder. Nothing. Not yet, anyway. I slumped down onto a chair, waiting for someone to approach me. It all felt too much like *Midnight Express*. A woman next to me smiled. *Undercover cop?*

After a few moments, I went to the toilet. I had to deal with the consignment. I couldn't sit through the six-hour flight to Amsterdam with this itchy bulk around me. I crept into the Ladies, sweating furiously, and put my bag down on the floor. I turned around to face the toilet bowl and heaved. Nothing came up. I heaved again. Liquid. I could smell the weed, a heavy pungent aroma. I could also smell myself.

I lifted up the kaftan, revealing the drugs, found the end of the cling film and started unravelling it. It had been wrapped round my body 12 times to secure it in place. I peeled each kilo packet off my sweaty skin and placed all three in my hand luggage, which was a plastic carrier bag. I had a cardigan with me to take the edge off the chill when I arrived in Europe and I placed this on top of the cannabis. I'd given up. I was on autopilot.

There it was in my bag, three kilos of class-B narcotics. I walked back into departures and waited to board the plane, still uncertain if I would get that far. Over the tannoy, the announcement came to start boarding the Amsterdam Schiphol flight. I went over to the queue at the allotted gate number, handed my boarding card to an usher and headed towards the minibus that would take us to the plane. Just before I managed to get myself onto the bus, a man's voice called me: 'Excuse me, miss. Excuse me . . .'

CHAPTER 24

AUGUST 2003

I boarded the plane and sat back. A nervous chuckle slipped out of my mouth when I thought about the man who had stopped me on the tarmac, calling 'Excuse me, miss!' only to tell me that the back of my jeans was trapped under my flip-flop.

I was overjoyed to feel the plane hurtling down the runway before tilting its snout upwards as it left African soil, but the thought of what was to come terrified me. I was relieved to be leaving Gambia, but I wasn't through with this journey just yet. I was still convinced the authorities had arranged to seize me when I arrived in Holland.

Amsterdam was cold and rainy. I scuttled through customs at Schiphol carrying the bag with the weed in my hand. I had resigned myself to whatever fate had in store. I flashed my British passport in the faces of the customs officers and they waved me through with barely a glance. I carried on walking. If it happened here, I was ready. I decided that if I got a tap on the shoulder, I wouldn't act dumb. I would put my hands up and confess straight away. I was emotionally screwed. I couldn't fight any longer. My nerves were destroyed. I wanted a drink. I wanted to sleep. I wanted to not be there – but there I was.

I had less than £10 to get me to Rotterdam, where a bus would take me the 40-minute journey to the Europort. From there, I would catch a ferry to Hull, where Jim would meet me. I paid £6 for the journey to Rotterdam. I shuffled onto the train, wondering if any of the people amongst the crowds were undercover police.

I hoped to God we would leave quickly. Time was ticking. There was one ferry a day, which left the port at 4.30 p.m. It was 3.30. I jumped off at Rotterdam Centraal and rushed through hordes of people. I started running, looking for an exit sign. My huge hold-all felt as though it was breaking my shoulder, but I had to keep going. *Where is the bloody exit?*

I was out of breath.

'Excuse me . . .' I was ignored. 'Excuse me . . .'

A man stopped. He looked local, briefcase in hand, newspaper under his arm. 'Yes, miss?' Luckily, he spoke English.

'Can you tell me how I get out of here, please? I need to find the bus stop for the Europort,' I panted.

I was close, he told me. I ran as fast as I could into the drizzling rain.

'Can you tell me where the bus that takes me to the Europort is, please?' I asked an official-looking man with a walkie-talkie in his hand. I didn't even think about the drugs I was holding.

'Europort?' He waved his arm vaguely. I didn't understand where I should go.

'There? Over there?' I snapped. I wasn't even sure where I was talking about. He nodded.

I ran roughly in the direction he'd indicated, and there in front of me were bus stops – but no one around. I stood still and looked at the first sign. That wasn't it.

I started squealing with anxiety. I rushed to the next stop. I couldn't find the stop to take me to the port. I saw a nearby sign: 'Politie' – 'Police'. I paused for a moment, remembering the weed, and I hesitantly walked over to the entrance, clutching my bag. I knocked on the door of the small office. Inside were two policemen, each of them speaking on a phone. I stood waiting, wet from the rain. They both looked at me and continued with their conversations.

HOOKED

'Hello,' I said apologetically. The two coppers ignored me. 'I'm sorry, excuse me, please.' I was angry. I needed them to help me out. 'Europort? The bus to the Europort?' Still no response. I spoke loudly in pidgin English and I wanted to cry with frustration. I wanted to scream for assistance. 'Where do I get the bus to the Europort, please?'

One of the men looked up, annoyed. 'You missed it,' he said, almost vitriolically.

'I missed the bus?'

'Yes,' he said, staring at me. I wanted to scream. The other copper ended his call, stood up and was milling around the office, getting on with his day as if I wasn't there. I couldn't believe I'd missed the bus. And surely if I'd missed one, there'd be another one soon? There wasn't, he told me.

I couldn't waste another moment. I went back outside and spoke to a woman who was smoking a cigarette. I remember her face was wrinkly and kind, and she looked older than she sounded. She showed me exactly where I needed to be.

'Do you go to the Europort?' I asked the bus driver when he pulled up.

'Get on,' he nodded.

I was elated. 'You go to the Europort, right?'

'I take you. Then you walk.'

I was puzzled, but I didn't think too much about it. I was on my way. Maybe, just maybe I could make the ferry. I had 25 minutes. 'I tell you when we are there, OK?' said the driver. He was helpful. That was all I needed in that moment. My panic wasn't quite over yet, but, for sure, I was on my way home. *Hallelujah!* I'd be back in Blighty by the next morning.

Minutes later, the driver called out, 'Europort!' I thanked him, but I was confused. I dragged my hold-all off the bus, never letting go of the carrier bag with the three kilos inside it. I had been to the Europort with my dad when I'd been small, but everything here looked unfamiliar. In fact, 'everything' consisted of some trees, grass and a motorway.

HOOKED

'Over there,' the driver said, pointing straight in front of him before turning off the road. *Huh? Where's the sea? Where are the seagulls? The boats? Where the hell is the ferry?*

It was starting to get dark and it was raining. I dragged my bag towards the junction and there, bold as you like, was a sign: 'Rotterdam Europort 18 km'.

CHAPTER 25

I wished myself dead.

This was *more* than the final straw for me. I'd missed the ferry. I didn't have any idea whatsoever what I was going to do. I was in Holland with no money and it was getting dark.

I dropped my bags onto the grass and slumped on top of them. I put my head down into my hands and wailed. 'God, *please*. Please help me,' I cried out loud. Tears poured down my face as I looked at the bruising sky, panic-stricken. 'Please help me,' I begged. 'Someone help me!' I screamed as I beat my clenched fists on my knees. I was hysterical. My body jerked with convulsions as I cried. Cars streamed past me.

I yelped loudly again, clenched my fists into a tight ball and started beating my head manically. There was nothing else on the planet – just me, alone, lost and totally isolated from everything and everyone. I screamed and screamed and screamed wildly.

Then stillness took hold. I looked up and relaxed my fists. My head was sore, but I felt calmer. I was resigned to my fate. Behind me there were bushes. I knew I needed to find somewhere to sleep through the night. They looked like my best option. I stood up to survey my surroundings, to check the density of the shrubbery, and then – a car horn. Someone wound down the window and a woman spoke to me in Dutch. She beckoned me over. I left my bags on the grass and ran towards her. The rain was blowing into the car. 'I only speak English. Sorry,' I said. Never in my life had I been more willing to make sense of another language.

'What are you doing? Where you are going?' she asked. The male driver leaned forward to take a look at me.

'I'm trying to get to the Europort.'

'Europort?' She scrunched her face up.

'Yes.' My head was virtually inside the car.

'That's way back there.'

'I know, the sign says eighteen kilometres but I'm too tired to walk. I've missed my ferry. I'll have to try and get there in the morning,' I said, waiting for their response.

'You can't walk it,' called out the man.

'Get in the car,' the woman said. 'Are they your bags?'

'Yes. Really, can I get in the car?' I asked exhilarated.

'Yes,' they both answered.

'We will take you to Europort,' the woman told me.

'Thank you! Thank you!' I called as I turned my back and ran to grab my bags. I was overwhelmed with gratitude for their kindness.

When we arrived, I thanked the couple profusely and ran towards the main entrance of the port. The rain was tumbling down. As I approached the terminal building, three women, P&O employees, came out. One of them turned around and began locking the door.

'Excuse me!' I shouted as I approached. They looked at me, a little afraid. I was panting. My arms were aching from the weight I was carrying. I slowed down as I approached and could see the worried faces of the women. I was speaking fast. I was cold, I was wet and I needed to make myself understood as quickly as possible. 'I was supposed to get the 4 p.m. ferry to Hull today and I missed it. I'm in a real mess because I don't have any money and I don't know what to do. Please can you help me? Please? Is there anywhere I can wait until the next ferry?' I pleaded with them.

The women looked at each other and started talking in Dutch. 'You were meant to get the ferry at four?' one of them asked in perfect English.

'Yes. I flew from Africa to Amsterdam today and I had to get a train from Amsterdam airport to Rotterdam, then get a bus from there to here, and I missed the boat. I couldn't get a taxi or anything cos I—'

'It's OK. It's OK.' They could see the stress in my face. They were standing just under the canopy above the entrance and I was standing in the pouring rain with my bags. I was fuelled by adrenalin. I was focused on survival, nothing else. Again, they talked amongst themselves for a moment. 'You can't stay in the terminal building,' one woman told me. 'I'm sorry. No one is in there right now. Come with me. I'll ask the security guard if you can sleep in the Portakabin.'

She opened the umbrella she was clutching and kindly told me to follow her. We sprinted in silence across the road and past two huge lorries. She knocked on the door of the cabin. A rotund middle-aged man opened the door. The woman spoke to him from under the umbrella. The man beckoned me inside.

'You will need to leave the cabin by 9 a.m. tomorrow, OK?' she said. 'I will be at work so come and see me. I will help you.' I smiled at her and thanked her again, and the man closed the door. He took me to the back of the large Portakabin and showed me a camp bed and a shower that I could use. At last I could wash and change my clothes. I no longer needed to look like a pregnant woman trying to hide her tummy under a huge billowy dress.

'Tea? You want tea?' he smiled.

He was kind and I was humbled. 'Yes, please,' I answered diffidently.

'Sugar?' I felt embarrassed by his thoughtfulness. I sat down on the camp bed and wiped my face dry. Moments later he brought me some milky tea. 'OK?' he nodded.

'Yes, thank you. I'm OK,' I answered, assuming he was asking about me, not the quality of his tea-making.

He let me use the phone to call Jim and tell him about the change of plan, then he went back to his work and I cried quietly.

*

HOOKED

I was on the ferry, penniless and hungry. I had to think quickly. I had to explain my financial situation to the ferry authorities to see if there was anything they could do, so I could get some food. I claimed that my purse had been stolen and they offered to lend me £20, which I agreed to pay back the moment we arrived at Hull docks. All I had to do was appear at the main reception area the next morning; a member of staff would escort me off the ferry and take me to meet Jim so I could repay the money.

I was still clinging on to the bag with the weed. I remembered scare stories about customs following single people coming from Holland because the majority, apparently, are drug smugglers. I'd heard that they particularly targeted single black people. What if the rumours were true?

At the designated time, I dragged my hold-all to reception on the blue deck and met the ferry employee who escorted me to the terminal building where I was meeting Jim. I wasn't feeling remotely like a drug smuggler – more like a lost child being taken to be reunited with her father.

My heart was racing once again. I wasn't sure about the security regulations walking through the port. Would I get searched? We got to customs, where I slowed down, ready to show my passport. My escort exchanged looks with the customs people and when they saw that my passport was British they let me through without another glance. But still I couldn't be sure that it was over. This could all be a ruse; they might be waiting to arrest me.

Jim was standing there and he didn't look happy. The first words out of my mouth after not seeing him for months were: 'Do you have twenty quid for this man, please?' I cringed. He looked at me blankly and thrust his hand into his pocket to pull out a £20 note. The steward thanked him and headed back where he'd come from. I wondered if he might have nodded to plain-clothes police to identify me as a drug smuggler.

'I'm sorry,' I said, fighting back tears. I'd sworn to myself that I wasn't going to cry again after what had happened at the roadside in Holland. I'd shed enough tears and was resolute in my decision that whatever life threw my way I was going to deal with it. But could I really deal with a prison sentence for smuggling drugs and bigamy? If I'd thought about that, I'd have collapsed there and then. All this so I didn't have to sell my arse and so I didn't disappoint a guy I'd had a holiday fling with.

'I need to call Faye. I need to see if I can stay at her place,' I said, trying to appear organised and as if I had a plan, although Faye was in London and I was in Yorkshire.

'Come on,' said Jim, putting his arm around my shoulders as I dragged my hold-all. 'Give me that.'

'No, I'm OK,' I said defiantly.

'Just give me the bag.'

'I can manage it, Jim.'

He grabbed the bag and started wheeling it to the exit of the terminal building. I would rather have had the safety of his arm around me and dragged the bag alone. I was still clinging on to the carrier bag with the drugs in it.

'Jim, let me try and call someone.'

'Have you got any change?' he asked me.

'No,' I answered with my head down.

Fuck it. There was nothing I could do. I didn't have the energy to pretend. I didn't have any change. I didn't have anyone I could call. I didn't have a place to stay. I didn't know what to do. I didn't have anything except a bag of clothes, a bag of drugs and two husbands; that was it.

I couldn't stay with Jim. He was living at his parents' place because he'd just sold his house and was in the process of building a living space at the back of his studio. Besides, his folks had never forgiven me for hurting their son when I'd left him. I couldn't ask my parents for help. I most definitely couldn't do that.

'I don't know what the fuck to do.' Panic was rising.

'Just calm down. Let's get out of here and we'll go to a café and get something to eat. You'll be all right, Katie. The worst-case scenario is that you'll have to stay in a hotel for a few days until you get yourself sorted out.' I could tell by his voice that he was more concerned than he wanted to show me.

'Jim, I can't fucking do that,' I snapped, waiting for him to reassure me that he would pay and make everything OK and that I wouldn't be stranded and that he'd help me resolve my plight. I had the weed I could sell. A drug dealer I wasn't, but a hooker I could be. The thought made me want to drown myself in Hull docks.

We headed to the city centre in silence. I needed money. I mean, that's why I'd brought back the weed. But did I even know who I could sell it to? I just couldn't think. Not then. First things first, I had to find somewhere to stay for that night.

Jim knew I was in a predicament. He also knew that I knew that he knew that it would take all my energy to crawl back from this. I stared out of the bus onto the streets of Hull, where Mr and Mrs Nine-to-Five, whom I'd always scoffed at, were getting on with their lives. However dull and dreary the place looked on that overcast day – people trotting around wearing hoods, carrying umbrellas, trying to dodge the rain – at that moment, I would have swapped lifestyles with any one of them in an instant.

London had once seemed so glamorous and fun. Now it felt like that had been another life. Before the rubbish outweighed the good, there was never a time when I could imagine living outside of the bustle of the cosmopolitan capital. But now the thought of London and what it offered me was frightening.

'We're getting off here,' said Jim as we approached the main bus station. I got out of my seat, consumed with sadness.

'Jim, I have to find somewhere to stay as quickly as possible. I don't know what the fuck I'm going to do otherwise,' I shouted, suddenly panicky.

'Katie, for Christ's sake, calm down,' he said angrily. 'We're gonna get you sorted, OK?' I could feel the tears starting to well in my eyes. 'You're in a fucking mess right now.'

'I know I am!' I screamed. 'I know I am.' I was fighting back tears.

'Come on, we need to sit down and chat about things.'

'I don't want to talk about things.' Tears were rolling down my face.

'Well, we're going to.' He was angry.

I followed him quietly, wiping my eyes. We sat down.

'So?' said Jim, looking directly at me. 'What's going on?'

I looked at him, wondering where the hell I could start. I didn't know what to say.

'Well, you look brown. You caught the sun at least,' he grinned, trying to make light of an obviously dire situation.

'Hmmm.' My tears had stopped.

'So, tell me about this Hassan geezer.'

'I can't. I've nothing to say.' I felt sick at the mention of Hassan's name. I didn't want to think about the marriage and the bigamy. I couldn't stand even the thought of anyone knowing about it.

'Well, how's your dad? Have you spoken to him recently? Did you keep in contact while you were away?' Jim was as serious as I'd known him. His accent was less broad; he wasn't teasing me with it that day.

'No, I haven't spoken to him for ages.'

'Katie, you're not making this easy for me. Tell me what I can do. I want to help you.'

He stroked my hand, his eyes piercing mine with concern. I wanted to die. To think none of this would have happened if only I'd stayed with him. That was what he'd wanted, but the problem was that when we'd been together I hadn't been able to decipher my arse from my elbow.

'I don't know what to do, Jim. I really don't know what to do.'

'I suppose you've been drinking a fair bit, then?' I nodded. 'I can see it in your face. It's pretty bloated, Katie. Look, do you want something to eat?' he asked gently.

'No thanks,' I answered quietly.

'Have something to eat, sweetheart. Come on, that'll help.'

'Really, I couldn't. You just said I look fat.'

'No, I didn't. I said your face has swollen; I can tell you've been drinking a lot. But eat something, baby, come on.'

'Jim, I've got bigger problems than feeling hungry, really.'

Neither of us said a word. I looked down. I knew Jim was staring at me.

'OK, this is the plan. We'll leave here and head back to York. Let's put you in a hotel for tonight, then I'll come and see you tomorrow and you can decide what you want to do after that. Let's just get you in somewhere so you can have a shower and a sleep in a comfortable bed for the night, OK, darling?' I was broken. 'You'll be all right. Everything'll be all right, Katie.'

'Do you promise?' I needed to hear his usual line that always comforted me.

'Like I told you when you were over there, so long as you haven't killed anyone, there's nothing that can't be resolved, OK?' He squeezed my hand. I wished I could scream and scream and scream from the depths of my lungs. I needed to release something.

'I'm not sure about that,' I said, as the tears rolled down my face.

CHAPTER 26

I felt a huge weight had been taken off my shoulders as I arrived at the train station in the Yorkshire town where my Auntie Flo lived. I wasn't at all anxious that I hadn't seen her in 12 years. Auntie Flo was 5 ft nothing and wider than a barrel. She was 20 stone if she was a pound, with a heart the size of a mountain. She'd smothered me with affection and love throughout my childhood. I knew that she would be the same as ever. Chatty, nosey, opinionated and bossy, a stoic Yorkshire woman who told it how it was, and if the world didn't like it, they were 'all bloody wrong'. I was excited to see her, but a bit embarrassed doing 'grown-up' things like smoking and drinking in front of her, regardless of the fact that she herself smoked 40 a day.

I arrived at her address and was sad that she had moved from the house that I had known as my second home when I was growing up. That had been Auntie Flo's *real* home, not here. Nonetheless, this was where she lived now, and I was just relieved that someone would have me. The old house was a stone bungalow built into the side of a hill. At the bottom of the garden across a quiet, leafy road was the mere, a large lake with three small islands in the middle of it breaking up the sheet of water. It was a popular walking area, with a lot of resident swans, ducks and the occasional fox dashing along the banks. Auntie Flo's was number nine. It sat next to an unkempt field where a few tired-looking horses lived, munching on the overly long grass. It was an idyllic place for a child to spend her formative years. Virtually every day after school and at weekends, my dad and I would visit Flo and spend time with her.

HOOKED

'Are you happy here?' I asked Auntie Flo, looking at her aged face and the stubble on her chin, which made me feel comfortable and safe. I couldn't remember a time when my aunt didn't have excess facial hair and a razor in the bathroom to shave it off with – although I suspect that was rarely used.

'I didn't have a choice, love. I had to move. I couldn't manage the garden any longer, and that bloody driveway – ooh, hell, I could barely get up it. I'd never noticed how steep it was until just before I moved. It must have been pushing 90 degrees.' She pulled a handkerchief from her hefty bosom and wiped her nose before stuffing the hankie back inside her nylon dress. 'So how long are you going to stay with me?' she asked. 'A while, I hope?'

'Yeah, if that's OK,' I smiled. I could breathe here with her. I felt safe and relished taking a step off my life's treadmill.

'Of course it is, love. You know that. You don't need to ask me. Make the spare bedroom your own, then I'll set you to work skinning the rabbits. My butcher brought me a few,' she said, pushing her glasses back onto her nose. She wasn't joking. She was very old-fashioned. If I were to invent a farmer's wife who lived off the land and tended to chickens and sheep, Auntie Flo would be a brilliant point of reference.

'I can do a lot of things—'

'What was that?' she shouted, interrupting me.

'I was saying I can do lots of things, but skinning rabbits and plucking pheasants wouldn't be top of my list of favourite activities.'

'Oh dear!' she said with genuine disappointment. 'Well, you used to help me do them when you were little. You used to love it. Remember gutting the trout? I bet you wouldn't want to do that for me now, eh?'

'Well, not really.'

'Are you afraid you'd chip a nail?' she teased.

'It's not that. Look at my nails, Auntie Flo! They're in a

227

right state! I haven't been able to have them done recently. I've had no money.'

'Aw, poor you!' she grinned. 'I was going to ask you about that. Are you going to sign on while you're here?' Most people would have asked if I was going to get a job, not if I was going to sign on. I got the sense she wanted me at home with her.

'I hadn't thought of it.'

'What was that, love?' she asked, straining to hear me.

'I was just saying that I hadn't thought of signing on,' I repeated, leaning towards her ear, her head tilted towards me.

'Well, you might as well, honey. Better you have the money in your pocket. You're entitled to it, you know.'

Not sure if I was, since I hadn't paid tax in my previous employment. I couldn't be bothered with signing on anyway. I'd been used to earning hundreds of pounds a day. I wasn't going to sign up for a measly £60 a week. Also, I didn't want to make the commitment; it would have made me feel like I was signing on to be a permanent local resident, the thought of which made my skin crawl.

Auntie Flo lit a cigarette and blew the smoke upwards, then offered me one without even asking if I smoked. 'Ah, go on, then.' I took a cigarette and lit it, keeping it beneath the table between puffs so it wasn't on display, while my aunt emphatically smoked in her usual style, both elbows on the table, staring into the garden, which was her pride and joy.

I trotted off to my bedroom. It was cold and felt damp, but I didn't care. I was safe. Here I could relax, clear my head and figure out what to do next. This type of normality was just what I needed. While I was there, I would do as much to help Auntie Flo as possible. It had come as a shock initially, seeing her as an elderly lady. She was certainly not the same woman I'd remembered. It made me sad that she had lived her life alone after her parents had died. Before that, she'd lived with them, taking care of them in the name of duty. She'd never married and never had children.

HOOKED

After a few days spent establishing that my relationship with my aunt was as sturdy as it had been before, I called Ivan, an old school friend who'd been part of the surrogate family that I'd acquired to compensate for not having many of my own blood relatives. Ivan and I were very close. We still are. I was close to his parents and he knew my dad and Auntie Flo. We'd gone through many life transformations together, from spotty teenagers to problematic adolescents, through Ivan losing his father and my dad marrying Elaine. We'd been good friends for 14 years and ours was a bond that time never altered. Ivan was a gentle and kind soul with a limited ego and a sensitive awareness of people.

'Ivan is coming round to see you,' I shouted towards my aunt, who was sitting back in her armchair, feet on the pouffe, holding a magnifying glass up to a crossword puzzle. The TV was on loud, even though no one was watching it. Naturally, she didn't hear a word. 'Auntie Flo!' No response. 'Auntie Flo!'

She looked up, startled, put the paper down and the magnifying glass in her lap. 'What's that, love? I can't hear a thing. That bloody television's on too loud,' she scowled as she fished down the side of her chair, searching for the large remote control so she could turn it off. She never turned the TV *down* – always *off*.

'Ivan's coming? Ooh, lovely! But I don't know why he'd want to see me,' she said in mock bewilderment, wanting me to reassure her of her fabulousness. 'Perhaps I can get him to go and quickly clean out those boxes that my butcher left those rabbits in.'

'You can't ask him to do that!'

'Why not? It won't take him a minute. You can stick the kettle on when he gets here. He can have it done by the time you've made us a cuppa tea. Oh, and there's some of that sponge cake you like. I baked one last week. You can get us all a slice of that and all.'

'I don't really eat sponge cake, but I'll get *you* some.'

'Rubbish,' she said, looking at me accusingly. 'It's your favourite! You can't get enough of it.'

'Auntie Flo,' I laughed. 'You're talking about when I was twelve years old.'

'I don't know if you were twelve years old . . . I think you were a lot younger than that. Have you finished now?' she asked, pretending to be annoyed. 'Can I get back to my puzzle and put *Emmerdale* back on?' I loved Auntie Flo. She could be a total pain in the arse but she made me laugh.

'I thought you weren't watching it anyway,' I teased.

'Well, I was,' she said, angling the remote towards the TV and attempting to turn it back on. She wasn't having any luck, so she handed it me. 'Do this for me, please, honey. It won't bloody turn on.'

'I'm not surprised. I've never seen a TV as old as that in my life!'

She laughed throatily, called me 'a cheeky sod' and told me to leave her alone so she could get on with her crossword. I walked out of the room smiling. We were both happy.

*

Ivan came round and was set to work washing out the pallets which had carried dead rabbits and a huge trout. Auntie Flo barked orders at him as he battled with the cold and the hosepipe to try and appease her.

'Just one more to do, Flo,' he shouted.

'That last one you did, there,' she said, wagging her finger in Ivan's general direction.

'This one?' he asked, holding up one of the white-plastic pallets.

'No! That other one!' she said, not being particularly clear. I stood behind her as she stood, holding a dishcloth, at the entrance to the kitchen, her voluptuous curves filling the space.

Ivan started to laugh, his face hidden behind his winter beard and his hair covered by a thick woolly hat. 'This one?'

HOOKED

He picked up a random pallet, hoping it was the one she was talking about.

'Aye! That one doesn't look properly clean to me, Ivan.' I started chuckling in the background. 'Bring it here,' she ordered, and Ivan, with a grin on his face, carried the suspect pallet towards her. 'Aye. I told you. It's still dirty, is that one,' she said, pointing to a single spot of congealed blood that was on the underside of the rim. 'There, look.' She was proud that she was right.

'Oh, yes, sorry. I'll give it another thorough going-over,' he said. She was cocky and sassy for a 77-year-old woman. Everyone was scared of Auntie Flo except Ivan, who seemed always to have known how to handle her. He just did exactly what she said without question.

Time passed and I drank steadily every day but rarely got drunk. Boring and steady – I knew I couldn't take it for much longer. I craved excitement. I craved mischief. My feet began to itch, and what does one do with an itch? That's it – scratch it . . .

CHAPTER 27

OCTOBER 2003

Petra and I cranked up 'Crazy in Love' by Beyoncé. It had come out that summer and Petra apparently couldn't get enough of it. We danced around her tiny top-floor flat. I'd sold the three kilos of weed to Luca. I wanted some money as quickly as possible. He got the deal of his life and I got rid of it, swapping it for an ounce of cocaine and £450. I then sold the coke to Petra. Luca didn't want to give me all cash, because it was cheaper for him to give me powder instead. But I needed more than 450 quid to help me get by. Since I had nothing else, I had to have money.

'God, I've missed you! I haven't seen you for ages!' Petra practically sang, in a rare moment of emotion.

'I've missed you too. I've missed going out,' I called out to her from the bathroom as we got ready to impose ourselves on London. I went into the lounge, where Petra had cut up some lines on the table. 'Not for me, babe,' I said. 'I'm just gonna drink tonight.' I was determined to try to help myself. I'd laid off the coke for a few months and I knew what would happen if I had a line. I'd be straight back to where I left off.

'Are you serious?' Petra sounded deflated.

'Yeah. Why do you think I sold you it? If I was doing it myself, I'd have hung on to it,' I laughed. 'I need to try to leave off that stuff. It's fuckin' with me. I'll end up worse than Luca within a year if I keep banging that shit up my nose,' I said, lighting a cigarette.

'Yeah, I thought it was a bit odd. I just thought you wanted to get some sniff off me for nothing and still have cash in your pocket. I think I should go a bit easier with it too, you know. Ever since the death of Maurice Gibb at the start of the year.'

'Who was that? One of those Bee Gee blokes?'

'Yeah. Well, you know how I love them, and since he died, the whole banging shit up my nose thing has started making me feel uneasy.'

'Yeah, but he didn't die from a fucking overdose, P.'

'I know that. But look at him and his success in life – I don't want to die before I make something of myself. One of my biggest idols dying just made me realise how vulnerable we all are.' Petra tipped her head so her glossy black hair hung down to the floor and she tied it into a high ponytail, saying no more.

She had bought a bottle of champagne, which we drank as she told me how business had been booming for her. She'd found a new madam, Juliet, who was mad as a hatter but only took 20 per cent of the £300 per hour fee. She was a 'cool chick', so I was told. *What a hideous expression.* But Petra was forgiven, as when she talked in her natural Irish accent even the worst phrases could sound almost endearing. Petra had arranged for me to meet Juliet for an interview the next day. Another 'interview'. *Pah!* Listening to her, she sounded practically in love with Juliet, who'd taken her to showbiz parties and had also introduced her to a couple of blokes who had become Petra's regulars.

I borrowed one of my friend's sexy black skirts, a tight wraparound top and some heels. I never dressed like this for a night out, but I was excited to be back out in London after everything that had gone on.

'Have you seen Felix, then?' I asked.

'Yeah, but I'm not that interested, especially now I've got Guy.'

'Guy?'

'My fuckin' boyfriend, Kate! I've just been talking about him.'

'Yeah, I know, calm down. I was only jesting. Is he out tonight?' Sometimes she was so sharp, she pissed me off.

'I'll call him and maybe we can meet him. He's got one or two fit friends, babe, and they're all fucking loaded,' she said proudly.

'Yeah? I could do with a bit of that!' I said, knowing that I wasn't fit to be anyone's girlfriend. Two husbands were enough for me to be going on with.

We had our usual night out, but I didn't sniff. The next day, my hangover was excruciating – endless agony. My body must have got used to watered-down Gambian moonshine. Now I was back in London and getting full-strength booze, I was definitely feeling the after-affects. I jumped off the sofa that had been my bed for the night, stubbing my toe on the bottom of the table that was nearby. Halfway towards the shower room, I yelled – a delayed reaction to my minor injury. My toe hurt. My head hurt. Everything hurt. *I need cocaine so I don't have to go through this shit.* It never occurred to me that drinking less might be the answer.

I pulled down the boxer shorts that I'd borrowed from Petra just in time. I had severe diarrhoea. I scowled as the smell rose upward and I leaned forward holding my cramping tummy. As the flow of liquid subsided, I started looking round the tiny bathroom. Then the thought of meeting Juliet made my bowels open mercilessly again. I wanted to meet her and wanted to get working again as quickly as possible; that way I would feel I was getting myself sorted. However bad my belly was, it was good, in a way, to be back in London, in company and on the road to making some cash. Fucking men wasn't looking so bad. *To hell with getting an office job*, I smirked, chuntering and tutting out loud as I justified my plan of action to myself. Then, suddenly, my bubble burst as the South Ken guy who had attacked me thudded into my thoughts. My skin turned cold.

*

Juliet was bitchy. I didn't like her. But she managed to get me a job for that evening. *Hooray!* I hadn't had sex or any male attention for some time, so I was ready for whatever was coming my way. I'd go for it and make sure I climaxed regardless of how he looked.

I arrived at the man's flat in a council block in an unfamiliar area. I rang the bell, wondering what I'd find behind the peeling, broken door. A moment later, a man with white hair, wearing a suit, stood in front of me. He was stooped over and must have been in his mid-to-late 70s. *Oh fuck.* My heart sank. *I can't go through with this.*

'Hello, love. Come in. I'm Willy,' smiled the old man, standing to one side of the door and making room for me to enter.

'Thank you. I'm Jasmine,' I said, wondering if the taxi had already pulled away. I was pretty sure it would have done. The flat looked like an old person's flat. It smelled like an old person's flat. It was an old person's flat, and I was here to have sex with the resident old person.

'Just turn left into the lounge, Jasmine, and take a seat. I'll be with you in a mo,' said the man as he shuffled along behind me. I smiled vaguely and turned into the lounge where the television was on mute. There was an old-fashioned lampshade that radiated a dusky, yellow light. In between two armchairs was a trolley, the kind I hadn't seen since I was a young girl, crammed with fairy cakes and round biscuits wrapped in silver and gold foil. I was touched; it all looked so lovely. I couldn't bring myself to shag this man. I'd eat his cakes but not his cock.

I carefully perched myself on the edge of one of the seats and texted Juliet to tell her that I'd arrived at the job and that I didn't know if I'd be staying because I wasn't feeling well. I needed to cover myself in case I had to leave. The old man shuffled into the living room with a teapot covered in a tea cosy, something I hadn't seen since I'd last seen one of those trolleys. I smiled at him as he said that he'd been waiting for me and how much he'd been looking forward to meeting me. My heart sank and I began to worry about what excuse I was going to use to explain my departure. There was no way, although I'd fucked old men in the past, that I was up for it tonight. And if he was, it would be a miracle.

'Right, my darling, first things first,' the man said, picking up an envelope. 'This is for you. A gift from me to you, to thank you for taking the time to come and see an old boy like me.' I wondered if he could see properly. As yet, we hadn't exchanged eye contact.

He held out the envelope to me and as I reached for it he clasped my hand in both of his, then kissed it. 'Aw, thank you,' I said. I looked at him. My suspicions were right; he was clearly partially sighted.

'Now I just want to make it clear,' he said, still holding my hand. 'I haven't asked you here for any funny business. I don't do that. I'm just happy if you can have a cuppa tea with me, and maybe a bun or two, and if you like you can hold my hand.' He chuckled as if he was being very naughty and risqué. I cooed with relief. I suddenly realised that this man was very lonely. He craved company, someone to chat to, someone to hold. He deserved that. He was a human being, with a need to feel the warmth of someone else's gentle words and soft skin.

'Come on, now,' he asked. 'What can I get you?'

I sat with him for nearly an hour and a half, listening to his life story. He told me about the loss of his wife years earlier and his sadness that the marriage had produced no children. I reached across and tenderly held the old man's frail hand, occasionally looking at the veins that protruded under the surface of his almost transparent skin. It was time spent with someone who, like myself, really needed an exchange of affection. And he was someone who wasn't too proud to admit it. Being with him made me feel hopeful that eventually I would be all right. I could still be kind; I wasn't too jaded; I could be patient and I could still show empathy for another human being. I left William with a kiss, a smile and his envelope, which I left on the trolley still intact.

CHAPTER 28

DECEMBER 2003

'Daddy, it's me. How's things?' I said, trying to be cute to hide my nerves. It was the first time I'd spoken to him in ages.

'Where have you been?' he asked sternly.

I was desperate to sound upbeat, but instantly felt down the moment I sensed my father's tension. 'I've been in Africa.'

'What do you mean? Whereabouts?' I could hear the worry in his voice, as if he expected me to tell him that I'd been searching for my mother in Zambia. *So what if I had? Why does that make him feel so threatened?*

'In Gambia. It was a wonderful——'

'Where? Zambia?'

'No, Dad, *Gambia*.' God, I felt awkward. 'Gambia in West Africa. I wanted to get out of London and try to find out a bit about African culture, that's all. I've just been trying to sort myself out while I've been there,' I lied. 'I didn't call you cos it didn't work' – I giggled, trying to make light of the matter – 'and I know how stressed you both get when things aren't really good in my life.'

'The only thing I can guarantee that you will do in your life is let me down and cause disaster.' A biting chill came down the telephone wire and slapped me in the face. He was hard and didn't know how else to be.

'Well, it's difficult when I have to cope with everything by myself. It's not like I can talk to you or Elaine, is it?'

'Kate, don't start all that again. Don't start any trouble, otherwise I'll put the phone down.'

There was no getting through to my father. He had barriers that would take more time than I could ever imagine to bring down.

'Oh, Dad, please. Not again. I'm sick of your threats. You always threaten to put the phone down,' I snapped out of frustration. 'I've just called to find out how you both are and already you're having a go.'

'Kate, I've already warned you . . .' He was starting his usual defensive panic attack, so I put the phone down on him. *Fuck it. To hell with them.* I fought back tears. I sat alone on the sofa in Petra's flat. I'd been sleeping on another friend's sofa, but I'd started to feel I was outstaying my welcome, and since Petra was on holiday with Guy, she'd offered to let me stay at her place for a week. I could do as I pleased without having to worry about anyone else. I'd been on a 36-hour vodka and cocaine bender with my new partner in crime, one of Guy's friends who loved coke as much as I did. I'd done a few long sessions with him, because there wasn't anyone else to cane it with – at least not to the extent that I was obliterating myself.

I'd been working like a carthorse, fucking hard and getting paid. I went into the bedroom, took my money from the back of the wardrobe and counted it. I had to justify my existence.

This was it, right there in my hand: £3,480. Who could fault me?

I took £1,000 out of the wad and placed the rest of the cash back in the wardrobe.

My phone beeped. A text: 'U in? Im bk! Im comin rnd. P. x.'

'Yeah, but the flats a mess. C U sn. x.'

I stuffed the mixture of 50s and 20s into my Chloé bag and decided to go shopping later that day if my shattered head allowed. I had no idea what to buy – I wasn't interested in much. I knew it was maybe wishful thinking, but at least I'd had the idea of going out instead of hibernating the day away as usual.

Within minutes, Petra came bounding in, lively and loud. 'Look at what Guy bought me while we were away! How fucking amazing!' were the first words to come out of her mouth in her excitable, posh voice.

'It's nice,' I said quietly, turning my head to look. It was a shiny silver Cartier watch. I didn't like it.

'I'm so freaking lucky. He's crazy rich, Katie. I really, really like him.' I'd noticed she'd been adopting a more transatlantic accent lately.

'That's good.'

'You're not interested, are you?' Petra said crossly.

'I am. I've just got a banging head and I feel like vultures are clawing at my brain.'

'That's an odd expression.' I ignored her. 'Yeah, actually, you look horrendous,' Petra scowled. She got the rise she was looking for.

'Oh, fuck off, P. Take it somewhere else. Don't be so mean. I can't be doing with your crap today, OK?'

'What do you mean take it somewhere else? This is *my* fucking flat, don't you forget, you ungrateful toerag. And look at the state of it! I didn't say you could treat the place like a shit tip!'

'You're angry because I feel like shit and don't give a flying fuck about your fucking watch, or Guy, who you clearly don't give a shit about either, and I'm not interested in your fucking bollocks today.'

'No, I'm fucking cross because recently all you do is just keep going on these fucking stupid benders for days on end.'

'It's not days on end. It's the odd time here and there, for a day or two,' I said, calmly defending myself.

'I'm sick of it, Katie! I'm fucking sick of you doing this.' I sat bolt upright and spun round so that my feet were on the floor. 'Look at the state of you!' Petra bellowed, furious.

I stood up. 'Petra, stop this now. I'm telling you. Fucking stop it now. Do you understand me?' I wanted to hit her.

She stood back and screamed, 'I won't calm down! I won't fucking calm down! Look at this place! I'm fucking sick of you! It's a mess, Katie! Look at how you're living!'

'Don't you ever, ever try and make out that you're better than me, do you hear me?' I screamed. 'I'm so fucking sick of you, you stupid fucking false bitch! I've got a banging head and you just keep going on like you're trying to persecute me! Drop it, Petra! Fuckin' drop it! I used to put up with this crap from Alex, I'm not gonna put up with it from you too.'

'I want you out!' she bellowed in my face. I couldn't tell if she was going to cry or attack me.

'I'm gone, babe. Don't worry about that,' I said more quietly. 'I can't be here with you another moment longer. I don't even fucking like you, Petra. And the sooner that idiot Guy realises what the hell he's letting himself in for, the better it'll be for him.' My voice was quivering.

'Just get out!'

After I'd dressed and got my things together, I said calmly, 'I'm going.'

'Go on, then,' replied Petra, while fiddling with her phone. She didn't look at me.

'Don't be like that,' I said, and as I looked at Petra I could see that she'd been crying. 'Come and give me a hug before I go.'

'No. Just go,' she hissed, still not moving from her seat.

'Give me a hug.' Petra ignored me. 'Petra, give me a fuckin' hug now,' I ordered her. She stood up at last. 'We're not going to see each other for a long time. We both know that. We're not good for one another. Look at the state of us. Neither of us was brought up to fuck men for money and drink and take drugs like we do. I'm going, babe, and listen, I wish you the best of luck. You need it like I do. Be careful out there, Petronella.' I took her raging face in my hands and kissed her cheeks hard. 'You take care. I love you.'

That was the first and only time I ever said that to her and meant it.

CHAPTER 29

As I left the flat, loneliness was throttling me again. I felt exactly the same as I had when I was by the side of the motorway in Holland. My heart was walloping my ribcage with every beat and my head was buzzing with jumbled thoughts. I took out my mobile, which I'd stuffed into the back of my jeans pocket, and started scrolling down the endless list of names, none of which meant anything to me. I couldn't figure out who my friends were. I found a café and ordered a cup of tea and a can of Coca-Cola while I tried to work out what I could do next. My head was in my hands and I cried out loud, not caring who heard. I wrapped my arms around my own shoulders. I was trying to comfort the child within me who was terrified of life and who couldn't articulate the pain she felt.

I moved into a room with an en suite in a hotel not far from Petra's flat. The room was clean and bright, and I felt safer there than trudging around the streets. No one knew where I was and I liked it that way; I wouldn't get any hassle from people forcing me to celebrate Christmas when all I wanted to do was die.

I'd spoken to Jim once on the phone since I'd been back in London, but for weeks I hadn't spoken to him at all. Time seemed irrelevant when I was lost in oblivion. I'd avoided his calls and after a few attempts he'd stopped phoning. He knew what I was up to. He wasn't stupid.

'Jim?' I said when he picked up the phone.

'Katie?'

'Yeah. It's me. Are you OK?'

'*I* am. More to the point, are you? What the hell's been happening? Are you OK?' He wasn't sounding remotely Northern.

'Yeah.'

'What you're doing isn't all right, Katie. One minute you're bouncing around London like you own the fucking place, next minute you've got no fucking money or anything else, then you disappear off the face of the planet. How do you think I feel? I suppose you never even think about it, do you?' He was hurt.

'I'm OK. Look, I'm really sorry about everything. I really am.'

'Fucking hell, Katie. This is shit, how you're living. Where are you? What are you doing with yourself?'

'I'm in a hotel. What do you mean what am I doing with myself?'

'You need to get out of London, Katie. That place is no good for you. I've always told you that.'

'It's not the place, Jim.'

'Maybe not.'

'But——'

'Just let me finish, will you? I don't care if you come back up north or not, but I'm telling you that you shouldn't live in London. There's too much tempation there for you.' My dad had been using the exact same phrase for years.

At times, I wondered how much of what he said was about him wanting me to be in Yorkshire, closer to him, rather than about London being a danger zone for me. Although he definitely had a point. There was a lot more on offer in terms of mischief-making in the capital than in the North.

'Jim . . .'

'Look, I know the problem is *you* and not necessarily the place you're living in, but it doesn't help when there's thousands of fuckin' arseholes around you trying to take advantage of a vulnerable girl. So you're living in a hotel now?' He was exasperated.

'Er, yeah.'

'Are you serious?' he said slowly. 'Jesus Christ! I won't ask.'

Silence. I felt ashamed of myself for being such a failure.

'The hotel isn't that bad, you know.'

'I don't give a shit about the hotel, for fuck's sake.'

'I know, but . . . it's quite nice. It's nicely decorated. Not everything I do is shit.' I was trying to keep it together, but I could feel myself cracking.

'I couldn't care less about the interior of the fucking hotel, Kate. Look, sweetheart, I just want you to be OK. How many times do I have to say this to you? I only want you to be all right. That's all. Nothing else. Just be all right. Not happy, necessarily – just steady. I can't tell you what to do. Your dad can't tell you what to do. Everyone's tried. For years, everyone's tried . . .'

'You always say that.'

'Well, I'll continue to say it and maybe one day you'll hear it. No one can tell you how to run your life. Well, they can, but we all know that you won't listen to a bloody word of it. You're an adult. You make your own decisions. But one thing I do know is that only rock stars and supermodels live in fucking hotels, and shall I tell you something else?'

'Go on, then.'

'You're not either.'

'Oh, for fuck's sake, don't start. You're talking to me like I'm an idiot.'

'Well, stop behaving like one, then.'

'Jim, please fuck off. I can't be doing with this now.'

'Oh, nice. You're telling one of the very few people who's got the time of day for you to fuck off. That's charming, that is. I love you, Katie. I always have and you know I always will. All I want is the best for you, but you won't let me speak.'

'I'm sick of hearing it, Jim. I'm sick of hearing what a fucking disaster I am!' I shouted down the phone.

'I didn't say that.'

'Maybe you didn't say those words, but that's what it amounts to.'

'You know I love you, don't you?'

This released a flood of tears. 'I'm in trouble, Jim. Please stop having a go at me. I'm not coping. I'm scared. Everything is wrong.'

His tone completely changed. 'Baby, what is it? Are you in immediate danger?'

'No,' I whispered, sniffing. 'I need to see you. Please come and help me. I'm not coping. I don't know what to do with myself. I'm cracking up. I'm cracking up.'

My guts wrenched. My thoughts flashed to Alex, the fact that I was homeless, I was selling my arse, I couldn't talk to my parents without us arguing, I'd been raped, I was a bigamist, I had no friends . . . and here was Jimmy, loving me regardless of my faults. I wanted to tell him I was sorry for the heartache I repeatedly put him through. My breathing got heavier and it became hard to draw breath.

'Look, are you safe?'

'Yeah, I'm in a small hotel. It's nice inside. It's got—'

'Katie, stop telling me about the bloody hotel, OK? I don't give a shit. Don't you get it? Look, so long as you've got a roof over your head at night and no one is trying to murder you for a fucking drug debt, or something . . .'

'I'm OK. Please calm down.' I was taking long, deep breaths.

'You have no idea how hard this is for me, do you? No, you don't. God, I just want you to be all right. I just want you to stop making yourself miserable. Can you do that? Please? Just stop hurting yourself all the fucking time.'

'I know, I know . . . No one's after me. The hotel's nice. Er, the thing is, I'm lonely. I'm really lonely.' Again adrenalin pumped through me. 'I don't know what to do. I'm scared. I just don't know what to do about anything.'

'I wish I could come down tomorrow, I do, but I just can't. I'm sorry. I've got a huge order being picked up and I have to finish some of the pieces before Christmas. But I'll come down as soon as I can, OK, sweetheart? I promise I'll be with you soon. Just stay in that hotel and relax. Have some food. Take a bath.' His accent was coming back. He was starting to calm down a little.

'I *can't* relax.'

'Well *try* to, OK? I'll come and see you after Christmas.'

'Will I be OK?' I asked, desperately searching for reassurance. I guessed what he would say next – and it never failed to comfort me.

'Have you murdered anyone?' asked Jim.

'No.'

But I've broken the law by being married to two people at the same time and I'll probably go to jail because of it and I've been having sex for money and . . . There was nothing in my life that I wasn't worried about.

'Well, you'll be fine then, Pushkin. Everything'll be all right.'

'Do you promise? I just feel . . .' *Shattered. Frightened. Alone. Anxious. Desperate.* I felt death would have been a comfort.

'I promise you, Katie, that everything'll be better than OK. Everything will be good. We'll talk when I'm there and we'll get you a flat sorted, OK? I love you, Katie. Don't worry, sweetheart. You're not alone.'

'I am.'

'You're not.'

'I am, Jim. My dad and I can't talk to each other normally. I don't have anyone else.'

'Well, thanks a lot. Do I mean nothing? You have me, you silly billy.'

'I know, but . . .' I felt confused. 'Thank you. I love you. Thank you.' I loved him. I meant that with everything I was.

'Don't thank me, pet. Thank yourself when you've pulled yourself out of all this shit. I'll give you a call tomorrow morning to make sure you're OK. Have you got money for food and fags?' His kindness sometimes broke my heart.

After we'd hung up, I could feel tears welling in my eyes again, but I didn't let them roll. I'd cried enough. I was sick of tears. I had to wait quietly for Jim to arrive. He'd said that he would help me in any way that he could, so I decided that things would be OK if he'd agree to sign his name on a lease and act as a guarantor. I wasn't asking him to pay the rent; I just needed him to say that he was willing to if I defaulted. I felt hollow and listless, but today more than ever, I had to try and hoist myself out of my depression. That or die.

I called Juliet, my boss. I hadn't worked for her for a while and I wasn't sure if she would take me back.

'I really need to work. I won't let you down, I promise. I mean, you've heard the feedback from the clients – I'm good at my job.' I winced hearing myself.

'OK, darling, we'll see.' She wasn't giving anything away.

I called the cross-dressing, lipstick-wearing masochistic teacher I'd met nearly two years before. We'd exchanged numbers to arrange a visit. How he remembered me was anyone's guess, but he sounded friendly enough. He suggested we meet at the Grosvenor House Hotel, Hyde Park. I was excited to be going out and to have the attention of a man – any man – for an hour.

While I was on the phone to the punter, I received a text from Petra. 'Buy *The Sun*. Page 16' was all it said. I was surprised to hear from her. I supposed there would be a photograph of her falling out of a club somewhere, showing off her tits to get in the paper. I went to the local shop for vodka and cigarettes to get myself geared up to meet the 'call me a cunt' teacher, and while I was there I picked up the newspaper. I turned to page 16. There was a large photograph of Alex hanging off the arm of a pretty tabloid darling.

CHAPTER 30

I creamed my body with heavily scented Floris Lily of the Valley body lotion. It reminded me of my childhood. My dad had once bought it for me and told me that it was his favourite scent. In a bid to cheer myself up, I decided to wear something that I normally wouldn't: a 1950s-style full black skirt with hand-embroidered cream flowers on one section at the bottom, a tight black fine-knit V-neck sweater, black leather pumps, my black wool coat and my Chloé bag. Minimal yet chic. I felt like I was going on a date.

Alex kept popping into my thoughts. *Fuck him*. He'd moved on. *Whatever*.

*

'Where're you off to, love?'

'Park Lane, please.'

'Ooh, very fancy. Who're you meeting? You got a hot date, all dressed up like that?'

What the fuck has it got to do with you? Nosy bastard.

'I'm not that dressed up,' I replied. 'Yeah, I've kind of got a date,' I said reluctantly. I looked at the driver, convinced that he knew what I was talking about.

'Well, you look lovely. I hope he treats you well.'

I stared out of the window and started thinking. Since my work with the agency seemed to have dried up, or was certainly drying up, I had to network. I had to make things happen for myself.

'We could always go on a date together,' I said suddenly. *What the fuck are you doing, you stupid slut?* part of me was thinking. The other part responded, *Don't worry about it, Katie. Who cares what he thinks? He can say no if he wants, it's up to him. He's an adult.*

'Who?'

'Me and you.'

'Yeah?' answered the driver, not too sure what I was talking about.

'Yeah, why not?' *This is fucking madness. What are you doing?* I looked at him blankly.

'Not sure the missus would like that very much, love.' *Fuck, I can't believe I just said that.* 'I'd have thought a pretty girl like you wouldn't have any trouble finding a man,' said the cabbie.

I felt tense but I was trying to keep it together. *He's interested; I can see it in his eyes. He's just trying to act coy.* 'Your missus doesn't have to know,' I said cautiously, waiting for his response. *Just shut up, Katie. What are you doing?*

The driver laughed, clearly embarrassed. He wasn't the only one. *I'm such a fucking idiot. What's wrong with me?* For the rest of the journey, we avoided eye contact and chatted about inane things that were of no interest to either of us.

I arrived nearly ten minutes later than arranged to meet the teacher, but I'd texted him to let him know. I scuttled quickly into the entrance of the hotel as though I was being watched.

I thought I looked good, despite my unkempt hair. My ego encouraged me to think that other people in the bar would be curious to know who this statuesque woman was. I had no idea that I looked tired and unhealthy. I was underweight, I had sallow skin, a perpetual frown and spots, and my nails were chewed to the quick.

In the long, ornate bar with its twinkling chandeliers, I started sweating with nerves. I peered round, feeling as though everyone was watching me. Almost as soon as I'd convinced myself that I looked fabulous, a wave of paranoia persuaded me that the clientele could tell what line of work I was in. I was certain I was the talk of the bar. There were a few chic, elderly couples who seemed to me to take a break from their cocktails to watch the black girl as I hesitantly searched as inconspicuously as I could for my client. The palms of my hands were moist. I took my phone out of my bag and tried to call him. His phone was off – *off!* The guy had stood me up. A *punter* had stood me up.

I headed for the exit. The doorman smiled at me and I suddenly felt quite elated. I beamed back at him. He was being friendly. I really appreciated it. He had a kind face and had shown me warmth. It didn't matter if he knew what I was up to or not. He'd been nice to me.

As I walked along Park Lane, the world closed in on me once again. I called Luca.

'Luca, it's Katie. Are you OK?'

'All right, darlin'. I'm OK, yeah. What can I do you for?'

'Where are you?' I asked.

'In the car, love. Where are you? Do you want me to meet you somewhere?'

'Yes, if you don't mind. I'm in Park Lane. I just had dinner with a friend,' I lied. I didn't need to explain myself to Luca, but I was so self-conscious about being stood up that I felt the need to make up a story.

'Well, it'll take me about half an hour to get into town.'

'OK, fair enough.' I was disappointed. Thirty minutes sounded a long time. 'Can you meet me near the Café Royal on Regent Street?'

'Is that where that club Elysium used to be?' he asked.

'Yeah. I'm gonna head down there. You're in the car now, right? Cos I don't wanna hang around by myself for ages, you know. It's not safe out there for a woman like me!' I said, trying to sound jovial, then immediately wondering why I'd said that. Had I just incriminated myself, given him reason to think I was a whore? *If only my head would stop persecuting me.*

'I just gotta drop something off to some guy at Fulham

Broadway station, then I'll be on my way over to you, all right, darlin'? How many can I do you for?'

'Two.'

'Sweet. See you soon, love.'

I put my phone back into my bag and my spirits suddenly crashed. In an instant, I felt acutely alone. I'd had a 'date' and the guy had let me down.

It was cold as I started walking in the direction of Green Park Tube station to meet the only person who seemed to be able to make me feel happy. I tottered down the street with my hands in my pockets, head down and suddenly feeling overdressed, with no place to go to and no one to go with. I wouldn't normally walk this distance, but I had nothing better to do. The chilly evening air snapping at my face prevented me from crying. It was a sharp contrast to the stagnant air in the hotel room, which I was getting too used to.

A car drove by and some young guys beeped the horn. One of them stuck his head out of the window and shouted something. I couldn't work out what had been said and I didn't really care. What I saw was a couple of young men in a car enjoying themselves and probably getting up to a little light-hearted mischief. They almost certainly had other friends to meet and more than likely weren't staying in a hotel room because they were homeless. Christmas was coming and fairy lights were twinkling everywhere. There's a special energy to the festive season; I could still feel it, but I had no one to share it with. I watched cars bombing to their destinations, no doubt to parties, dinner, drinks with lovers or family. There were couples passing me, clinging to each other, striding out purposefully into the night. I passed Pangaea, a club I used to go to in happier times, when I loved my lifestyle and felt comfortable(ish) with the choices I was making. There were hordes of people outside.

I felt a great sadness and a longing for the old days when I'd swanned around feeling like Lady Muck, with heaps of money and cocaine and the means to buy whatever drinks I wanted. I'd always prided myself on never relying on men to buy my drinks.

I carried on walking, past a white limousine. A huge group of women who appeared to be on a hen party were getting out of it, laughing and screaming drunkenly with their friends, all of them dressed up and ready for a wild night of fun.

I knew the cool places to go to, but that was only surface stuff. Inside, I'd always felt like an impostor. I'd never been one of the über-glamorous chicks I was fascinated by and wanted to be. I'd mimicked other people's lifestyles but had never found what I'd been looking for, which was a man who was intelligent, kind and had money, someone who would take the time to understand me and not condemn me or walk away from me because of my insecurities and neuroses. I wanted to be with a man I could trust. The marriages dropped into my thoughts and I told myself out loud to 'Stop it! Stop it! Stop it!'

I carried on walking through the city, heading towards the Café Royal, past the Ritz, where the doorman could be seen in his top hat and tails opening doors for people who I supposed didn't have a fraction of the problems I had. Seeing the bright lights and the swanky cars pulling away outside this ornate epitome of English sophistication, a world that I had wanted nothing more than to be a part of, I felt isolated and invisible. I'd been trying so hard to find a place for myself where I felt at ease and comfortable, and that was where I'd wanted to be: right opposite, walking into the Ritz as if I belonged there, on the arm of a man I loved and who loved me, with no worries. I wanted to be stoned on coke or drunk on anything, and laughing with someone, preferably not a punter, but if that had been all that was on offer, I'd have taken it.

My heart was thumping and anxiety besieged me. I felt as exposed and self-conscious as I would have done if I'd been walking down the street wearing little more than a flower in my hair. Nevertheless, I continued to walk on. The marriages popped into my head again. 'Stop it! Stop it! Stop it!' I told myself again to stave off a panic attack. Meeting Luca to get my drugs was the only thing that was keeping me going. At that moment, there was nothing else in my life.

As the cars glided down Green Park towards Piccadilly, I realised I could disappear off the planet and no one would notice. I passed two young men getting out of a slinky black Porsche, and wished I was part of that scene again, even though I had never felt as though I was really part of it. I felt empty. I swallowed deeply, feeling my throat blocked, and sadness squeezed my spirit out of me. 'This is fucking bollocks!' I said out loud, fed up of constantly feeling lonely. 'I'm not doing this any more,' I grunted out loud, talking to myself.

'Katie!' called a male voice. My heart leapt. I was paranoid. Who was it? Who was it calling my name and interfering with my private thoughts? I turned around and couldn't see anyone, so I carried on walking. I heard my name called again and ignored it, thinking that someone must be calling another woman called Katie. Suddenly, behind me, I heard fast footsteps. It was Felix.

Fuck. I couldn't be arsed with talking to him.

'How you doing, girl? I haven't seen you for time.'

'I know,' I smiled as he leaned in to kiss my face, thinking about what he'd just said. *What's wrong with 'for a long time'? Not cool enough for you?*

'Where've you been? I asked Petra where you were, but she said that you two aren't talking or something.'

I wanted to be away from there. I didn't want to be having this conversation.

'Anyway,' he said, politely changing the subject, 'this is my mate Frankie.' Frankie and I smiled and said hello. 'Come for a drink with us.'

'No, I've got to meet someone.'

'Go on,' both boys said at the same time. I was taken aback by Felix's friendliness.

HOOKED

'It would be nice to hang out. We've never really got to know each other before. I always felt that Petra didn't like me talking to other women, even her friends,' Felix smiled.

He looked radiant and relaxed. I'd never noticed him like this before.

'You gonna come with us, babe? We're just heading to Pangaea,' Frankie piped up.

'Come on, just call your friend and get her to come down here as well,' Felix said, taking my arm.

'Ahh, that's really sweet, babe, thanks, but I really can't, not now. Maybe later.'

'Aw, pity. All right, sweetie. I'm not gonna try and force you. But take my number if you want to come down to the club later.'

I took my phone out of my bag and stored Felix's number. I was bewildered by his warmth. Had I spent all this time hating him for nothing? We said our goodbyes and I turned my back to continue walking down to the Café Royal.

Again I was alone. Why hadn't I just gone with Felix and his friend? *What's wrong with me? I'm always by myself and then when someone asks me to hang out with them, I don't do it.* I didn't realise then that my often self-imposed isolation was partly to do with my feelings of inferiority. I checked my phone. Nothing. No one was trying to contact me, no one at all; so I tried to make contact. I dialled Luca. He didn't pick up. *Where the fuck is he? What's going on?*

Was he ignoring me now? If so, why? 'Fuck this,' I said out loud as I put my phone back in my bag. I was cold from lack of food during the day and my anxiety was replaced by anger. I just wanted to get the coke and go home. I needed anaesthetising.

It would help if I could have sex; better still, if I could fuck a punter, that would be a double whammy. I'd get the attention I craved, the feeling of being wanted, of being desired, and also some cash to help ease the pain of loneliness on leaving the client. I wanted a man to fuck me and take me out of my reality for a while. I didn't care who it was, so long as I wasn't alone.

The man who had raped me dropped like a weight into my mind and for a very brief moment I even entertained the thought of being with him. I'd be with someone that way. At least I wouldn't be alone. 'Stop it! Stop it! Stop it!' I repeated out loud, as I felt my hatred towards my attacker bubbling in my veins.

If I had been in the hotel, I'd have masturbated. The more shit I felt about myself, the more I wanked. I found comfort in sex, whether it was fantasy or for real. I hadn't got involved with another man since Alex, and I wasn't in the habit of having one-night stands for free.

Luca rang. 'Where are you, love? I'm here.'

'All right, Luca. I'll be there in five minutes, OK?' There was laughter in the background.

'What you laughing at?'

'What? Me? No, it's my mate here laughing at something.'

'Oh, right.' I was convinced that they were laughing at me. 'I'll see you outside the Café Royal, then.' Luca rang off.

I felt tense and angry. These feelings were consuming me all too often and I was sick of it. Anger was the default emotion I used to cover up everything else I felt.

'Where are you? I'm here.'

'I can see you. My mate's flashing the car lights. Can you see me?'

'No.' Was he winding me up? Were they taking the piss out of me?

'Straight in front of you, Katie,' he said, laughing again. This time I knew he really was laughing at me. He was parked about 20 yards from where I was standing.

'Hiya,' I chirped, getting into the back of the car. I couldn't decide how much of an act I was willing to put on to make him feel comfortable. He was used to me being upbeat, but it was so draining. I'd become bored with trying to sound happy in front of people just to make them feel more at ease. I shut the car door and felt my momentary blast of cheerfulness expire.

'All right, darling. Merry Christmas, sweetheart. This is my mate Mac,' Luca said, nodding at the guy in the driver's seat.

'I know. We've met before. But I'm not surprised you can't remember, Luca.'

'How's it going? Merry Christmas,' Mac said, pulling away from the kerb.

'It's not going that great, really.' I wondered why I'd just said that. They couldn't care less how I was doing. They just wanted my cash.

'There you go,' said Luca from the passenger seat, leaning back and handing me two small wraps of coke. 'So, got any plans for Crimbo?' *Fucking 'Crimbo'.* 'Your family's up north, ain't they? You going up there to see your ma?'

'I've told you loads of times, I don't know my mum,' I said, taking the wraps and placing them in the side compartment of my bag. I handed him two £50 notes.

'Aw, ran off with the milkman, did she?' he laughed, scrabbling about in his pockets, searching for £20 change. He took out a £10 note and handed it to me. He continued rummaging in his pocket as we approached Charing Cross Tube station.

'Something like that. He was actually a lorry driver.'

'Well, I hope she's well shot of him now, anyway, sweetheart.'

'Fuck's sake, I wish you wouldn't call me sweetheart all the time. It gets on my nerves.'

'What do you mean?'

'Nothing, forget it,' I tutted. Then I continued: 'The way you talk sometimes gets on my tits. Listen, don't worry about the other tenner. I'll get out here, it's OK.'

'Hey, what's with the attitude, babe?'

'My attitude? There's lots of things wrong with my attitude, Luca. If there wasn't, I wouldn't be buying this fucking junk off you on such a regular basis, would I, eh? And if you had any fucking integrity, you wouldn't be selling it. Look, I'm gonna jump out here,' I said, gripping the handle on the inside of the car door.

'I don't understand what you're going on about.'

'No, I don't suppose you would. Well, now I'm telling you that I hope not to see you again. I'm bored of all this sniffing bollocks. I hope you understand that.'

I closed the car door, my mind on crossing the road safely before jumping into a cab to take me back to the hotel. I was confused as to why I'd just said what I'd said to Luca, but it seemed right. I was fed up of talking to and being around people whom I didn't care about and who cared nothing for me. I felt like I was losing the ability to be around anyone unless I was fucking them; even then, I wasn't certain how I'd perform.

Back at the hotel, I sat staring blankly at the walls, thinking nothing, in between attempts to sleep away my pain. The days passed, Christmas came and went, and I remained in my room, alone.

I couldn't stop thinking about Alex, analysing everything that had happened in our relationship. I hated myself for having tolerated a relationship with a man whom I knew had never cherished me. I'd thought sex had been enough.

CHAPTER 31

FEBRUARY 2004

Jim could be domineering at times, but he was always true to his word. After Christmas, I'd moved into a one-bedroom flat and he'd agreed to pretend to be the tenant, since I couldn't pass the necessary credit checks. I'd finally got one of the things I'd really wanted and I convinced myself that it would change everything. I desperately wished Jim could be with me so that I could give him a big thank-you hug. I knew that saying thank you wasn't nearly enough, but that was all I could offer. I wanted to feel his strength around me, but I knew that if he was with me, the way I was feeling, I wouldn't want to let him go – that is, until I started to feel better, and that wouldn't be fair on him.

When I moved in, I had no intention of facing life outside my flat for a few days. I couldn't do it. I sat on the sofa . . . and sat . . . and sat. I thought of Alex. I wished Freddie was there to make my flat feel friendlier. I wondered how he was surviving without me. *Probably better than if he'd been with me.*

Shadows seemed to follow me. I'd sit still, rigid with fear because I'd heard a noise. But the most frightening thing was the movement in my peripheral vision. There was no escaping the shadows.

There was no one to visit and no one would visit me. Faye was clearly fed up with me. Petra could piss off. I had friends in Yorkshire, but the thought of going to Yorkshire without seeing my parents seemed too depressing. I had never been one for staring at the television, unless *Columbo* was on, but the stupid channel had stopped showing him for a while. I'd never in my life watched a film all the way through and the parts of films that I did manage to watch, I could never remember. I had nothing to do except sit alone and listen to my goblin battling with Nice Kate. Nothing that was good for me was allowed freedom to flourish. Goblin Kate would always smack it down with phoney justifications or unadulterated anger. The only thing I could think of doing was to get some drugs.

I couldn't continue like this. Something was going to have to change. Faye was right. *No, she isn't. Yes, she is. No, she isn't.*

I decided to call Luca and ask him to deliver half an ounce of charlie. I was nervous as hell after the way I'd spoken to him the last time I'd seen him, but I needed what he had on offer. I would apologise and have done with it. The local dealer's gear was crap, so if a little squirming was in order to get what I wanted, so be it. I made up my mind to tell him that I was at a friend's house. I didn't want him to know where I was living and definitely didn't want him to invite himself in, if, that was, he was still willing to sell me the stuff. I sat back for a moment pondering and decided that he would definitely sell me it. Pride wasn't high on his list of personal attributes. Not many people would ask him for a half ounce of charlie and I knew he'd want the cash.

'Is Luca there? It's Katie.'

'Nah, he ain't. I got his phone, Katie. It's Mac. Luca ain't around tonight.' I was relieved but a bit worried. Would I get my drugs? 'What is it you're after, love?' Niceties over with, down to business. Yay! He had the powder.

'Half,' I said, trying not to be too obvious over the phone.

'Half an ounce?' He just came out with it. 'Right then, nice one. Er, I'll be there within the next two hours.'

'Two hours? That's a bit long, isn't it? Can't you make it any quicker? Anyway, where's Luca?'

'He's in hospital.'

'Hospital?'

'Yeah, he collapsed the other day. He ain't well. He had a fit and fucking started foaming at the mouth, so me and my mate called an ambulance cos we couldn't move him, like.'

'Fuck. Is he all right?'

'Nah, not really, babe. I don't know, to be truthful. He's in intensive care at the minute. Listen, I'll see you in a couple of hours and tell you more then, all right?'

'All right. Well, when you get here, call me and I'll come out, OK? I'll text you the address now.'

'Nice one, mate. See you in a bit.'

'Oh, and Mac . . .'

'Yes, love?'

'Bring me a couple of two-litre bottles of Diet Coke as well, will you?' I'd forgotten to buy a mixer.

'Fucking hell,' he laughed. 'Anything else, darlin'?'

'Oh yeah, thanks for reminding me. You got any sweets?'

'Yeah. Which ones do you want?'

'I don't care. Just bring any.'

'Youse lot are having a bit of a party over there, ain't ya? Right, I'll be with you as soon as I can.'

I had a plan: I was going to get absolutely, totally and uninhibitedly out of my head.

What. Are. You. Doing. Now? Nice Kate was thinking.

Fuck it. No one even knows if you're dead or alive, apart from Jim. Your parents don't care. Why should you? There's nothing else to do, snapped the goblin.

Jim's just come down here to help you, and as soon as his back is turned you're sniffing and drinking like a maniac again. It's not right. Why are you doing this? Nice Kate.

Why not? Give me one good reason why I shouldn't do it?

LEAVE ME ALONE! I couldn't stop the constant barrage in my head. Would I ever be free of myself?

Ha! There isn't one reason why I shouldn't get wasted. Goblin Kate.

This is all so wrong. Nice Kate.

Look at you. You're weak. You're indulging me by calling the dealer, you fool. I've been a part of your life for too long. I'm not going to just go away. You've been nurturing me for years, remember. You've made me into the stronger, more powerful part of you that I am today. It wasn't through anyone else's doing. Nope. It's your own mind alone that's created me. Goblin Kate.

Katie, you are indulging that sick, destructive part of yourself by getting some charlie. Cancel him. Just call him and tell him you had to go out. You're going to fuck yourself up completely if you let him bring round that gear. Nice Kate.

Yeah, right, like I'm gonna tell Mac not to come round. Fuck it. I just wish he'd hurry up. I'm waiting! Goblin Kate.

BE QUIET!

I continued to sit on the sofa and wait. Mac rang nearly three hours later. I grabbed my bag and keys in case the door shut behind me and virtually ran to the car. I jumped into the back and gave him the money and he gave me the drugs.

'You all right, love?' Mac asked, nodding at me.

'I'm fine. Nothing's up with me. So, what's happening with Luca?' I wished I hadn't asked. Truth be told, I didn't care. I just wanted to get inside the flat with the drugs.

'He just fucking collapsed when he was on a session the other day.'

'He's always on a session.'

'Exactly. Anyway, the poor guy dropped to the floor like a fucking sack of spuds, like, and started convulsing. Fuck me, mate, he even had blood coming out of his ear. I thought he was fucking dead for real.'

'Shit, sorry to hear that,' I mumbled, feeling creeped out that the last time I'd seen Luca I'd told him that I hoped never to see him again.

'Cheers for this, Mac. Look, I'm off back in the flat, my friends are waiting.'

I avoided eye contact. I couldn't face any more chat. I had

an agenda that I was determined to carry out. Yeah, I felt bad for Luca – but I felt worse for myself.

*

As the days went by, I disintegrated into my own paranoid world. I stopped crying. I paced around my flat, usually naked, checking behind doors, through blinds and in drawers for anything suspicious that might be there to harm me. Peace was staring into space. Normality was searching and drinking and sniffing and smoking – *lots*. I didn't have the imagination to wank. It was pointless. Too much cocaine numbed me anyway. The shadows moved around my peripheral vision. They had the power to make me freeze perfectly still for as long as they saw fit. Only occasionally did I have the confidence to speak out and ask them to leave me alone, and when they didn't, I'd beg.

Finally, I picked up the phone.

'Jim, I need help.'

'What is it, darling? What's going on?'

'I'm sick, I'm not well. Please, please. I can't manage.'

'Baby . . . Come on, what is it?'

'I need help!' I suddenly raised my voice, becoming hysterical. 'Please can you help me? Please. I don't know what to do.'

'What have you been doing?'

'I've been in the flat for a few days by myself. Jim? Jim?' The shadows were there by my side.

'Doing what, baby?'

'Everything. Please, Jim. I'm scared. I'm frightened. I'm scared of being alone, of myself, of my thoughts. I'm not OK. Please, please help me!' I really was losing it.

'I will. I will, sweetheart. Just tell me what you want me to do and I'll do it. I'm here for you.'

I paused. My head was swimming. I wanted to die. I had no other option: 'Take me to rehab.'

CHAPTER 32

At long last I'd truly decided that I no longer wanted strangers and misery as my constant bedfellows. I knew I could no longer continue to exist as I had done. I wanted to live, but I couldn't change my life without help. In May 2004, Jim and I took the train from Paddington, chatting as we headed towards the 12 Step rehab centre I'd chosen. The hum of his voice was neither irritating nor comforting. It was just there, blending into the background of my increasingly overwhelming sadness. But my tears had gone.

I was screwed. I'd built my adult life on lies and I knew I was heading to a place where I would have to face those lies. I would feel safer away from London, away from drugs, away from booze, away from punters. I knew I was resilient, in spite of all my tears before arriving at this point. There was a part of me that was extremely tough. Jim described it as 'a spine of steel encased in putty'. I was exhausted emotionally, physically, spiritually. The process of trying to fight my demons alone had brought me to my knees.

*

'How much have you been drinking recently?' the counsellor asked after introducing herself.

'I dunno,' I answered, my head down. 'Maybe the equivalent of a couple of bottles of wine a day.'

'What else?' she asked abruptly.

'At night maybe a couple of vodkas or brandies . . . it varied.'

HOOKED

I looked at her face to see if she was satisfied with the answer. She grinned. 'What else?'

'Cocaine.'

I was sure the counsellor felt she was hitting the jackpot. 'How much coke did you do?'

'How much? God! I don't know . . . maybe a couple of grams whenever I went out.' I smiled to myself. I'd noticed that already I was talking about my activities in the past tense.

'How often did you go out, Katie?' She lowered her glasses.

The woman looked battered, as though she'd had a hard life. *Why don't I just tell her what really went on and have done with it? Not yet.* It was too soon to fling crap across the desk in her direction. Besides, I couldn't think of anyone who really knew everything I got up to, not even my closest friends. I was a perpetual liar. Hell, I couldn't admit some of my antics even to myself.

'Most nights. I went out most nights.'

'Doing what?'

I sat there feeling as if I was under a magnifying glass. *I've just got into this rehab, for Christ's sake. Give a girl a break.* 'What do you mean doing what?' I asked uneasily. 'Drinking, sniffing coke, you know . . .'

I watched her scribbling her notes manically, wondering what was being written down. I hadn't really told her *anything* yet. The counsellor took off her glasses and put them on the desk along with her pen. This all felt so serious and I was tired.

'You didn't drink what you're telling me you did, and you didn't sniff two grams of charlie.' I couldn't hold eye contact with her. 'What did you *really* take? OK, so you *bought* two grams? But what about the party after the club? What about the blokes you were partying with? They must have had coke too, right? You must have had them queuing up offering it to you. I bet you sniffed a bit of their stuff as well, eh?' To me, she sounded victorious, not stopping for breath, as if she thought she'd cornered her new patient.

HOOKED

Is she getting off on this interrogation? I wondered, unable to let go of my hostility and fear. *Is it turning her on, the thought of me being taken into a toilet cubicle by a stranger in a nightclub and sniffing a line of coke off his cock?*

'A *couple* of vodkas or brandies? Come on, now! You're talking to an addict and alcoholic here, sweetheart.'

Sweetheart? Fuck off, you old trollop!

'Tell me who the hell you know who drinks *just a bit* of anything when they're hoovering up charlie all night? You look like a party girl, Katie. You know what goes on in these places on these nights out, girl, and here is the place for you to be able to get honest and start dealing with all that stuff that's in your mind. I mean, what about the comedowns? What did you take to deal with those?' she asked in her Scouse accent, baiting me, waiting for my response.

I looked at her and nearly started to grin, then decided not to. I wasn't going to prove her right. But I also felt that I'd given her enough information to be going on with. Yeah, I used sleeping pills to try and help me with my coke comedowns, but I wasn't a prescription junkie. *Jesus! The cheek of the woman, accusing me of not telling her the whole truth!* It seemed rude that she should doubt me without even knowing me. But credit where credit's due: seven out of ten – she was on the ball and I was getting pissed off.

'We can make this a difficult and long-drawn-out process, or you can just tell me everything, right now, and make it simpler.' She sounded like a policewoman.

'I'm not sure I'm ready for you to accuse me of being an alcoholic coke-whore,' I said to her, rolling my eyes and tugging at my white T-shirt, which had suddenly started to feel uncomfortably tight.

But I knew she was right. I had to take this opportunity to stop fucking around and try to get my life on track. If I wasn't ready now, I never would be and I was likely to find myself in an asylum.

I excused myself to use the bathroom, where I looked at

my spotty face in the mirror. The peculiar, dim yellowish light made my skin look sallow. I looked closer. I could barely recognise who I was. I stared and stared. I was my father's daughter. I had a mum. I didn't know her, but I had a mum. I was joined to people – friends, acquaintances, family – but who was I? Who had I become? It was time for me to stop trying to kill myself. I was emotionally destroyed and willing to take instruction from anyone about the basics of living. I couldn't cope with myself and what I had created any longer.

From that moment, I humbly decided that I would wave the white flag on my life and try, genuinely try, to construct a new one. I was shitting it, though, cos I'd lived with my crutches for so many years I could barely imagine life without them.

It's almost impossible to explain how painful the process of releasing the veil that I'd used all my life to hide from myself was. The very things that I had used in an attempt to ease the discomfort I'd felt at being me had let me down. Drugs and drink had shown me a false promise of hope that I had embraced, believing that I had found the answer to my unease. I had freely taken them as my friends, before they had taken me hostage.

Now I was fighting back.

I stayed in rehab for 12 weeks and every day we had two 90-minute group-therapy sessions and 30 minutes of one-to-one therapy. The experience was vastly different from my first time in rehab. I was a different woman. This time, I was broken. I had given up my fight. I had done so many more things to erode my soul that my sanity was the only thing left for me to lose.

One of the first questions I was asked by my therapist was: 'You only ever mention your dad. Why's that? Where's your mum?'

'I don't talk about my mum,' I replied.

'Why not?'

'Because I don't,' I snapped, desperate not to have to open that Pandora's box.

HOOKED

I was furious that someone was attempting to intrude into my private world of hate. It had become so ingrained that I didn't even know if I wanted to let go of it. What would I do without the anger? I tried to ignore the therapist's instructions when she told me that she wanted me to write a letter to Mum that I wasn't to post, just something to enable me to express some of my feelings. But she wouldn't let it go. Eventually, I wrote the letter, six sides of A4. I could have written more, but I had been told that I would have to read it out loud in front of other people, so I left it there.

During that group session, we sat in a circle and all eyes were on me as I started to read the letter out loud. I was angry and afraid about saying the things I had to say, embarrassed, feeling I was exposing secrets. I'd never vocalised anything about my mother, so I had no idea how I would feel and how I'd react. I tried to be blasé. Just past the first half of page one, I broke down.

I wept, shaking as I released a little of the anger I'd locked inside me for years. The room was silent. No one moved. I have never cried so freely in front of other people and I don't suppose I ever will again. For a few precious minutes, I forgave my mother and myself for letting down Kumba, the child who lived within me.

That moment, right there, the flood of tears and the release of my anger, was the beginning of my real journey to recovery.

EPILOGUE

I had to learn over time to forgive myself for the misery I caused my dad and Elaine, and Jim, my most constant ally. But I also have to try to forgive myself for putting my body and mind through physical and emotional torment.

I would never wish to go through the first 18 months of recovery ever again. It was a heavy-hearted battle; every moment was a journey of self-discovery and a welcome to reality that I wouldn't wish even on someone I dislike.

I have no contact with Petra these days. We haven't spoken for nearly five years now. We have nothing in common, and finally I am able to admit that. She's still working as a hooker. I've seen her on the agency website. I have little or no feelings about that. If she manages to cope with it emotionally, then so be it. I imagine she is with some boy, who, like all the others, thinks the sun shines out of her pert bottom.

Faye is now living abroad. Although we're both lame at keeping in contact, I rest comfortably knowing that she's been with her girlfriend for more than two years and they are blissfully happy. We will always be friends.

I know nothing of Luca. Bizarrely, he called me a few months after I left rehab and asked me what I was up to. The call made me feel vulnerable and very anxious, but I told him that I'd taken a detour and had no intention of using his services again. Then I cringed, remembering that he'd heard that from me before. He laughed as if to say, 'We'll see.' He'll be waiting a long time. I considered changing my phone number but decided against it. I can't keep running from people and things; that's what I've spent my whole life doing. I've never heard from him since.

HOOKED

As for Alex, I bumped into him on Oxford Street one sunny afternoon. We arranged to meet for coffee, which we did. I realised that nothing had changed. Yeah, he's handsome. So what? So is my neighbour's spaniel. We had our time together, albeit brief, and now, although I will never forget the intensity of our relationship, I will never yearn for what could have been.

My beloved Auntie Flo died last year. I managed to tell her how much I loved her, but she was busy trying to turn the television down, so I'm not sure she caught everything I said. I know she will watch me from wherever she is, being the nosy and wonderful woman that she was. I love her more than I was ever able to express.

As for Jim, my dear, dear Jimmy, whom I continue to adore to this day, is creating masterpieces in a studio in a tiny village in North Yorkshire. He designed and built a gallery that is a credit to his brilliantly creative mind and is currently painting frescoes in a chateau in France. He gets more and more eccentric as the weeks tick by, and he is happy.

My relationship with Dad and Elaine has transformed more positively than I ever imagined possible. They no longer worry about me. If I miss their early-morning calls, they no longer suspect that I have been drinking or using drugs the night before. We laugh, we talk, we hug. We've left the past behind us and look to the future.

And as for me, well, I'm sober, clean of drugs, divorced (twice) and single.

I say this casually now, but at one time I thought I'd never be rid of those dastardly marriages. The idea of dealing with two divorces at once was a huge mental hurdle, and it often kept me awake at night. I was consumed with anxiety and I considered confessing to the police. Terrified of the consequences, I was persuaded not to by a close friend.

I didn't want to go to jail. I discussed my crime with a lawyer, who was openly baffled by my case. He'd never dealt with this situation before. As well as promising that he

HOOKED

wouldn't shop me to the police, he suggested that I deal with each divorce separately, as if there was nothing unusual or illegal about my situation. 'Do one, then the next. And don't panic. I'm sure you'll be all right,' he said kindly.

I approached my local county court and applied for a divorce petition. I hadn't had contact with my first husband for more than five years, so I didn't need his permission or signature on the papers. And since we had no property or children together, the process was surprisingly simple. It was over within three months.

Although I was pleased, I wasn't done yet. I still had the illegal marriage to Hassan to contend with. First, I contacted a lawyer (via the Internet) who lived in Gambia, who agreed to represent me in a Gambian court. I was terrified by the thought of revisiting the scene of the crime, convinced I'd be thrown into jail the moment I stepped onto African soil, so I claimed that because of work commitments I couldn't attend court. I had to sign power of attorney over to a friend, who flew to Gambia for a week. He went to court to represent me and the case was adjourned. Two days later, and within thirty seconds, he received my decree absolute.

The next day, he flew back to England and it was all over. I held both divorce papers in my hands and took a moment to thank God and feel some relief. It wasn't as overwhelming as you might expect. I had a helluva lot of work to do on myself and I knew that, although this was a momentous step forward, it was just one of many practical things that I had to deal with.

I no longer hate myself for my past choices. I see them for what they were: a misguided attempt to get through life. People say all the time that your past experiences make you the person you are today. I'm comfortable being myself these days, but would I go through it all again to gain the insight that I have today? *Hell, no.*

Would I change the past if I could? *Damn right I would.*

Do I accept that I can't? *Yep.*

HOOKED

What have I learned? *To be honest about my feelings.*

Am I happy? *I'm getting there and I'm happy with that.*

What about my mother? *She breaks my heart.*

Do I love her? *Right at this moment, as I write this, yes, I do. Other days, I hate her still, but I try to work on that. She is the blood that runs through my veins. However hard I've tried, I can never flush her out of my system. But one thing is for certain, I do understand that sometimes we've all got to swim upstream.*

When I asked one of my therapists the question 'Why me? Why did all this happen as it did?', she answered pragmatically, 'Why not?'

Can't say fairer than that.